The Structure of Post-Keynesian Economics

This book is a major contribution to post-Keynesian thought. With studies of the key pioneers – Keynes himself, Kalecki, Kahn, Goodwin, Kaldor, Joan Robinson, Sraffa and Pasinetti – Geoff Harcourt emphasises their positive contributions to theories of distribution, pricing, accumulation, endogenous money and growth. The propositions of earlier chapters are brought together in chapters 6 and 8 in an integrated narrative and interpretation of the major episodes in advanced capitalist economies in the post-war period, leading to a discussion of the relevance of post-Keynesian ideas to both our understanding of economies and to policy-making. (Chapter 7 is concerned with theories of growth from Adam Smith to the present day.) The appendixes include biographical sketches of the pioneers and an analysis of the conceptual core of their discontent with orthodox theories. Drawing on the author's experience of teaching and researching over fifty years, this book will appeal to undergraduate and graduate students interested in alternative approaches to theoretical, applied and policy issues in economics, as well as to teachers and researchers in economics.

G. C. HARCOURT is Emeritus Reader in the History of Economic Theory, University of Cambridge, Emeritus Fellow of Jesus College, Cambridge and Professor Emeritus of the University of Adelaide.

The Structure of
Post-Keynesian Economics

The Core Contributions of the Pioneers

G. C. Harcourt

CAMBRIDGE
UNIVERSITY PRESS

CAMBRIDGE UNIVERSITY PRESS
Cambridge, New York, Melbourne, Madrid, Cape Town, Singapore, São Paulo

CAMBRIDGE UNIVERSITY PRESS
The Edinburgh Building, Cambridge CB2 2RU, UK

Published in the United States of America by Cambridge University Press,
New York

www.cambridge.org
Information on this title: www.cambridge.org/9780521833875

© G. C. Harcourt 2006

First published 2006

Printed in the United Kingdom at the University Press, Cambridge

A catalogue record for this publication is available from the British Library

ISBN-13 978-0-521-83387-5 hardback
ISBN-10 0-521-83387-6 hardback

Contents

v

Figures

Preface and acknowledgements

While writing this book, I have had in mind two sets of readers: first, undergraduate and graduate students who may be looking for alternative approaches to thinking about theoretical, applied and policy issues in economics. By presenting a structure of the thought (and its origins) that I have found so helpful over my working life I hope to at least interest and possibly even enthuse this first set. Secondly, I also hope that what I have written may interest teachers and researchers in economics, not so much perhaps for the details of the analysis, with which many will be familiar, but for the way in which one person at least sees the inter-connections and interrelationships which have emerged as our discipline has evolved and developed.

The ideas in the book themselves have evolved and developed for me over the past fifty years, in both lectures and research. My model is not exactly Dennis Robertson's three volumes of lectures on Economic Principles in Cambridge, Robertson (1957, 1958, 1959); but I suppose it has something in common with them, even with his admission that 'if it is all wrong, it can't be helped now' (Robertson 1957, 7). I trust, though, that I have not written in quite as querulous a tone as that into which Robertson sometimes lapsed, for I remain, as ever, a happy and enthusiastic, even optimistic, person who nevertheless is willing to admit that he may be wrong.

I wrote the first draft of this Preface in April 2005, in the fiftieth year since I first came to Cambridge in September 1955. Half my working life has since been spent here (the other half in Adelaide, most happy years) and I count myself most fortunate to have studied and taught in such a stimulating and satisfying, even if sometimes–no, often–so cantankerous an environment.

Much more than this, though, this year Joan and I will celebrate our Golden Wedding anniversary on 30th July. As ever, her love and support have made possible the writing of the book, much of which occurred in the study she imaginatively prepared for me in our New Square home when, having had three years' grace over and above the obligatory seventy years' constraint, I no longer had a room at Jesus. I would like to dedicate the volume to her with my love.

I am much indebted to many cohorts of pupils who have listened to my lectures, to my graduate students and colleagues in Adelaide, Cambridge and Toronto and to friends in many countries who have contributed greatly in discussions and their own writings to my understanding of economic issues. I hope I will not cause offence if I thank explicitly the people who have most directly influenced what I have written here: Mauro Baranzini, Stephanie Blankenburg, Wylie Bradford, Giuseppe Fontana, Prue Kerr, Tom Russell, Sean Turnell and the anonymous readers of the manuscript for Cambridge University Press.

Finally, may I thank Rhona Watson for her generous and efficient searches and for answers to my obscure queries, and Susan Cross, Frances Thomson, Frances Flood, Debra Armstrong and Janet Nurse who cheerfully typed the manuscript and never once complained about my atrocious handwriting.

Thanks are also due to Macmillan for the extract from Joan Robinson's *Essays in the Theory of Economic Growth* (1962) reproduced in chapter 3.

GCH
Cambridge
October 2005

1   Introduction: why post-Keynesian economics and who were its Cambridge pioneers?

Maynard Keynes, Richard Kahn, Richard Goodwin, Nicholas Kaldor, Luigi Pasinetti, Joan Robinson and Piero Sraffa all started initially, at least in some degree, within the mainstream of their time. They all moved well and truly outside it, attempting to create either a revolutionary alternative or to rehabilitate the classical–Marxian tradition, in most cases in the light of the Keynesian revolution. The one exception is Michal Kalecki, whose personal history and independent mind combined to place him virtually always outside the mainstream. This volume, though, is not principally concerned with why and how the discontents that led them to change their minds arose. Rather, its principal object is to set out the structures of their alternative approaches in order to suggest modes of thinking about theoretical and policy issues in political economy.[1]

The structures presented here are based on over forty years of teaching and researching under the rubric of what is now called post-Keynesian economics. I certainly was not aware that it was so called when I started on this track in the 1950s. In fact, I have much sympathy with the stance of my old friend, the late Athanasios (Tom) Asimakopulos, who declined an invitation to be included in the first edition of Philip Arestis and Malcolm Sawyer's admirable *A Biographical Dictionary of Dissenting Economists* (1992), because he regarded his views and contributions as belonging fully within the tradition of economics proper, not in a dissenting stream. It was only in order to provide a suitable tribute to his influential contributions and splendid personal example as a teacher and human being that his widow, Marika, allowed the entry on Tom to be included in the second edition of Arestis and Sawyer (see Harcourt 2000). However, it must be admitted that at the time of writing (August 2004), though something of a backlash/comeback may be discerned (see

---

[1] Some of the reasons for their discontent are given in the appendixes to the volume: these contain short intellectual biographies of the main contributors (appendix 1, pp. 158–76) and a sketch of some of their principal arguments (appendix 2, pp. 177–84).

Harcourt 2001a for reasons why), the views and approaches taken in this volume still continue to be regarded by the bulk of the profession as those of dissenters.

The most succinct definition of post-Keynesian economics comes from Joan Robinson (1978; *CEP*, vol. V, 1979b, 210)[2]:

> To me, the expression *post-Keynesian* has a definite meaning; it applies to an economic theory or method of analysis which takes account of the difference between the future and the past.   (emphasis in the original).

I obviously have no quarrel with this; but, as I try to be ever-mindful of historical developments, I also wish to stress that the approaches to political economy which reflect post-Keynesian thought are there partly for historical reasons and partly because of logical associations. Post-Keynesianism is an extremely broad church. The overlaps at each end of a long spectrum of views are marginal (*sic*), often reflecting little more than a shared hostility towards mainstream neoclassical economics and methodology, *IS/LM* Keynesianism and the 'fix-price' Keynesianism of the 'New Keynesians' and certain French economists. Some post-Keynesians are working actively towards a synthesis of the principal strands.[3] Others regard the search for a synthesis, for a general all-embracing structure, as a profound mistake: to quote Joan Robinson (1974; *CEP*, vol. V, 1979b, 119), a founding mother, a misguided attempt to replace 'one box of tricks' by another. Post-Keynesianism should be a situation-and-issue-specific method of doing political economy, a 'horses for courses' approach, itself an all-embracing structure at the methodological level (see Harcourt 2001a, Essay 19).

The principal object of analysis is the advanced capitalist economies of the twentieth and twenty-first centuries. The central aim is to provide a framework within which to understand and explain their macroeconomic and/or microeconomic processes over time. It must be admitted that the tradition within which they are presented objects vigorously to the microeconomic/macroeconomic dichotomy of mainstream economics (see Joan Robinson 1977b; *CEP*, vol. V, 1979b, 4–5 for a typically

---

[2] The Convention in this book is to separate by a semicolon the date of the cited work from the date of the collected work(s) where it is reprinted. 1978 here is therefore the publication date of Joan Robinson's 'Keynes and Ricardo', which is reprinted in vol. V of her *Collected Economic Papers* (*CEP*) in 1979 (*CW* is the siglum for Keynes' *Collected Writings*).'
[3] The deepest and most profound example of the attempts to provide a coherent synthesis is the splendid monograph by Heinrich Bortis, *Institutions, Behaviour and Economic Theory: A Contribution to Classical–Keynesian Political Economy* (1997). Reading successive drafts of Henry's book taught me so much. If I were ever to be persuaded that a synthesis were possible, it would be because of his arguments.

forceful argument why). Basically, neither individual nor group/class behaviour may be understood without making explicit the economy-wide structures and relationships that provide the backdrop to their behaviour. Similarly, economy-wide structures and relationships not only influence but also are influenced by individual and group/class motivations and behaviour. Thus the microeconomic foundations of macroeconomics must always be complemented with – indeed, it could be argued, dominated by – the macroeconomic foundations of microeconomics, see Crotty (1980).

The particular subsets of the mainstream literature that this happy band became increasingly dissatisfied with were the theory of distribution, especially the marginal productivity theory in its aggregative form (but also the supply and demand approach in general, see Bharadwaj 1978); the theory of pricing at the level of the firm and the industry, principally as it came down from Marshall and Pigou; the theory of investment behaviour and expenditure that is implied in Marshall and Pigou and, and more explicitly, in the writings of Irving Fisher; and the theory of growth, to which is allied the theory of the trade cycle (the business cycle to our North American cousins), as it has been developed in the post-war period by leading neoclassical economists (some of whom, such as James Meade, Robert Solow, and Trevor Swan were/ are also leading Keynesians). In doing so, they were inspired and stimulated – even irritated – by Roy Harrod's and Evsey Domar's seminal contributions in the late pre-war and early post-war years. The final objective of the volume is to show how the alternative theories of the post-Keynesians under each of these heads may be combined into an overarching general framework that may then be applied in explanations of post-war happenings in the advanced capitalist world. This same framework, together with its constituent parts, may be used to rationalise various policy proposals which tackled, or should have been used to tackle, some of the major malfunctions of these economies in the same period.

An equally important aim of the volume is to rescue the pioneering contributions of this first generation from the benign neglect and misunderstandings that are starting to occur as the time from their respective deaths lengthens. It is important to have recorded for posterity the background and the nuances to the making of the theories by people who knew these pioneers personally and who were present for at least part of the time when the ideas were developed, not only to restore them to their correct place in the narrative but also to correct the misconceptions and often neglect they suffer or experience as the third and even fourth generation of post-Keynesians increasingly come to constitute the post-Keynesian literature and canon. I do not mean to denigrate the contributions of the latter groups; but I would like to restore to their rightful place the fundamental pioneering contributions of the first contributors.[4]

The structure of the volume is as follows: In chapter 2 I discuss post-Keynesian macroeconomic theories of distribution. I start with Kaldor's 1955–6 paper, as it is the best known. I use it and its characteristics as the backdrop to discussions of Kalecki's earlier contributions, including his review of Keynes' *General Theory*, Joan Robinson's eclectic approach and Frank Hahn's macro theory of employment and distribution which was initially developed in his PhD dissertation at the LSE in the later 1940s and early 1950s.

Post-Keynesian theories of the determination of the size of the mark-up are discussed in chapter 3. Adrian Wood's 'Golden Age' model is taken as the benchmark against which are assessed the 'historical time' model developed by Peter Kenyon and myself and the choice of technique in the investment decision in both the orthodox and the post-Keynesian approach. The chapter closes with a discussion of why internal finance is usually preferred to other forms of finance of investment expenditure. Kalecki's principle of increasing risk is taken as the most insightful explanation.

Chapter 4 is concerned with macroeconomic theories of accumulation. It starts with a critique of the details of Keynes' theory in *The General Theory* and after. The critique stems from the writings of Kalecki, Joan Robinson and Asimakopulos. All the ingredients involved in it come together in Joan Robinson's well-known banana diagram, an exposition of which ends the chapter.

Chapter 5 contains a brief discussion of money and finance – whether they are exogenous or endogenous in theory and real life. In chapter 6 all the previous developments are brought together in an explanation of post-war inflationary episodes, drawing on the conflict inflation models of Steve Marglin (1984a, 1984b) and Bob Rowthorn (1977).

Theories of growth from Adam Smith to 'modern' endogenous growth theory are discussed in chapter 7. We start with Smith and Ricardo's theories, move on to Marx and then to Harrod's theory. The reaction to Harrod's findings and problems by Solow and Swan, on

---

[4] Paul Davidson (2003–4) has written a most idiosyncratic review article of John King's history of post-Keynesian economics since 1936 (King 2002). It was entitled 'Setting the record straight. . . '. I was tempted to write a reply with Luigi Pasinetti entitled '*Really* setting the record straight' but desisted after I read the courteous but powerful replies to Davidson by Marc Lavoie and King himself.

the one hand, and Kaldor and Joan Robinson, on the other, are then discussed together with Richard Goodwin's eclectic theories and Pasinetti's grand synthesis. The chapter closes with discussions of Kaldor's later views in which he scraps many of his earlier ideas, and of endogenous growth theory, emphasising how it relates to previous discussions from Smith on.

The concluding chapter 8 uses the approaches developed in earlier chapters to examine their application to policy issues. It discusses how 'vision', approach and method interrelate with policy recommendations. It closes with a proposed 'package deal' solution to a crucial dilemma raised by Kalecki in his classic 1943 paper on the political aspects of full employment, especially how it may be permanently sustained as opposed to attained from a deep slump.

The volume ends with two appendixes: biographical sketches of the pioneers and an account of the conceptual core of the post-Keynesian discontent with the orthodox theories of value, distribution and growth.

2   Post-Keynesian macroeconomic theories of distribution

Kaldor's 'Keynesian' theory

We start with Nicky Kaldor's 'Keynesian' macro theory of distribution (Kaldor 1955–6), not because it was the first – that honour belongs to Kalecki in the late 1930s and even earlier, as Kaldor argued, to Keynes in 1930 – but because it is the most well known. It is, moreover, a good reference point because it has some idiosyncratic features, not least that it is a long-period, full-employment model, seemingly a most strange work to come from the pen of such an eminent Keynesian economist as Kaldor. This even led Paul Samuelson to dub him 'Jean Baptiste Kaldor' (Samuelson 1964, 345). The model itself comes at the end of a long article which reviews theories of distribution from Ricardo on, and which finds most of them either out of date or severely wanting. The starting point of Ricardo is significant because Ricardo's theory emphasised the distribution of the surplus of production after the *necessaries* of production – the (subsistence) wages of the wage-earners and the replacement of the means of production – had been taken into account. Ricardo's theory reflects the early years of the British industrial revolution when real wages were still very low (in Ricardo's model due to the workings of the Malthusian theory of population and the classical theory of rent) and relatively constant, at least in the long-term sense, so that as technical advances, mechanisation and industrialisation occurred, the surplus to be distributed grew both absolutely and relatively. In Ricardo's view – it should be remembered he was himself a member of the landed gentry by then – the rising share of rent in the distribution of the surplus was a 'waste', for it was only the agricultural and industrial (and commercial?) capitalists who reinvested the major part of their share (profits). The landowners consumed most of theirs. (Ricardo's friend, Thomas Robert Malthus, thought this a good thing because it kept at bay contractionary and deflationary forces that otherwise would operate, a not very well explained source of autonomous expenditure – hence Keynes' view that Malthus was 'the first of the Cambridge economists' (Keynes 1933; *CW*, vol. X, (1972, 71), that is to say, the first to think like Keynes.)

By the time we get to the mid-1950s when the 'Golden Age of Capitalism' was already in full swing, the advanced capitalist economies were experiencing full employment and growth, real wages were far above subsistence and so it was possible in Kaldor's view to make an 180° turn and allow the profit-receiving capitalist class to have first bite of the cherry, as it were, leaving wage-earners to receive the residual after profits, accumulation (and rentier consumption) had been accounted for. (Arthur Lewis 1980, 257 told a not dissimilar story but used a neoclassical approach to analyse the distribution of income between profits and wages in the phase of development when there were no longer unlimited supplies of labour.)

Despite arguing that only a fully employed economy could continue to grow over the long term, Kaldor nevertheless called his theory 'Keynesian', for at least three reasons. First, he located the origins of his theory in Keynes' analogy of the widow's cruse in *A Treatise on Money* (1930; *CW*, vol. V, 1971, 125), whereby the more profit-receivers spent, the more profits they received:

If entrepreneurs choose to spend a portion of their profits on consumption . . ., the effect is to *increase* the profit on the sale of liquid consumption goods by an amount exactly equal to the amount of profits which have been thus expended . . . Thus, however much of their profits entrepreneurs expend on consumption, the increment of wealth belonging to entrepreneurs remains the same as before. Thus profits, as a source of capital increment for entrepreneurs, are a widow's cruse which remains undepleted however much of them may be devoted to riotous living. When . . . entrepreneurs are making losses . . . by saving more, the cruse becomes a Danaid jar which can never be filled up.

(emphasis in original)

Secondly, Kaldor took the Keynesian view that (planned) investment led and saving, determined by income and its distribution, responded. Thirdly, he argued that the Keynesian multiplier was a short-period concept in *The General Theory* model, with changes in income needed to bring planned investment and planned saving into equality, because money-wages and prices were sticky in the short period. In the long period, however, the multiplier applied to the distribution of long-period, full-employment income, principally because, in the long period, prices were relatively more flexible than money-wages, and the marginal propensity to save out of profits was greater than the marginal propensity to save out of wages.

We should also see Kaldor's contribution within a context of the development of the peculiarly Cambridge (England) contributions to growth theory, stimulated by Harrod's 1939 article and 1948 book and by the awakening of interest in the post-war period in development itself. This meant that Kaldor, in tackling the problem of Harrod instability (see chapter 7, pp. 102–9 for a discussion of Harrod's model and problem) and the processes by which the warranted rate of growth, g_w, and the natural rate of growth, g_n, were equalised, assumed for his theory of distribution that planned investment, if realised, was such as to give the economy over the long term the necessary capacity to allow it to grow at g_n. This required forces at work which took g_w to equality with g_n and allowed planned investment to become actual investment.

The value of the share of investment in long-period, full-employment national income was therefore predetermined in Kaldor's model. In later models he attempted, not ever successfully, to show *why* the economy should be at full employment and the share of investment in national expenditure should be endogenously determined at the share consistent with producing g_n over time.

Kaldor assumed that the long-period equilibrium position of a growing capitalist economy is a full-employment one, Y_f. He assumed simple proportional saving functions with $s_\pi > s_w \geq 0$, where s_π is the marginal propensity to save (*mps*) of profit-receivers and s_w is the *mps* of wage-earners. Let Π be total profits, W be total wages.[1] Then Keynes' saving–investment equilibrium condition determines the *distribution* of Y_f rather than the level of actiivty and income.

Thus:

$$S = s_\pi \Pi + s_w W = \bar{I} \tag{2.1}$$

where $\bar{I}$ is given, autonomous:

$$s_\pi \Pi + s_w(Y_f - \Pi) = \bar{I}$$

i.e.

$$\Pi = \frac{\bar{I}}{s_\pi - s_w} - \frac{s_w}{s_\pi - s_w}Y_f$$

and

$$\frac{\Pi}{Y_f} = \left\{\frac{1}{s_\pi - s_w}\right\}\frac{\bar{I}}{Y_f} - \frac{s_w}{s_\pi - s_w} \tag{2.2a}$$

[1] Subsequently, the distinction between saving from different classes of income – profits, wages – and by different classes of persons – profit-receivers, wage-earners who save – was analysed explicitly by Pasinetti (1962) and followed up by Kaldor (in, for example, Kaldor 1966a). See also Harcourt (1972, chapter 5).

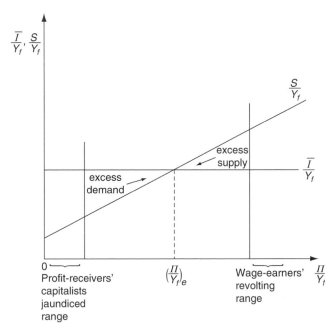

Figure 2.1. Kaldor's 'Keynesian' theory of distribution.

As

$$s_w \to 0, \frac{\Pi}{Y_f} \to \frac{1}{s_\pi} \frac{\bar{I}}{Y_f} \qquad (2.2b)$$

clearly the Keynesian multiplier relationship.

We now use a simple diagram (see figure 2.1), to illustrate Kaldor's arguments.[2] (In lectures, I have always tried to use words for the poets, algebra for the mathematically inclined and geometry for the in-betweens.)

On the vertical axis is measured the share of (given or autonomous) investment, $\bar{I}$, in long-period, full-employment national income, Y_f, and the share of (planned) saving, S, in Y_f. On the horizontal axis is measured the share of profits (Π) in Y_f. Because $s_\pi > s_w$ and prices are more flexible than money-wages in the long term, if the economy is not initially at the distribution of Y_f where planned saving and planned investment are equalised

<hr>

[2] The diagram was suggested to me by the late Hugh Hudson, who edited the first two volumes of Kaldor's collected papers.

$$\left(\frac{\Pi}{Y_f}\right)_e$$

there are zones of excess demand to the left of the intersection of $\frac{S}{Y_f}$ and $\frac{I}{Y_f}$, and of excess supply to the right. These impact on prices relatively to money-wages and redistribute the *given* level of Y_f so as to raise (to the left) or reduce (to the right) the share of profits, thus changing the share of saving appropriately.

$$\left(\frac{\Pi}{Y_f}\right)_e$$

is therefore a stable equilibrium position, for if the economy is not initially there, appropriate signals and processes will take it there. At that point the value of

$$\frac{S}{Y_f}(=s)$$

is such as to make

$$g_w\left(=\frac{s}{q}\right)$$

(where q is the desired incremental capital–output ratio) equal to g_n. The economy thus has the desired amount of investment expenditure and capacity creation to allow it to grow at g_n, realising its full-employment potential by employing all its labour force and the expanding capacity of its stock of capital goods over time.

Kaldor provides two provisos: the share of profits must not be so low as to make the profit-receiving capitalists feel that accumulation and profit-making are not worth the candle (this is shown in figure 2.1 as the profit-receivers' capitalists' jaundiced range. It corresponds to Ricardo's argument that there must be at least some minimum rate of profit received to keep capitalism going.) Correspondingly, the share of profits must not be so high as to entail a share of wages and a level of real wages that are unacceptable to the wage-earners, who are assumed passively to accept whatever residual of national income is left for them after the profit-receivers have received their share. In this situation, the wage-earners no longer passively accept the residual but respond by causing a wage–price and wage–wage inflationary spiral and the distribution of income will no longer be determined by the Kaldor process. This range is designated as the wage-earners' revolting range in figure 2.1.

That in outline is Kaldor's 'Keynesian' macro theory of distribution. The other theories we now examine share much of what he argues – that investment leads and saving responds, that $s_\pi > s_w$ – but they do not confine themselves to the long period nor to a situation of long-period full employment. By contrast, they allow distribution *and* employment to be determined together.

Kalecki's 'degree of monopoly' theory

We illustrate Kalecki's theory first with his theory of the simultaneous determination of employment, output and the distribution of income in the short period, a contribution that dates from the 1930s: see Kalecki (1938; *CW,* vol. II, 1991). Indeed, a version of it was already present in Kalecki's review of *The General Theory* in 1936. Unfortunately, the review was published in Polish and a full English translation did not become available until December 1982 (see Targetti and Kinda-Hass 1982). Kalecki's review is discussed on pp. 21–5; here we use Joan Robinson's exposition of his theory. It exploits a very simple, clever and illuminating diagram (see figure 2.2), on which generations of Cambridge undergraduates were brought up by Joan Robinson herself and then, later, by me. It appeared in print in Joan Robinson's Michal Kalecki Memorial Lecture in the Oxford *Bulletin* memorial issue in honour of Kalecki in 1977 (Joan Robinson 1977a; *CEP*, vol. V, 1979b, 191).

In Kalecki's writings on capitalism two principal forms of price formation are recognised: Marshallian market-determined prices for raw materials, and mark-up pricing for industrial products. The size of the mark-up is determined by what Kalecki called 'the degree of monopoly', a portmanteau term to take in the factors determining the degree of discretion in price-setting that imperfectly competitive firms in different industries have: patents, barriers to entry, dominance as a price leader and so on.[3] In Joan Robinson's version it is the second form of pricing that is used, combined with Kalecki's view that in the short term the cost curves of individual firms are reverse L-shaped – that is to say, marginal costs are equal to short-term average variable costs up to capacity output.

---

[3] Peter Kriesler (1987) has written the definitive account of the development of Kalecki's views on these and related matters.

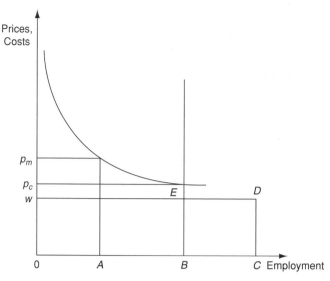

Figure 2.2. Joan Robinson's diagram of Kalecki's model.

Joan Robinson uses this assumption, a not unrealistic one, of course, to introduce a very neat measuring trick. All quantities in the short period concerned in her analysis are measured in terms of the labour required directly and indirectly to produce one unit of the consumption good. (We have a two-sector model, the consumption goods sector and the investment goods sector.) This implies that the wage cost per unit of production and the wage cost per unit of labour employed coincide, as do the price per unit of production, employment and the amount of value added per unit to be shared between profits and wages. We deal with a closed economy without a government so that all intermediate purchases net out and only values added of the private sectors are considered.

On the vertical axis of figure 2.2 we measure prices, costs, profits and wages per unit. On the horizontal axis we measure employment in terms of the units defined above. The vertical line indicates capacity output/maximum employment offered in the consumption goods trades.

Though it may not be found as such in any of his writings, it is well known that Kalecki's macroeconomic theory of distribution may be neatly expressed in the aphorism that wage-earners spend what they earn and profit-receivers receive what they spend. To see this, consider the simplest case where wage-earners do not save and profit-receivers do not consume. Write the national accounts:

$$E \equiv C + I \equiv Y \equiv C + S \equiv W + \Pi$$
$$C \equiv W \text{ by assumption}$$
$$\text{So } S \equiv \Pi$$
$$\text{and } I \equiv \Pi$$

Kalecki argues that profit-receivers *as a class* (as well as individually) can always decide what to spend on investment (up to a financial constraint) but not how much as a class (or individually) they will receive. Therefore causation must run $I \rightarrow \Pi \rightarrow S$. In equilibrium, planned I is not only realised but it is also equal to planned S and an equivalent level of Π created by the level of I and its consequent effect on employment and income (and its distribution). Y (and its distribution) must be such as to give a level of $\Pi(=S)$ to match the injection of planned and now realised I.

Moreover, it may be shown that the profits of the consumption goods trades are equal to the wages bill of the investment goods trades. The wages bill of the consumption goods trades, even when fully spent, covers only the wage costs of the consumption goods trades, that is to say, itself. In order to receive profits there must be an injection of spending from outside the sector, that is to say, the spending from the wages received by the wage-earners in the investment goods trades. Profit *per unit* in the consumption goods sector will be determined by the size of the mark-up in that sector.

As it is a short-period analysis, we may provisionally take the level of planned investment as given. (Of course, Kalecki spent the whole of his professional life improving his theories of investment and accumulation because he always stressed that accumulation was the most important process at work and to be explained in an analysis of the motion of capitalism over time.) The given level of planned investment implies that we know the amount of employment needed to produce the corresponding amount of investment goods. For simplicity, and also because it is not a bad first approximation, we assume that all investment goods are made to order and that agreed prices, and so profit margins, the mark-ups over wage costs in the investment goods sector, have been agreed upon between buyers and sellers.

The amount of employment needed to make the investment goods is shown as BC in figure 2.2; B is the point where capacity working $(0B)$ occurs in the consumption goods sector. The money-wage is also assumed to be given and, again for simplicity, is assumed to be the same in both sectors. Wage costs per unit and the wage itself are shown as $0w$. The rectangle $BCDE$ therefore measures the wages bill in the investment goods sector. We draw a rectangular hyperbola which subtends the same area as $BCDE$ under each point on the left-hand side of the vertical line with a vertical axis starting at w and a horizontal axis emanating from w as shown. The rectangle $0ABEw$ is, therefore, the maximum wages bill payable by the consumption goods trades if all available capacity there were to be operated. The area under the rectangular hyperbola may be thought of as the 'marzipan icing' on the consumption goods sector's wages bill Christmas cake, the thickness or thinness of its spread depending on the size of the mark-up set, itself determined by the intensity of the degree of monopoly ruling in the short period concerned.

If free competition ruled in the consumption goods sector, excess supply pressures would mean downward pressures on the now market-determined margin until full-capacity working prevailed and the competitive price of $0p_c$ with a profit margin of wp_c were established at the intersection of the rectangular hyperbola with the vertical line. Notice that there is no suggestion that just because prices of consumption goods have been assumed to be flexible and market-determined that full employment of labour and capital automatically results. The combined wage bills of both sectors would have to provide enough demand to absorb the available labour force. But if the given level of investment was 'low' – due, say, to sluggish 'animal spirits' of the investors – then there still could be involuntary unemployment occurring overall even though there is full capacity working in the consumption goods sector.[4]

Suppose, though, that the existing 'degree of monopoly' implies a mark-up of wp_m. Then employment and production in the consumption goods sector will be $0A$ and, again, demands and supplies will match in both sectors with $W = C$ and $\bar{I} = \Pi = S$. Moreover, we have now determined simultaneously output, employment and the distribution of income between wages and profits in the short period without the need to assume full employment for the mechanism to 'work'. So Kalecki's adaptation of Marx's schemes of production and reproduction has allowed him to present both the production and expenditure aspects and interrelationships of capitalism, and to make explicit the role of price-setting behaviour in macroeconomic processes. This is a major reason why Joan Robinson came increasingly to prefer Kalecki's approach to Keynes' more Marshallian framework, which she thought required indirect and rather convoluted arguments to make points which are crystal clear in Kalecki's exposition. (An example of what she had in mind may be obtained by comparing the structure of Kalecki's model with Keynes' passages about the widow's cruse which we quoted on p. 7.)

---

[4] We discuss all this more fully in chapter 4.

Kalecki's framework also allows another fundamental aspect of the workings of indeed any economy and social system to be brought out. For not only are employment and output determined by aggregate expenditure on investment and consumption, they are also directly related to the productivity of labour in the two sectors and to the real wage in the following sense. Given the productivity of wage-earners in the consumption goods sector and the value of the real wage (which is determined once the prices of consumption goods have been determined, the money-wage being taken as given for the current short period),[5] the surplus of consumption goods per unit of labour over and above the real wage is known. Then, given employment in the investment goods trades, enough units of labour must be employed in the consumption sector to 'feed', as it were, themselves and to provide enough consumption goods from the surpluses simultaneously created to 'feed' the investment goods wage-earners as well.

The framework may be used to analyse both developing economies and democratic socialist economies as well as capitalist economies. For example, Kalecki argued that in a democratic socialist society, the planners should decide the level of consumption per head and overall for a fully employed labour force, possibly through deciding money-wage levels and the relative wage structure, and by a judicious use of sales taxes added to labour and material costs to set prices. Those wage-earners not required in the consumption goods sector would be available for the investment goods sector. There, the composition of the total production of investment goods would be decided by socialist managers following rational rules for the choice of technique, given the allocation of available resources between the combination of various capital goods to make both consumption goods and capital goods themselves.

Kalecki himself always advocated a modest rise from period to period in the level of consumption goods per head. Citizens then would have more jam today rather than being fobbed off with promises of more jam in tomorrows that never came, as tended to happen too often in Stalinist regimes, not least in Kalecki's own country, Poland. There, when he returned to Poland in the late 1950s, he was soon sidelined as far as policy was concerned, just because of his progressive democratic socialist views (see Steindl 1981, 592).

---

[5] In a short-period by short-period analysis such as Kalecki developed in his model of cyclical growth over time, the money-wage may also be made an endogenous variable. Thus, wage-earners react to realised real wages in any period by bargaining for money-wages in the following periods that are designed to obtain the real wages they wish to have, the pressure of real wage resistance, for example. These and related themes are taken up again in chapter 6.

Kalecki's views and approach had, as we noted, an increasing influence on Joan Robinson's approach to theory, not least in her *magnum opus*, *The Accumulation of Capital* (Robinson 1956). We illustrate this in the context of the discussion above of the creation, extraction and use of the surplus of the consumption goods trades in the accumulation process. Joan Robinson's 1956 book precipitated a number of comments and reviews, two of which are relevant for the present discussion: Harry Johnson's 1962 note in *Osaka Economic Papers* and David Worswick's 1959 article in *Oxford Economic Papers*. Johnson noted that the technical surplus of (consumption goods) output per worker over subsistence in Joan Robinson's basic model is

$$\frac{1}{l_c + l_m m_c} - \bar{w}$$

where l_c is labour employed per unit of output of consumption goods, l_m is labour employed per unit of output of machines, m_c is machines employed per unit of output of consumption goods, $\bar{w}$ is the real wage rate, and the expression is measured in consumption goods per worker. Johnson derived the result as follows: l_c units of direct labour and $l_m m_c$ units of indirect labour produce one unit of consumption goods. In consumption good units the total cost of producing one unit of consumption goods is $(l_c + l_m m_c)\bar{w}$. The surplus is $1-(l_c + l_m m_c)\bar{w}$ for $(l_c + l_m m_c)$ labour units and

$$\frac{1}{l_c + l_m m_c} - \bar{w}$$

consumption goods per worker.

Johnson's result brings out the saving aspect of accumulation – the forgoing of immediately consumable goods in order to make possible the construction of new and additional machines. The same result can be obtained by approaching accumulation from its investment aspect. The surplus over subsistence per worker can then be regarded as net investment per worker, that is

$$\frac{M - R}{L}$$

where M is the number of machines produced per period, R is the number of machines required to replace the existing stock, L is total labour employed and the expression is measured in machines per worker.

$$\frac{M - R}{L}$$

can be written as

$$\frac{1}{l_m} - \bar{w}\left[\frac{l_c + l_m m_c}{l_m}\right]^6$$

This can be converted to consumption good units per worker by multiplying by

$$\frac{l_m}{l_c + l_m m_c}$$

the ratio of labour time per machine to labour time per consumption good, to give

$$\frac{1}{l_c + l_m m_c} - \bar{w}$$

the original result.

The two approaches serve to emphasise two important factors stressed by Joan Robinson: first, the need to specify the *units* in which economic quantities are measured, and, secondly, that accumulation has both a *saving* and an *investment* aspect. The result is quite general and relates to the surplus of consumption goods per worker over the real wage rate, whether or not the latter is the subsistence one. It also illustrates the dependence of the rate of growth of capital goods on the level of the real wage rate that we noted above. The lower is the real wage rate, the

---

[6] This result is derived as follows: assume that wage-earners spend all their wages on consumption goods and that profit-receivers spend all their profits on machines; then

$$L = \frac{Cp_c}{w} = \frac{p_c}{w}\frac{L_c}{l_c} = \frac{1}{\bar{w}}\frac{L_c}{l_c}$$

where C is the quantity of consumption goods produced in a period, p_c is the price of consumption goods, w is the money-wage rate and L_c is labour employed in consumption goods production. $L_m = L - L_c = (1 - \bar{w} l_c)L$, where L_m is labour employed in machine production.

Now

$$M = \frac{1}{l_m}L_m = \frac{1 - \bar{w} l_c}{l_m}L$$

and $R = m_c C = \bar{w} m_c L$. (Machines are assumed to last for one period only and the gestation periods of machines and consumption goods are assumed to be equal.)

$$I = M - R = \frac{1 - \bar{w}(l_c + l_m m_c)}{l_m}L$$

where I is net investment

$$\frac{M - R}{L} = \frac{1}{l_m} - \bar{w}\left[\frac{l_c + l_m m_c}{l_m}\right].$$

greater is the surplus of consumption goods available per worker for employing workers in the investment goods sector on net investment, and the greater is the command of any given surplus over labour time in that sector.

Johnson's model may be used to illustrate the technical limitations on the growth of capital goods, supposing there is to be available an unlimited supply of labour, and that production each period is planned by (say) Worswick's dictator.[7] Assume that the dictator is planning the production of the current period, t, and that he wishes to maximise the rate of growth of the stock of machines over time. He has available from period $t-1$, a stock of machines (M_{t-1}) which is the gross investment of the previous period. M_{t-1} machines allow the employment of L_c wage-earners in the consumption goods sector and the production of $C = \frac{L_c}{l_c}$ consumption goods. If wage-earners receive a given money-wage w, all of which they spend, the dictator will choose a price of consumption goods, p_c, such that the resulting real wage rate, $w = \frac{w}{p_c}$ will be the subsistence one.

The technical surplus available for gross investment (S) – that is, the consumption goods available with which to employ wage-earners in the investment goods sector – is

$$\frac{I_c}{I_c} - L_c\bar{w}$$

i.e.

$$S = L_c\left[\frac{1}{l_c} - \bar{w}\right] \cdot \left[\frac{1}{l_c} - \bar{w}\right]$$

is consumption goods production per person employed in the consumption goods sector less the real wage per person. The surplus buys

$$\frac{L_c}{\bar{w}}\left[\frac{1}{l_c} - \bar{w}\right]$$

units of labour time in the investment goods sector, and makes possible gross investment (M_t) of

$$\frac{L_c}{l_m\bar{w}}\left[\frac{1}{l_c} - \bar{w}\right]$$

---

[7] Allowance being made for the assumption that machines last for one period only, the results of the following three paragraphs are identical with those of Worswick (1959, 128–30).

machines. Net investment (I) is

$$\frac{L_c}{l_m \bar{w}} \left[\frac{1}{l_c} - \bar{w} \right] - M_{t-1}$$

machines. (Machines are assumed to last for one period only, and the gestation periods of machines and consumption goods are equal.) It is clear that the smaller is the real wage rate, the greater are both gross and net investment.[8] Establishing the subsistence real wage rate maximises total employment (L), employment in the investment goods sector ($L-L_c$), and the production of machines in period t.[9] (It is assumed that machines are made by labour alone.)

The rate of growth of capital goods (g) may be derived as follows:

$$g = \frac{I}{M_{t-1}}$$

This can be written as

$$\frac{\frac{L_c}{l_m \bar{w}} \left[\frac{1}{l_c} - \bar{w} \right]}{M_{t-1}} - 1$$

Now

$$M_{t-1} = m_c C = m_c \frac{L_c}{l_c}$$

---

[8] Both

$$\frac{\partial M_t}{\partial \bar{w}}$$

and

$$\frac{\partial I}{\partial \bar{w}} = -\frac{L_c}{l_c l_m} \frac{1}{(\bar{w})^2} < 0$$

The use of the calculus may be questioned, since two different situations, rather than changes over time, or at a point in time, in the one situation are being compared.

[9] From n. 5

$$L = \frac{1}{\bar{w}} \frac{L_c}{l_c}$$

As

$$\frac{\partial L}{\partial \bar{w}} = -\frac{L_c}{l_c} \frac{1}{(\bar{w})^2} < 0$$

L will be greatest when $\bar{w}$ is as small, as is consistent with wage-earners either staying alive or being willing to work in the industrial sectors of the economy.

Therefore

$$g = \frac{1}{m_c l_m} \left[\frac{1 - l_c \bar{w}}{\bar{w}} \right] - 1$$

That is, g is inversely related to the real wage rate and to the indirect labour cost per unit of consumption goods.[10] The rate of increase of the stock of machines depends upon both the real wage rate and the real amortization element of consumption goods. With a given real amortization element of consumption goods, the rate of increase is greatest when the real wage rate is the subsistence one.

In conclusion, two points can be noted. First, as the current period's production of machines and consumption goods become available only at the *end* of the period, it must be assumed that wage-earners carry, on average, a stock of consumption goods equal to half the current period's production.[11] If the stock of machines is growing, this cannot be done; in these circumstances, M_{t-2} will be less than M_{t-1} and, therefore, C_{t-1} will be less than C_t. This difficulty can be overcome by supposing that the dictator offers for sale on the first day of the current period the consumption goods produced in the previous period. Simultaneously, he offers employment and pays money-wages in the two sectors. Employment in the consumption goods sector is still determined by the stock of machines there (M_{t-1}) and, provided that the dictator chooses a price of consumption goods such that the subsistence real wage rate is established, the surplus of consumption goods, total employment in the investment goods sector, gross and net investment, and the rate of growth of the stock of machines will still be maximised. However, the surplus of consumption goods must now be regarded as the difference between the stock of consumption goods accruing from the previous period and the real wages bill in the consumption goods sector established at the beginning of the current period.

The second point is that the above results depend upon the dictator directing production. There is no guarantee that the decisions of private businesspeople would bring about the same total employment, production, and rate of growth of machines each period. For this to occur, businesspeople in the investment goods sector would have to plan to produce the quantity of machines implied in the equation for M_t above; businesspeople in the consumption goods sector would have to buy

10

$$\frac{\partial r}{\partial \bar{w}} = -\frac{1}{m_c l_m (\bar{w})^2} < 0$$

[11] Johnson (1962, 28.)

this quantity, offer sufficient employment to keep M_{t-1} machines running and, supposing w to be given, set the price of consumption goods which establishes the subsistence real wage rate. Failure to do any of these would mean frustration of plans and lower levels of employment and production.

Kalecki's review of Keynes' *General Theory*

Before Kalecki published his macro theory of distribution in *Econometrica* in 1938, he wrote in Polish a quite extraordinary review article of Keynes' *General Theory* (Kalecki 1936). Unfortunately, as we have seen, the review was not available in full in an English translation until 1982 (see Targetti and Kinda-Hass 1982).[12]

The review shows conclusively that Kalecki had derived independently the principal propositions of Keynes' book, albeit by a different route: for it seems beyond the bounds of credibility that anyone could have written such a masterful account of the new theory and display such a complete command of the issues unless either he had derived them independently or, as in the case of, for example, David Champernowne (1936) and Brian Reddaway (1936), who also wrote remarkable reviews, had been Keynes' pupils when *The General Theory* was being written.[13]

Kalecki's title in English is 'Some remarks on Keynes' theory' – Kalecki was never one to waste words. He thought the book was 'without any doubt, a turning point in the history of economics' (245, all page references are to the 1982 Targetti and Kinda-Hass translation, unless stated otherwise). Kalecki identifies two fundamental parts to the theory. The first is the determination of short-period equilibrium with what he calls 'a given production apparatus' (245), once the level of investment (per unit of time) is given. The second is the determination of the volume of investment itself (this was the principal preoccupation all of his life in Kalecki's writings on the capitalist economy). Kalecki judged that Keynes had solved the first point 'very satisfactorily', though Kalecki in the review decided to give his own interpretation and follow

---

[12] Ferdinando Targetti was a research student of mine in 1972–3 in Cambridge and Bogulslawa Kinda-Hass is a Polish economist who married Targetti. I asked them to translate the review and write a commentary on it for *Australian Economic Papers (AEP)*, of which I was then a joint editor. I regard Kalecki's article as the most important article we ever published in *AEP*.

[13] Austin Robinson also wrote a most perceptive review for the *Economist* (Robinson 1936). It is the only signed review ever to appear in the *Economist* and, even then, it was only his initials, EAGR. Austin complained to Keynes that the journal had changed the title, making it too narrow ('Mr. Keynes on Money') and had altered some of the text. Keynes said it served him right for publishing in the yellow press.

a different path to arrive at Keynes' basic conclusions. Kalecki detected serious deficiencies in the construction as well as the exposition of Keynes' arguments under the second heading, leaving problems that remain still at least partly unsolved. We discuss the second part of Kalecki's essay in chapter 4 on accumulation, in which we set out Keynes' theory of investment and the deficiencies in it as revealed by Kalecki's and others' criticisms. Here we concentrate on the first fundamental part of Keynes' contribution, assuming, as we did above, that the level of planned investment is given.

Kalecki starts by clearing out of the way some preliminary issues: first, the concept of a given production apparatus. Because actual accumulation will change the inherited production apparatus – the stock and capacity of existing capital goods – over any period of time (unless it is assumed that we are in a stationary state), we must choose a period of analysis that is short *enough* to allow us to ignore the effects of a change in the apparatus on output, employment and so on. As output and income are measured per unit of time, they are independent, Kalecki argues, of the length of the period we choose. Kalecki says that Keynes considers a closed system, an economy without either an overseas sector or a government sector. Kalecki follows suit and further assumes that wage-earners do not save so as not to 'obscure some typical characteristics of the functioning of the capitalist economy in general' (246).[14]

Kalecki refers to Keynes' use of the wage unit as his *numéraire*. Though he adopts it for expositional purposes in the review, he is not happy about using it because, in his opinion, it eliminates from the analysis one of the most important factors in the working of the economy – the general movement of prices. Probably he had in mind the proportional movement in prices when money-wages change in the short period.

Kalecki also follows Keynes', in many ways unfortunate, procedure in the light of subsequent interpretations of *The General Theory*, of assuming a constant money-wage. He also assumes that there is a reserve army of labour.[15]

Now the analysis proper begins. The level of production, Kalecki argues, depends upon employment and its allocation to particular

[14] This was always a characteristic of Kalecki's procedures – make simplifying assumptions that allow us to bring out starkly and clearly the processes at work without leaving out essential determinants of the economy's behaviour which are relevant for the particular issue being analysed – surely the mark of an inspired theorist and an example of how important is the role of judgement in the making of a really great economist.

[15] On the face of it, this is a strange assumption to make for though, of course, it – unemployment – was very much in evidence then – and now – yet one of the aims of the analysis of both Keynes and Kalecki was to explain *why* it was there.

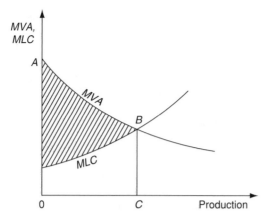

Figure 2.3. Kalecki's firm in the short period.

sectors of the production apparatus. We then go to the basic unit of analysis, the firm.[16] In every firm the level of production (and so the
employment offered in each short period) is determined by the intersection of the curve of marginal revenue which, Kalecki points out,
is horizontal in a freely competitive market – that is to say, the firm is
a price-taker. It is significant that Kalecki, as with Keynes and, later on,
Paul Davidson, Jan Kregel and Nina Shapiro (see, for example, Shapiro
1997), felt then that the new theory of effective demand was independent of the market structures of the economy. Kalecki confirms this by
saying that he will 'deal with a more general case, which includes also
imperfect competition' (247). Raw material costs and depreciation
(which is associated with use) are deducted in order to construct the
curves of marginal value added (*MVA*) and marginal labour costs
(*MLC*), see figure 2.3. Production is determined by the intersection of
the two curves, with all quantities measured in wage units.

Kalecki defines short-period equilibrium as the state where none of
the curves of all the firms moves. The position of the *MLC* curve is

---

[16] It is significant that Lorie Tarshis, who was Kalecki's contemporary and Keynes' pupil,
also always argued that the firm should be the basic unit of analysis. Tarshis' Ph D
dissertation, written in the second half of the 1930s for Cambridge (Tarshis 1939), was
an independent discovery of Kalecki's theory of distribution. It drew on Joan Robinson's
The Economics of Imperfect Competition (1933a) and Kahn's lectures on the economics of
the short period, embedding their findings in the system of *The General Theory*. It is a
tragedy that it was never published; for the reason why, see Harcourt (1982, 1995a;
2001a).

settled because of the assumptions of a given money-wage and production apparatus. So the *MVA* curves when they no longer shift are responsible for equilibrium. 0*ABC* is the total value added provided by the firm when it is producing 0*C*. The shaded area formed by the two curves is the income of the capitalists-entrepreneurs and rentiers, those we called profit-receivers above. *Σ*0*ABC*, the sum of the values added of all firms in the economy, is the national income measured in the wage units; the sum of all the shaded areas is the capitalists' income, profits; and the sum of all the unshaded areas is the global income of the wage-earners, the wage bill.

But social income, Kalecki argues, is the value of consumption (*C*) plus investment (*I*) and because wage-earners are assumed neither to save nor to borrow, the sum of the non-shaded areas coincides with the value of the wage-earners' consumption. The sum of the shaded areas coincides with the profit-receivers' expenditure on consumption and investment – they receive what they spend.

A spontaneous change in the wage-earners' spending cannot occur because they spend what they earn, neither saving nor able to dissave. A spontaneous change in spending by capitalists is possible because they can spend their reserves, or contract new debt, or issue new shares. Suppose they raise their expenditure per unit of time. This will shift the *MVA* curves up to the point where the sum of the shaded areas matches the higher value of their expenditure and 'will force' a higher income of the same amount for them. (The same process could be illustrated in Joan Robinson's diagram above, see p. 12, by supposing that there is a higher level of investment planned so that the wages bill of the investment goods sector is greater and the rectangular hyperbola corresponding to it moves out to subtend the greater area associated with this greater wage bill.)

In the new resulting short-period equilibrium, employment and income of the wage-earners and the value of consumption will be higher, activity having expanded in all branches of industry. It is though, Kalecki stresses, the level of capitalists' spending that is the crucial factor in the determination of short-period equilibrium. The new level of investment also 'forces' saving, the value of which is equal to the value of this investment (even though the capitalists who do the investment are not necessarily those who save – the latter's saving arises from, is created by, the investment of the former). Kalecki adds a proviso: to determine short-period equilibrium in all its details the composition of the magnitudes of consumption and investment needs to be known, but this is a minor consideration relative to the determination of the overall levels of employment and income.

Kalecki writes, therefore, $Y = f(I)$ and $\frac{dY}{dI} = f'(I)$, where $f'(I)$ is the Kahn–Meade–Keynes multiplier. Investment is therefore the factor which decides both short-term equilibrium and the amounts of employment and social income *at a given moment*. Hence why we have high or low levels of employment and production depends on the analysis of the factors governing the amount of investment.

Kalecki stresses that saving does not determine investment but that investment creates saving so that the 'equilibrium between demand for "capital" and supply of "capital" always exists', whatever determines the rate of interest (250).

Kalecki also discusses the effect of a change in the wage unit on short-period equilibrium. He supposes that businesspeople do not infer immediately the consequences for the expected profitability of planned investment of, say, a fall in the value of the wage unit (the relevant case to consider in a situation when the conventional wisdom saw cuts in money-wages as *the* cure for unemployment). They do nothing immediately, prices therefore fall in the same proportion as the wage unit and the 'improvement' in profitability turns out to be 'illusionary' (251).[17] It would be an interesting thought experiment to do Kalecki's case in reverse by considering the impact of a rise in the value of the wage unit.

Summing up, Kalecki's review article is a remarkable contribution both then and now. It sets out succinctly, clearly and persuasively, a theory of the determination of the levels of employment, income *and* the distribution of income in the short period.

The eclecticism of Joan Robinson

Though Joan Robinson was to end up adopting Kalecki's framework, especially in short-period analysis, nevertheless over the years she took a most eclectic stance on the issues of distribution, especially when considering the long period. In the 1930s, while already an enthusiastic Keynesian, when she came to extend the system of *The General Theory* to the long period (Robinson 1937), she was still content to use a neoclassical framework for the distribution aspects of her long-period model. (There is, of course, nothing that surprising about this – both Keynes and Joan Robinson were brought up on Marshallian–Pigovian concepts and approaches.) Joan Robinson exploited the then highly fashionable concept of the elasticity of substitution between capital and

---

[17] If it is asked: 'what about the Pigou or real balances effect?' it should be recalled that Kalecki devastatingly criticised it in 1944, see Kalecki (1944; 1990-7).

labour to determine the distribution of the product between profits and wages and so, because of the different values of the marginal propensities to save from the two income sources (and correspondingly classes), the overall rate of saving.

Even in the 1950s, though she was by then criticising both neoclassical methodology as she saw it and marginal productivity theory, in a wide-ranging article published initially in French and reprinted in English in her second volume of *Collected Economic Papers* (1960), she used a straightforward neoclassical argument, together with arguments related to Harrod's theory of growth and Kalecki's and Kaldor's macroeconomic theories of distribution, to illuminate some possible long-period and longer-term theoretical possibilities and happenings. She did conclude with an enigmatic statement – 'It is at the points where the theory breaks down that it begins to become interesting' (Robinson 1960, 158). Moreover, she also used Kalecki-type arguments for short-period analysis as well as considering the role of bargaining in the labour market between capital and labour as a major determinant of distribution in specific situations. In addition, she examined the link between the determinants of the rate of exploitation in Marxian analysis and the distribution of income between profits and wages in both a Keynesian and a Sraffian framework. Her suggestions here have been most simply and persuasively exposited by one of her younger colleagues, Donald Harris, in his article in the *American Economic Review* (Harris 1975) and, more fully, in his later book (Harris 1978).[18] Her final views are to be found in a joint article with Amit Bhaduri (Bhaduri and Robinson 1980) where, significantly, it is Marx, Kalecki and Sraffa who are named as the key inspirations.

Here we concentrate on the short period, in particular on an especially pithy paragraph in an article Joan Robinson wrote in the *New Left Review* on Piero Sraffa's 1960 book:

In any given situation, with given productive capacity in existence, a higher rate of investment brings about both a higher level of total gross income (through a higher level of employment and utilization of plant) and a higher share of gross profit in gross income (by pushing up prices relatively to money-wage rates). Thus, within reason, investment generates the saving that it requires.

Joan Robinson (1965b; *CEP*, vol. III, 1965, 177)

---

[18] The details of this synthesis are presented in Chapter 7 (pp. 119–21), where all the strands of the discussions above, not only on the distribution of income but also on theories of price-setting and accumulation, are brought together.

We draw on this paragraph to help us make a link between the macro-economic theory of distribution and the underlying theories of the determination of the size of the mark-up that come with it, already sketched in terms of Kalecki's 'degree of monopoly' theory on pp. 11–15. Kalecki's theory of increasing risk, discussed in chapter 3 (p. 51), is to my mind the best explanation of why firms prefer, if they can, to finance their investment expenditure from retained profits. Suppose we ally this insight with the notion that decision-makers in oligopol-istic or imperfectly competitive industries have some discretion as to the level at which they set their prices and so what sizes of mark-up they use. A variant of these ideas became an integral part of Kaldor's analytical structure in the post-war years – oligopolistic firms following a leader-cum-price-setter. Then we may postulate that a dominant determinant, in our simplified model *the* determinant of the size of the mark-up, is the financial requirements of the current programmes of accumulation occurring. Thus, given what finance may be expected to be raised externally, either from banks or capital markets, and what dividend and interest commitments are, prices are assumed to be set so as to ensure the required flows of finance through retained profits.

This, of course, is a description of possible behaviour by individual firms. What are the systemic effects?

We suppose that each time the rate of planned accumulation in the economy takes on a higher level there is a corresponding rise in the mark-ups and in prices determined by the factors outlined above. (Strictly speaking, we should say that each possible level of planned accumulation in the given conditions has associated with it corresponding levels of mark-ups and prices.) As a first approximation and supposing, for the moment, that the money-wage is given for the short period concerned, there will be a given level of saving associated with *any given level* of income, its value being greater, the greater is the value of planned investment, because the share of profits in each income level will be greater.

A very simple diagram (see figure 2.4) can illustrate this story (the algebra behind the diagram may be found in Harcourt 1972, 210–14). On the horizontal axis we measure *real* income, on the vertical axis *nominal* planned saving and investment. We consider four possible levels of *real* planned investment expenditure, supposing that the absolute difference between them is a constant *real* amount. However, because each higher level of planned investment will be associated with a higher price level, the *nominal* investment lines, P_1I_1, P_2I_2, P_3I_3, P_4I_4, are separated by larger and larger amounts. The corresponding saving lines fan out, reflecting the higher levels of saving from each income level as we consider higher levels of prices set.

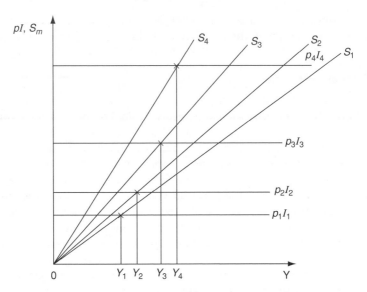

Figure 2.4. Accumulation and internal finance: systematic effects.

It is immediately obvious (*ex post*, all things in economics are obvious when someone else has explained them) that a higher level of accumulation need not necessarily be associated with a higher level of income such as we have come to expect from the operation of the simple Kahn–Meade–Keynes multiplier analysis (and has occurred in figure 2.4). Whether income will be higher, the same, or lower obviously depends on the respective sizes of the movements upwards in the nominal planned investment and corresponding saving schedules. The equilibrium condition is as ever saving equals investment, but now saving may be changed by both the higher level of income and the higher share of profits at any given level of income. Indeed, the result is the private sector near-equivalent of the balanced budget multiplier theorem in the public sector.[19] By itself, a higher level of planned investment has an expansionary effect; by itself a higher level of planned saving out of a given level of income has a contractionary effect, an example of the old-fashioned paradox of thrift.

---

[19] My former graduate student Jorge Araujo even went so far as to dignify this seemingly negative multiplier result with the title 'the *Harcourt effect*' (see Araujo 1999, 338, emphasis in original!).

Hahn's finest hour: the macroeconomic theory of employment and distribution of his PhD dissertation

In the late 1940s, early 1950s Frank Hahn wrote a PhD dissertation at the LSE.[20] He was supervised for a short while by Kaldor and then by Lionel Robbins. His contribution is in some ways the most satisfying version of the Keynesian macro theory of distribution that we have (see Hahn 1972).[21]

The inspirations for Hahn are not only classical – the subtitle is *An Enquiry into the Theory of Distribution* – but also the Keynesian revolution, Samuelson's *Foundations* and the then current theories of entrepreneurial behaviour in situations of uncertainty. The method is Popperian – theory must produce inferences that may be empirically falsifiable, at least in principle. It is an early example of the attempts to provide microeconomic foundations for macroeconomics. It emphasises the Keynesian forces of effective demand and the analysis is set emphatically in the short period, for Hahn will have no truck with long-period equilibrium as a guide to an explanation of the level and changes in the level of the share of wages in the national income. With this volume he stakes a just claim to being an originator of the Keynesian macro theory of distribution. He recognises that Kalecki was there first, but dismisses his theory once we are not analysing the distribution of income in a depression in which there is an unlimited amount of excess capacity, as 'not very helpful when net investment is positive, for then there is no reason why [Kalecki's] basic assumptions [that there is continuous excess capacity, that marginal "overhead" costs are small enough to be ignored and that the concept of an average degree of monopoly is meaningful] should hold' (Hahn 1972, 44–5). Neither does he like Kalecki's 'degree of monopoly' determination of the size of the mark-up because it does not predict the observed changes in the share of profits over the cycle.

The basic tools are the *IS/LM* version of the Keynesian model, used by Hahn to build up the aggregate demand side of the story. The aggregate supply side is built up from the behaviour of the principal decision-makers in the economy, those who decide on the levels of output and employment and on rates of accumulation in the short period,

---

[20] It was not published until 1972 in the Weidenfeld & Nicholson series of famous dissertations unpublished on their immediate completion.

[21] I often teased Frank that it is the best thing he ever did, that it has been downhill ever since.

operating in an environment of uncertainty and having suitably specified utility functions to reflect this. Simply put, the decision-makers
must expect to receive more profits, both absolutely and as a share of
higher levels of national income, in order to offset the increasing disu-
tility associated with organising higher levels of output and employment
and of accumulation to provide the capacity to make these higher levels
possible. This leads, through complicated aggregation procedures, to a
simple relationship between the share of wages in short-period national
income and levels of activity – income – themselves.

On the aggregate demand side, the *IS/LM* construction is adapted to
take into account the distribution of income and accompanying differences in the marginal propensities to save from wages and profits, assuming prices to be more flexible than money-wages in the short period (for
simplicity, money-wages are assumed to be constant). Expected levels of
income play two roles. First, they induce certain rates of accumulation
once the level of output is such that existing capacity cannot produce it,
making allowance for some extra capacity to cope with unexpected
events. There is then a relationship between the share of wages in each
level of income and income itself, such that both the levels of income and
their distribution are such as to provide overall levels of saving that are
just offset by the injections associated with the rates of accumulation
that have in turn been induced by each level of income. Unrealistically,
though Hahn is in good company with Harrod at this point, current
accumulation also provides the capacity needed to produce the current
income that induced it. (The factors behind the *LM* curve do not really
get a look in, at least explicitly.)

The two relationships are shown in figure 2.5. On the vertical axis
we measure the share of wages in national income, on the horizontal
axis, income itself. The *SS* line shows the supply side of the story, the
IS line the demand side. Where they intersect, we have a stable short-
period equilibrium position, with the share of wages (and therefore
profits) being such as to justify both the production of the associated
level of income (aggregate supply) and to provide sufficient aggregate
demand for it. It is a stable equilibrium position, because to the right
of the intersection the forces of excess supply resulting produce
signals that take the economy back to the intersection; similarly, to
the left of the intersection excess demand situations bring about the
same result.

To sum up, all the approaches examined in this chapter share many
of the same ingredients - though each, of course, takes its own unique

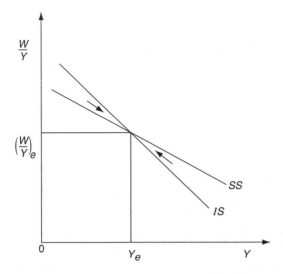

Figure 2.5. Hahn's short-period model of income distribution and activity.

slant on the issues involved. What is clear is that all these macroeco-nomic theories of distribution are consistent with quite different postu-lates about individual firms' behaviour and motivation. What is missing from them, at least explicitly and with the exception of Kalecki's contri-bution, is a theory of the determination of the size of the mark-up, the subject of chapter 3.

3   Post-Keynesian theories of the determination of the mark-up

Wood's 'Golden Age' model

There are a number of papers on the determination of the size of the mark-up in the post-Keynesian literature – Ball (1964); Eichner (1973, 1976); Harcourt and Kenyon (1976; Harcourt 1982); Wood (1975), for example. I concentrate here on the contributions of Adrian Wood and Peter Kenyon and myself because each in their own way reveals the strengths and the limitations of the analysis. James Ball's contribution must be accorded a pioneering role and his contribution has been shamefully neglected in subsequent discussions. The other contributions are relatively well known, with Alfred Eichner's articles and books probably the most widely known. However, I shall not discuss his particular version of the theory, while acknowledging its originality and influence, because it is dependent upon Keynes' theory of investment expenditure, the *mec* and all that as set out in *The General Theory*. As we argue in chapter 4, there are serious flaws – or at least unnecessary limitations – in the details of Keynes' theory. Subsequently, these have been removed by the criticisms and contributions of Abba Lerner, Kalecki, Joan Robinson and Tom Asimakopulos.

We use Wood's model and then Harcourt and Kenyon's model because Wood's analysis is explicitly 'Golden Age', logical time analysis, while Harcourt and Kenyon attempt to make an analysis set in historical time, as advocated by Kalecki (implicitly) and Joan Robinson (explicitly).

Both procedures have their place in the development of theories as Kahn (1959) and Joan Robinson (1962a) have argued – the need to flex intellectual muscles by doing the necessary preliminary work of 'Golden Age' analysis before tackling the more complex task of process analysis, that is to say, an analysis in historical time. Kahn puts the issues extremely clearly:

when one speaks of a Golden Age being preferred [to another one], it means that it would be preferable to be in it . . . to be in it involves *having* been in it for a long time past, and enjoying the legacy of the past in terms of the accumulated stock of capital and the degree of mechanisation. The desirability of a movement from one . . . to the other, and the manner in which it might be smoothly negotiated is . . . [an] important and difficult [problem]. What I have said in this paper . . . is no more than prolegomena to the solution of real problems.

(Kahn 1959, 206–7, emphasis in original)

'Golden Age' analysis allows definitions of concepts and relationships to be set out precisely and exactly, valuable mind-clearing exercises. Historical time analysis, by its nature, is often more fuzzy and vague but has a closer hold on the processes that are actually observed in real life economies.

Joan Robinson (1962a, 23–6) speaks of:

two kinds of economic arguments, each of which is useful in analysis provided that it is not stultified by being confused with the other.
[The first] proceeds by specifying a sufficient number of equations to determine its unknowns, and so finding values for them that are compatible with each other . . . The other . . . specifies a particular set of values obtaining at a moment in time, which are not . . . in equilibrium with each other, and shows how their interactions may be expected to play themselves out. . .
There is much to be learned from *a priori* comparisons of equilibrium positions, but they must be kept in their logical place . . . cannot be applied to actual situations . . . a mortal certainty that . . . particular actual [situations are] not in equilibrium. . .
A model applicable to actual history has to be capable of getting out of equilibrium . . . normally not . . . in it. To construct such a model . . . specify the technical conditions obtaining . . . and the behaviour reactions . . . and then, so to say, dump it down in a particular situation in historic time and work out what will happen next. . .
At any moment in logical time, the past is determined just as much as the future [, there is no causation] . . . In an historical model, causal relations have to be specified. Today is a break in time between an unknown future and an irrevocable past. What happens next will result from the interactions of . . . behaviour . . . Movement can only be forward.

Both Wood's and Harcourt and Kenyon's contributions are written in a Marxian vein, involving a vision of capitalist society and especially of the role of the firm in capitalism as an institution in which accumulation, growth and profit-making are ends in themselves for the decision-makers in charge. In order not only to survive but also to dominate, price-setting and attempted sales are necessary means to these ends. Both sets of authors postulate a direct connection between price-setting on the one hand and the supply of finance through internal funds, given the availability of external funds, needed for planned accumulation on the other.

So what determines the size of the mark-up over costs in such a regime – or, in Wood's case, the rate of profit in sales revenue or target profit margin? Wood's analysis is explicitly long-period in the sense of Joan Robinson's discussion and refers to a price-leader firm in an oligopolistic industry in which the firm's expectations of the future for all respects and purposes are fulfilled.[1] The firm's aim is to maximise the growth of its sales revenue subject to certain constraints – the growth in the demand for its product, growth in its capacity and the availability of finance.

Wood takes growth in aggregate demand as exogenous so that the growth in demand for the product of the firm relates to the effects on such growth of its selling policies *vis-à-vis* those of its competitors. Wood formulates these constraints as two frontiers – the opportunity frontier (*OF*) and the finance frontier (*FF*).

First, *OF*: the opportunities of the firm for growth may be related to sets of alternative pricing, investment and sales policies. Each set is associated with a given average profit margin, a particular rate of growth in sales revenue and a particular level of planned investment expenditure. At some point the firm must encounter a trade-off between a higher profit margin, on the one hand, and a higher rate of growth of sales, on the other. This trade-off is the *OF* of the firm; its position and shape depends upon the efficiency of the firm in controlling its costs.

Investment expenditure is the clue to growth by providing additional capacity and lowering costs (by embodying the latest best-practice techniques through investment in the capital stock). This means that for a given rate of growth of sales revenue, a higher profit margin may be achieved; for a given profit margin, a higher rate of growth of sales revenue may be achieved. For every possible investment coefficient or incremental capital–output ratio, we may define a unique opportunity frontier, *OF*, see figure 3.1, where p is the profit margin and g is the rate of growth of sales revenue. Once the frontier has been reached, the firm has either to cut its price and/or increase its selling costs, both of which actions imply a squeezed profit margin, in order to increase the rate of growth of its sales revenue.

The other constraint is the finance frontier, *FF*, the ability to finance investment expenditure both internally and externally. In figure 3.2 we show the increasing level of p needed to finance the provision of capacity required to make possible a given rate of growth of sales revenue, defined for a particular investment coefficient.

---

[1] 'Long-period equilibrium is not at some date in the future; it is an imaginary state of affairs in which there are no incompatibilities in the existing situation, here and now' (Robinson 1962b; *CEP*, vol. III, 1965, 101).

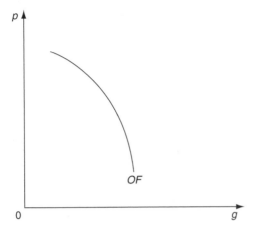

Figure 3.1. Wood's opportunity frontier.

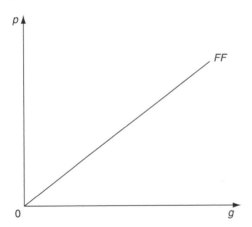

Figure 3.2. Wood's finance frontier.

So the objective of the firm is to maximise g, subject to these two constraints (see figure 3.3). The area *within OF* satisfies the first constraint and the area *above FF* satisfies the second constraint. Where they intercept gives the highest growth possible in the existing situation, g_1, and so p_1 is the chosen profit margin.

So far, we have arbitrarily supposed there to be only one best-practice technique (k) available to the firm at any moment of time. Suppose, though, that there is a complete set of ks available. Then we may

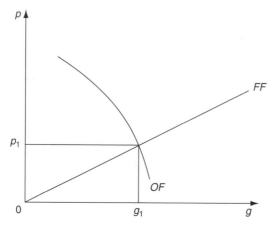

Figure 3.3. The optimum p, g combination.

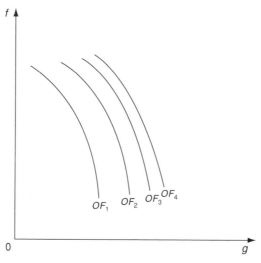

Figure 3.4. The family of opportunity frontiers.

postulate that higher valued ks – more investment-intensive, labour-saving techniques – push the OF out to the right by reducing the average cost of production. This occurs, though, at a decreasing rate, so that for a given rise in investment expenditure we get closer and closer OF curves in the family of OFs (see Figure 3.4).

As for the FF lines, higher values of k imply a rise upwards, or rather a fanning outwards, in the frontier. This is proportionate, as a given proportionate rise in k requires a given proportionate rise in p in order

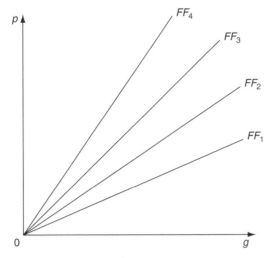

Figure 3.5. The family of finance frontiers.

to finance the rising capacity needed to sustain a given rate of growth (see figure 3.5).

By putting the two frontier families together in the one diagram we generate a concave curve of p, g consistencies (see figure 3.6).

g_4, with corresponding profit margin p_4, is the highest growth rate attainable. k_4 (which defines the positions of the two frontiers labelled 4) will be the chosen technique of production to be embodied through investment in the capital stock of the firm.

The choice of technique in the investment decision: orthodox and post-Keynesian approaches

Wood argues that his account of how the choice of technique puzzle is solved is consistent with a number of different methods or rules followed in both theory and practice – for example, discounted cash flow (DCF) rules, the pay-off period criterion (*POPC*), the accounting rate of profit rule. But in fact this is not so: according to which choice of technique rule is followed, a different technique will be chosen. I illustrate this using some very simple examples. The exercise not only bears on Wood's conjecture but it is also an example of how post-Keynesian and orthodox methods and analysis may result in different answers to real world problems. The orthodox analysis starts from the axiom that we are examining the outcome of an *optimising procedure*. Post-Keynesian analysis starts from observations of real world behaviour which is then simplified

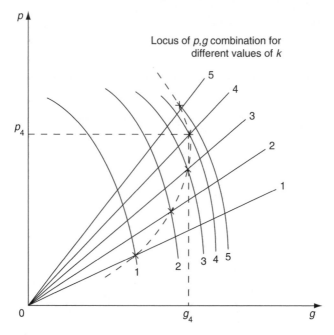

Figure 3.6. Choice of technique in Wood's model.

(hopefully not in a misleading way) in order to make the observations and the analysis of inferences drawn manageable.

We consider three possible choices of technique rules: the net present value rule (*NPV*), the internal rate of return rule (*IRR*) and the pay-off or pay-back period criterion (*POPC*). The first two rules are examples of DCF procedures and are derived from the axioms of profit-maximising and cost-minimising behaviour. They are also taught in business schools, increasingly so in the post-war period. Nevertheless they belong within the canon of the mainstream axiomatic approach and constitute explicit optimising behaviour in themselves and for microeconomic and macro-economic models. The *POPC* is the rule of thumb that business practice has developed to help it cope with decision-making in an environment of inescapable uncertainty. In one form or another, the object is to try to ensure that the outlay on an investment project will have been recouped long before the project itself, and the activities associated with it, have become obsolete, driven out by technical advances and price and cost changes which at the moment when the investment decision is made could not be known.

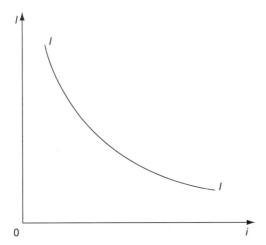

Figure 3.7. The best-practice isoquant, with constant returns to scale.

We consider a simple, constant-returns-to-scale isoquant of best-practice techniques (see figure 3.7, where l is labour input per unit of (unit) output and i is investment input per unit of output). We assume that the length of life of the machines associated with each point on the isoquant is an arbitrary given constant, $\bar{n}$. The question posed is: which points on the isoquant will be chosen by the use of each choice of technique rule? Can we say anything about their order – that is to say, which rule will result in the choice of the more (or most) invest-ment-intensive, less (or least) labour-intensive technique, for example.

The equation of the isoquant is $l = f(i)$, where $f'(i) < 0, f''(i) > 0$.

The NPV rule instructs us to choose the technique that maximises NPV.

Write $V = (p - w_m l) B - i = (p - w_m f(i)) B - i$

where $B = \{(1 + r)^n - 1\}/r(1 + r)^n$ is the present value (PV) of £1 a year for $\bar{n}$ years, p is the expected price assumed to be constant for (at least) $\bar{n}$ years, w_m is the expected money-wage also assumed to be constant for (at least) $\bar{n}$ years and r is the money rate of interest. The first term on the RHS is the PV of expected net receipts from each technique over the lifetime of the investment project, using the money rate of interest as the discount factor. The first-order condition for the choice of the technique with the maximum NPV is:

$$\frac{\delta V}{\delta i} \left(= -w_m B f'(i) - 1 \right) = 0$$

i.e. $f'(i) = -\frac{B'}{w_m}$ where $B' = \frac{1}{B}$.

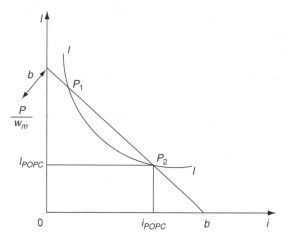

Figure 3.8. Choice of technique by the *POPC*, by Bob Rowthorn as told to Geoff Harcourt.

As $\bar{n} \to \infty$, $B' \to r$ from above.[2]

The *NPV* rule thus tells us to choose the technique that entails that the slope of the isoquant, the marginal rate of substitution of investment for labour inputs, is equal to the ratio of the expected prices of the services of labour and capital goods. w_m is self-explanatory; $B' = \frac{1}{B}$ is the annual expected rental on the relevant capital good, the PV of which over its length of life $\bar{n}$ is equal to i.

One version of the *POPC* is the instruction to choose that technique that maximises expected net receipts over the pay-off period, b, measured in years and much shorter than $\bar{n}$, subject to the constraint that the firm may at least expect to get back its outlay on the project by the end of the pay-off period, i.e. subject to $b(p - w_m l) \geq i$.

This constraint (as an equality) may be written as:

$$l = \frac{p}{w_m} - \frac{1}{bw_m} i$$

(shown as the straight line $b\,b$ in figure 3.8). Anywhere along $b\,b$ the equality form of the constraint is satisfied. Now consider figure 3.8.

In figure 3.8, the $b\,b$ line cuts the isoquant $l\,l$, at P_1 and P_2 (the other possibilities are either a tangency solution or no intersections – in the

---

[2] The same result may be obtained by finding the first-order condition for minimising expected costs (C). Write $C (= w_m f(i) + B') = 0$, i.e. $f'(i) = \frac{B'}{w_m}, \to \frac{r}{w_m}$ as $\bar{n} \to \infty$.

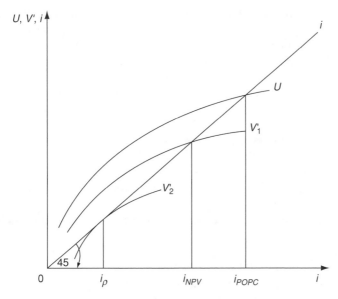

Figure 3.9. Choice of technique, by three different rules.

latter case, no techniques are chosen). P_1 satisfies the constraint but not the instruction to maximise expected net receipts over the pay-off period. So P_2 shows the choice of technique by the *POPC* by satisfying both requirements.

Can we say anything definite about the respective orderings of the investment-intensity resulting from the use of the two rules? The answer is 'yes and no', a typical two-armed economist's answer. To illustrate, suppose that the pay-off period b is five years, an order of magnitude often found in practice.

Then

$$f'(i) \leq \frac{1}{5w_m}$$

at P_2 in figure 3.8. But we know that the value of $f'(i)$ corresponding to the *NPV* rule is

$$f'(i) \geq \frac{1}{5w_m} \left(= \frac{20\%}{w_m} \right)$$

So in this case – one, moreover, most likely to be found in practice – the *NPV* rule results in the choice of a less investment-intensive (more labour-intensive) technique than does the *POPC*. In order to show though that this result is not, alas, general,[3] consider figure 3.9. The U

line shows the (*undiscounted*) value of the sum of the expected net receipts associated with each possible point on the isoquant (and expenditure on investment) for the pay-off period, b. Where U cuts the $0i$ line, a $45°$ line (that ubiquitous tool of our trade) showing i plotted against itself, the sum of expected net receipts for the pay-off period is maximised and the constraint that the project at least 'pay for itself' over the same period is met. i_{POPC} is therefore the technique chosen (see figure 3.9).

Assume for the moment that $\bar{n} = b$. The curve V' shows the *discounted* value of the sum of the expected net receipts associated with each point on the isoquant. The distance between V' and $0i$ (NPV) is maximised at the level of investment expenditure where the two curves are parallel to one another – this is the choice of technique chosen by the NPV rule (see i_{NPV} in figure 3.9). Clearly, in this case, it is less investment-intensive than i_{POPC}.

But clearly we cannot suppose that $\bar{n} = b$, in general it will be greater, often much greater. This implies that as we consider higher and higher values of $\bar{n}$, the V' curve rises and must eventually reach a position where it is parallel to $0i$ to the *right* of the intersection of the U curve with $0i$, so that the ordering of choice is reversed.

Finally, what can we say about the respective orderings implied by using the internal rate of return (ρ) rule: choose the technique associated with the highest internal rate of return (IRR), where the IRR is that rate of interest which, when used as a discount factor, makes the PV of the sum of the expected net receipts of an investment project just equal to the initial outlay on the project? To find the outcome of this rule in figure 3.9, consider higher and higher values of r. This will lower the V' curve but not in a parallel manner, as the higher values of the rate of interest have greater effects on the PVs of the expected net receipts of the more investment-intensive techniques. When the curve has fallen so that all of it except one point lies below $0i$, that point being a point of tangency (see V_2' in figure 3.9), we have found the choice of technique by the IRR rule (see i_ρ in figure 3.9). It clearly is a less investment-intensive, more labour-intensive technique than those chosen by the other two rules. So in practice we may say the ordering is most likely to be, in terms of investment-intensity, $POPC > NPV > \rho$.[4]

---

[3] Many years ago I thought that it was, but Jim Mirlees found a mistake (a wrong sign) in my algebra!

[4] In long-period perfectly competitive equilibrium with no uncertainty, the choices of technique by the two DCF procedures coincide and, because there is no uncertainty, the *POPC* is irrelevant.

Harcourt and Kenyon's model in historical time

We set out the attempt by Peter Kenyon and myself to model 'pricing and the investment decision' in historical time (see Harcourt and Kenyon 1976; Harcourt 1982).[5] If anything of interest is to be said about actual economic behaviour, the post-Keynesian theory of the firm must be constructed by setting out initial conditions; the firm's current stock of capital goods; the current price(s) of its product(s); the existing money-wage rate; the structure of the industry; and the extent of vertical integration. The next moves are to specify the expectations of the firm with regard to its costs and the demand for its product(s) in the immediate and more distant future. We then need to specify an objective function – the aims of the firm – and some rules for pursuing them. We are then in a position to follow causal sequences in historical time, at the same time allowing the story to unfold with appropriate feedback effects on expectations.

There are at least three aspects of, dimensions to, the investment decision of a firm: first, the amount of extra capacity to be installed each period; secondly, the sort of investment to be done (the choice of technique decision); thirdly, the cost and method of finance.[6]

Consider a manufacturing firm that is a price-leader in an oligopolistic environment. We suppose that it produces only one product. The methods of production are fixed in the short period, with given input–output coefficients determining the technique of production for each vintage of plant laid down by past accumulation. We have constant wage and raw material costs up to the point of technically determined, full-capacity utilisation of each vintage of plant. We suppose that the firm

---

[5] The paper had a long gestation period. I wrote a first draft in Cambridge in 1966 and submitted it to the *Bulletin* of the Oxford Institute of Economics and Statistics. It was rejected because of a logical flaw in the argument but the referee liked the approach. So when Peter came to work with me in Adelaide for a Master's degree in the early 1970s, I suggested to him that he work in this general area. In 1974, he gave a progress report on his research to a seminar at Adelaide University. I had just spent three weeks in hospital following a major operation and I went to the seminar literally on my way home from hospital. No doubt the rarefied atmosphere of the hospital and the seminar cleared my head. Listening to Peter, I suddenly saw the solution to the logical flaw. As soon as I returned home after the seminar, in a state of a great excitement, I set out the skeleton of the structure of the model. I subsequently asked Peter to put the flesh of research and scholarship on it. We had to wait a couple of years before the paper was published. (I tell the story why in George Shepherd's absorbing volume *Rejected*, Shepherd 1994, 75–6.) Unfortunately, during my various moves since then, I have lost the file relating to this narrative so that I cannot now remember what the logical flaw was!

[6] We abstract here from the choice of new products, the production of which is preceded by investment, clearly an increasingly important aspect of the investment decision.

wants to maximise the growth in the value of its sales revenue, subject to a minimum profit constraint, that it wants to retain the bulk of its profits and that the greater part of current investment expenditure is financed from internal sources. Our firm, therefore, is in many respects identical to Wood's firm (and to Kaldor's typical firm).

There are no forces pushing the firm to full-capacity utilisation of plant (such as there are in the competitive market structures analysed by the classical economists and Marx, and in Joan Robinson's competitive case in her exposition of Kalecki's model, see chapter 2, p. 14). In fact, having surplus capacity that allows firms to pounce when there is a sudden unexpected increase in demand is a good strategy for oligopolists to pursue. (That is why Hahn's criticism of Kalecki's analysis as depression economics rather misses its mark, see chapter 2, p. 29).

The firm has to decide on its price, its mark-up on costs and its desired level of productive capacity. These decisions are related to the three aspects of the investment decisions outlined above. The firm has a double objective in setting its price and mark-up – first, to be consistent with its expectations, in general terms, of the demand for its product and, secondly, to provide enough retained profits to finance its investment. When the firm is successful in setting a mark-up and price which yields sufficient retained profits to allow capacity to expand in the desired manner in step with the growth in market demand, a stable interaction is possible in which investment keeps capacity growing in step with demand in a tranquil world of stable market shares (the ultimate outcome of Wood's analysis, of course).

Now we make the analysis more formal, considering, first, the case of a single 'best-practice' technique available at any moment of time. (We discuss below, pp. 49–50, the choice of technique when there are several 'best-practice' techniques known at a point of time.) We divide time into price-setting and investment-planning periods, periods that are much longer than those appropriate for short-period production.[7]

There is no reason why the two periods should coincide in length, but sometimes both decisions are made on the same 'day' even though price decisions may be revamped in the light of additional information before the investment plans have been fully implemented. Investment plans, too, may be revamped in the light of new information, a characteristic that featured prominently in Kalecki's analysis of investment decision-making. However, for simplicity, we assume that both periods

---

[7] In *The General Theory*, price-setting was done by the competitive market, not by individual firms, but the production and employment decisions correspond to our procedures.

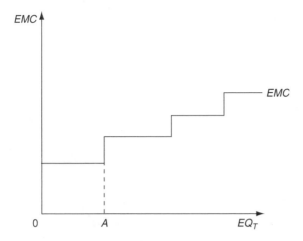

Figure 3.10. Expected marginal costs of production of existing vintages.

are of the same length, that both decisions are made on the same 'day' and are held for that period. The firm has expectations about prices, its costs as well as its own sales and quantities and likely scrap values of its equipment. It also knows *now* the capacity that will be in operation by the start of the current period.

We can draw an expected marginal cost curve (EMC) for existing vintages of the firm's stock of capital goods for the next period (see figure 3.10). On the vertical axis we measure expected costs (EMC), on the horizontal axis, expected total quantities (EQ_T). We have a step function, EMC, each step of which shows the amount of output that can be catered for by the different vintages installed in previous periods. Each marginal cost is the marginal cost of production plus scrap value (for simplicity, assumed to be zero). For example, $0A$ is the output that can be catered for by the most recently installed capacity, the outcome of the investment plans and expenditure of the previous period. We assume that the latest vintages are always associated with lower prime costs.

From this EMC function, and given the scrapping rule in operation and the firm's expectation of demand at various prices, we can find the amounts of new capacity that would have to be provided for the next period at the various possible prices.

So we have an expected sales, expected price relationship, *dd*, drawn as a near-vertical line to indicate the *relative* independence of expected quantities – 'normal' quantities – over a range of possible prices (see figure 3.11). This reflects the extent of the firm's discretion in setting prices. We take it that output rather than price is more likely to fluctuate

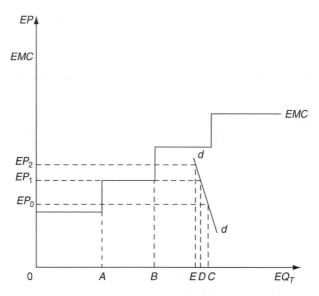

Figure 3.11. Price, output and output shortfall.

over the cycle, and that the firm has in mind 'normal' output growth and a price which allows enough capacity to be installed to cope with 'normal' output growth.

If the price were set between EP_0 and just below EP_1, existing capacity would cater for production of $0A$ and production between AC and AD would need to be catered for by the investment plans of the current period, assuming that existing plant is scrapped (or retired to emergency standby when $EMC \geq$ the set price). If the price were between EP_1 and EP_2, $0B$ would be produced by the (then) existing capacity and BD to BE by new plants. This information allows us to draw the expected price, output from *new* investment (EP_N) relationship as p_1p_1 (see figure 3.12), where we plot expected prices against the expected quantities corresponding to these prices.

If there is only one 'best-practice' technique at any moment of time then, given expectations with respect to marginal costs and demand during the current period, pay-out ratios and the proportion of investment expenditure that can be financed externally, the firm will have a definite set of expectations concerning the flow of retained profits over the current period available to finance investment expenditure. This is the relationship, p_2p_2, in figure 3.13. It shows what extra capacity can be installed at each possible price level.

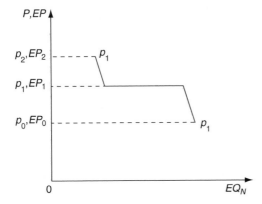

Figure 3.12. Price, quantity from new capacity.

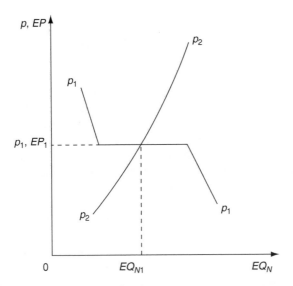

Figure 3.13. Determination of extra capacity needed.

$p_2 p_2$ and $p_1 p_1$ intersect to give a price of p_1 and an output of EQ_{N1}. Only at this point are the two sets of expectations consistent – that is to say, what is to be produced with the new capacity (together with the old) can be sold at that price and the price provides the finance to 'pay' for it. Anywhere else, there are either insufficient funds or more than sufficient

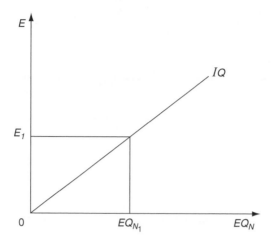

Figure 3.14. Determination of investment expenditure.

funds relative to the finance required for the investment to provide the extra capacity to produce the extra output which can be sold at that price.

It should be noted that we are dealing with both current prices and expected prices and that there is a two-period coincidence between this period's price and the next. But that price may be inconsistent with the demand conditions of the period following it. This is an implication of 'sharpening up' the analysis by including discrete points and periods in time. In general, the price set will be consistent with raising funds and with demand conditions in the future, until conditions so change that decisions concerning prices and investment have to be revised.

When there is only one 'best-practice' technique there is a unique relationship (IQ) between investment spending (E) and expected output to be catered for (EQ_N). This is shown in figure 3.14. For example, with expected output of EQ_{N1} we need investment expenditure of E_1. We suppose that the firm knows the prices of investment goods either because it is a price-taker or that it is a monopsonist that sets the price when it orders the required equipment, or when it constructs the equipment itself.

The pay-out ratio is given in any short period (it reflects the strength of merger movements, the standing of the firm's shares on the stock exchange and so on). The price set by the firm will be both a maximum and a minimum price; while the firm will not wish to prejudice further sales by charging a price higher than is needed for the finance of its

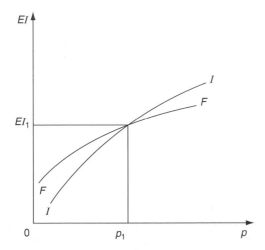

Figure 3.15. Determination of price and investment expenditure with choice of technique.

planned investment expenditure of the next period, it cannot charge a lower price and meet its immediate goals.

When we introduce the choice of techniques into the analysis, we have a problem. There are now a number of ways of producing a level and a unit of output, and therefore differing levels of investment expenditure will be needed for each level of output and so different prices will be needed to raise the funds to finance them. Moreover, which technique is chosen will not itself be independent of price, regardless of the investment-decision rule used (except in a very special case of the *NPV* rule). p_2p_2 in figure 3.13 is not now a unique relationship but one of a *family of such relationships* which depend on price and the investment-decision rule used. There are three possible relationships between two variables, EP and EQ_N. EQ_N determines the extra capacity required, which in turn depends upon the rule and the price. But EQ_N also depends upon price, which in turn depends upon the investment-decision rule, given the pay-out ratio and the proportion of investment expenditure to be financed from external funds.

We have assumed that expected levels of output are relatively independent of price over a certain range of prices (see *dd* in figure 3.11). We can define two relationships, one concerning what can be spent, the other what can be raised. The first is between investment expenditure and price, taking as given the investment-decision rule used, the current price of investment goods and the *level of output* to be catered for by new capacity. This is the *II* curve in figure 3.15, where investment expenditure is plotted on the vertical axis and price on the horizontal axis. The second relationship is between price and funds *available* for investment expenditure, taking as given the firm's expectations with respect to costs, sales during the current period, the pay-out ratio and sources of external finance. This is the *FF* curve in figure 3.15. There is a family of *FF* curves, each of which corresponds to a specific level of output to be catered for. We show only one here, as we take output as given.

There is no reason why the two curves should coincide because the relationships are independent of each other. We now show that there are reasons why they will always diverge either side of the intersection at the point EI_1, p_1 in figure 3.15.

With the *POPC* as the investment-decision rule, with higher and higher prices, the investment intensity increases but at a decreasing rate. The isoquant, *ll*, in figure 3.8 (p. 40) is convex to the origin and so given rises in price mean smaller and smaller distances between the intersection of *ll* and the constraint line, *bb*. The funds available for financing investment will rise at a decreasing rate, giving the *FF* curve its shape. However, at low prices, relatively low investment-intensive techniques will be chosen while the flow of internal funds generated at that level of output will be greater than that which is needed to finance them. Exactly the opposite is the case for high prices – the funds generated will be less than are needed for the relatively high investment-intensive techniques chosen. Hence we get a unique intersection of the two curves.

If the price so indicated falls within the range at which output may be regarded as independent of price, that is the end of the story. If not, then the pay-out ratio and/or the investment-decision rule will have to adjust until a price is found which serves both to finance investment expenditure and be consistent with the expected level of output; or the expected level of output will have to change until a price is found which will do the financing task – *II* and *FF* have to change until we have a price compatible with all expectation sets and goals of the firm.[8]

Why is internal finance to be preferred?: Kalecki's theory of increasing risk

We have already talked a lot about the desire of firms for internal funds – retained profits – as the preferred means of financing their investment

---

[8] With the *NPV* rule as we have set it out, we have a horizontal *II* line as different price levels do not affect the choice of technique. The V' curves in figure 3.9 are moved up or down in a *parallel* fashion by different levels of price.

expenditure. The best explanation of why firms want them that I have found in the literature is Kalecki's famous article, 'The principle of increasing risk', first published in 1937 and later republished as 'Entrepreneurial capital and risk' in his 1971 *Essays* (and reprinted in a revised form in vol. I (1990) of his *Collected Works*, Kalecki 1990-7). Kalecki starts by saying that (at the time when he was writing) two factors are usually mentioned as limiting the size of firms. The first is diseconomies of large-scale production. The second is the limitation of the size of the market, so that expansion of sales by a firm sooner or later requires either unprofitable reductions in price or unprofitable increases in selling costs (we have already met these factors in our discussion of Wood's model, see p. 34).

Kalecki is not convinced by the first reason. He argues that once a plant with minimum costs in the existing situation has been discovered, it may be duplicated, giving rise to lumpy rather than smoothly continuous advance, but possible nevertheless. He concedes that limitation by the size of the market is real enough, but then poses the question: why do we have large and small firms operating in the same industry – should they not all be the same size?

So what is the reason? Kalecki singles out the amount of *entrepreneurial capital*, the amount of capital owned by the firm itself, as being a factor of 'decisive importance' (Kalecki 1971, 105). He argues that access to the capital market, the amount of rentier capital a firm may hope to obtain from the stock exchange, is determined to a large extent by the amount of its own (entrepreneurial) capital. Why? Suppose that the firm tries to place a bond issue that is 'too large' in relation to its own capital. It would not be subscribed in full. Even if the firm were to offer a rate of interest higher than that currently prevailing, that in itself could give rise to misgivings concerning the firm's solvency.[9]

There is also what Kalecki calls 'increasing risk' associated with the expansion of the firm. The greater is the amount of investment in relation to the size of existing entrepreneurial capital, the greater will be the reduction in the entrepreneur's income in the event of an unsuccessful business venture. Suppose that an entrepreneur fails to receive any return at all on his/her business in a particular period. If only part of his/her capital is in the business, the other part being in first-rate bonds, the entrepreneur will receive at least some net interest income. But if all of his/her capital is invested in the business, he/she gets nothing.

---

[9] Similar arguments were made in the 1980s by Stiglitz and Weiss in a series of papers on credit rationing and the theory of markets when price and quality are interrelated, negatively in this case (see, for example, Stiglitz and Weiss 1981, 1983).

And if there has been borrowing, there is a net loss which, if it continues, will eventually drive the firm out of business. (Kalecki wrote at this point with personal feeling, for his father's business had gone into bankruptcy when Kalecki was a university student.)

The size of the firm therefore depends on the size of its entrepreneurial capital, both through its influence on capacity to borrow and through its effect on the degree of risk. Differences in the sizes of firms arise from differences in the sizes of their entrepreneurial capital. Those firms with large entrepreneurial capital can more easily obtain funds for large investment projects, while those with small entrepreneurial capital may not – indeed, below a certain size they may have no access at all to capital markets. (Kalecki may have had in mind the so-called 'Macmillan gap' in the UK capital market at that time, see Henderson 1951). There is a hint here of a cumulative causation process, first identified in the Gospel according to Saint Matthew, chapter 25, verses 28 and 29. Jesus concluded the parable of the talents as follows: 'For unto everyone that hath shall be given, and he shall have abundance: but from him who hath not shall be taken away even that which he hath.'[10]

The principal corollary of the preceding discussion is that the expansion of the firm depends principally on its accumulation of capital financed out of current profits. This allows the firm to undertake new investment without encountering obstacles of a limited capital market for its financial assets and 'increasing risk'. Saving from current profits may be directly invested in the firm and the consequent increases in the size of the firm and its entrepreneurial capital in turn makes it possible to contract new loans.

What then of joint stock companies (Kalecki was criticised for not dealing explicitly with this institutional form in the original version of his views, see Kalecki (1990–7; CW, vol. I, 516)) Kalecki argues that if a company issues debentures, the situation is much the same: the greater is the size of the issue, the more the ability to pay dividends (and retain profits) is impaired in the event of an unsuccessful business venture. The same argument may be applied to the issue of preference shares because they constitute a fixed return with a prior claim on profits before dividends.

What may we say of ordinary shares, what are the limits associated with their existence and issue? First, in a typical example of Kalecki's wry

---

[10] We discuss cumulative causation processes, which are increasingly a hallmark of the post-Keynesian approach, in more detail below, (see chapter 8, pp. 145–7). I am indebted to Jonathan Collis who provided me with the quote above from the Authorised Version of the Bible.

irony, a joint stock company is not a 'brotherhood of shareholders' (Kalecki, 1971, 107) but is more likely to be managed, or at least dominated, by a controlling group of large shareholders. The rest of the shareholders therefore do not differ from a category who hold bonds but bonds with a flexible rate of interest (as opposed to a fixed rate with a prior claim on profits).[11] If the first group are to keep control, the company cannot sell an unlimited amount of shares to the public (though the device of a holding company does give the controlling group some extra flexibility). Nevertheless, the problem of retaining control provides *some* restraining influence on their behaviour.

Moreover, investment financed by an issue of shares may not increase profits as much as the issue increases the company's share and reserve capital – that is to say, marginal returns may well be less than existing average returns. If this were to be the case, the dividends of the old shareholders in general and the controlling group in particular would be squeezed. The risk will be greater, the greater is the size of the new issue, a further example of the operation of the principle of increasing risk.

The amount of shares issued is also restricted by the limited market for the shares of a given company. Because people and institutions diversify their portfolios (it will be remembered that Jim Tobin received the Nobel Prize, as he told reporters who asked him to explain his contribution in simple terms, for discovering that you should not put all your eggs in one basket), it is not possible to place more than a certain amount of shares of a given company at a price which satisfies the old, already existing shareholders.

So joint stock companies also experience definite limits on their expansion, and they too depend on financing accumulation out of their current profits. Increases in entrepreneurial capital are not confined in this case only to undistributed profits because new shares could also be sold to the controlling group of shareholders and bought from their

---

[11] It was usually at this point in the argument when I lectured on Kalecki's article, that I told the story of the classic 1956 film, 'The Solid Gold Cadillac'. It starred Judy Holliday, who was given the seemingly non-job of agony aunt in the company after she had asked some, on the surface, simplistic but in fact deeply disturbing questions at an annual meeting of shareholders. Needless to say, the directors were all crooks (with the exception of an honest hero played by Paul Douglas). Through her subsequent correspondence and contact with small shareholders, often widows and orphans, Judy acquired their proxy votes which accumulated to a majority of votes. This allowed her to outvote the crooked directors and, with the help of our hero, now her's too, to outwit and disgrace them and so to drive off into the sunset, with her beau, of course, in a solid gold Cadillac. This closing scene was the only time when the film was shot in Technicolor. I suggested that the film should be required viewing for those who wished to understand the true nature of corporate capitalism.

own saving. This in turn allows expansion of the share issue without disturbing or weakening their control.

The growth in the size of the firm through internal accumulation reduces the risk associated with a *given* amount of shares sold to the public in order to finance new investment. Investment in the firm without resource to the public widens the effect of the firm's shares on the stock market, for the larger in general is the firm, the more important is its role in the share market.

Kalecki (1971, 109) concludes:

The limitation of the size of the firm by the availability of entrepreneurial capital goes to the very heart of the capitalist system. Many economists assume, at least in their abstract theory, a state of business democracy where anybody endowed with entrepreneurial ability can obtain capital for starting a business venture. This picture of the activities of the 'pure' entrepreneur is, to put it mildly, unrealistic. The most important prerequisite for becoming an entrepreneur is the *ownership* of capital.

The above considerations are of great importance for the theory of determination of investment. One of the important factors of investment decisions is the accumulation of firms' capital out of current profits.   (emphasis in original)

Hence our emphasis above on pricing and the investment decision and the role of prices in raising finance for investment through retained profits.

4   Macroeconomic theories of accumulation

Keynes' theory: right ingredients, wrong recipe

Keynes himself was never comfortable with the analysis and the presentation of his theory of investment in chapter 11 of *The General Theory*, 'The marginal efficiency of capital'. He much preferred the freedom from formal constraints to be found in his exposition in the exhilarating chapter 12, 'The state of long-term expectation'. It contains some of his finest and most memorable passages – for example, on the nature and operation of the stock exchange and the consequences for the behaviour of the economy when enterprise and speculation change places:

> If I may be allowed to appropriate the term *speculation* for the activity of forecasting the psychology of the market, and the term *enterprise* for the activity of forecasting the prospective yield of assets over their whole life, it is by no means always the case that speculation predominates over enterprise . . . Speculators may do no harm as bubbles on a steady stream of enterprise. But the position is serious when enterprise becomes the bubble on a whirlpool of speculation. When the capital development of the country becomes the by-product of the activities of a casino, the job is likely to be ill-done. The measure of success attained by Wall Street, regarded as the institution of which the proper social purpose is to direct new investment into the most profitable channels in terms of future yield, cannot be claimed as one of the outstanding triumphs of *laissez-faire* capitalism.   Keynes (1936; *CW*, vol. VII, 1973, 158–9, emphasis in original)

His change of mood as between the two chapters was explained succinctly in a letter to Gerald Shove (21 April 1936):

> But you [Shove] ought not to feel inhibited by a difficulty in making the solution precise. It may be that a part of the error in the classical analysis is due to that attempt. As soon as one is dealing with the influence of expectations and of transitory experience, one is, in the nature of things, outside the realm of the formally exact.   Keynes (1973; *CW*, vol. XIV, 1973, 2).[1]

---

[1] Shove had written to Keynes (15 April 1936) that he had 'enjoyed reading the *General Theory* very much'. Shove thought Keynes was 'too kind to the 'classical' analysis as applied to the individual industry and firm . . . [Shove] been groping all these years after a

As the writings on the links between Keynes' philosophy and his economics of the last twenty-five years and more have made clear, Keynes felt that in a subject such as economics there was a whole spectrum of languages available and appropriate, according to the issues, or aspects of issues, being discussed. They ran all the way from intuition and poetry through lawyer-like arguments to mathematics and formal logic. He attempted to use the last set of languages in chapter 11. However, though the ingredients of his arguments are surely correct, the recipe he provided for mixing them together is not, as subsequent criticisms by Kalecki, Joan Robinson and Anathanasios (Tom) Asimakopulos have made clear. Even those who are more in agreement with the mode and content of analysis of chapter 11 – for example, Paul Davidson and Luigi Pasinetti – have nevertheless changed significantly the exposition of Keynes' theory (see Davidson 1972; Pasinetti 1997).

Before we discuss their criticisms, let us briefly remind ourselves of the essence of Keynes' theory in chapter 11. His principal object was to determine the rate of planned and actual expenditure on investment goods in a given macroeconomic short period. His principal concept was the marginal efficiency of capital (*mec*). (As we argue below, it should have been the marginal efficiency of investment, (*mei*, ρ). The *mec* is then a special case of the *mei* when gross investment expenditure serves only to maintain the given stock of capital goods intact – that is to say, is confined to replacement expenditure alone.) Keynes defined the *mei* as the rate of interest which, when used as the discount factor, brought the present value of the sum of the expected net receipts over the lifetime of an investment project into equality with the outlay on the project. For simplicity, assume that the outlay occurs at the start of the project (*S*) and the expected net receipts (expected additional sales revenues less expected additional variable costs per year), $q_i, i = 1 \ldots n$, are expected to come in over a period of n years in the future. (We ignore any scrap value at the end of the project.) Then the *mei*, ρ, is defined as follows:

$$S = \sum_{i=1}^{n} \frac{q_i}{(1 + \rho)^i} \tag{4.1}$$

Keynes gave two reasons why the higher was the rate of planned investment in any given situation, ρ, both individually and overall, as it were, would be expected to be lower. The first reason was a short-term one. The higher is the level of production in the capital goods trades in the

re-statement of it . . . stressing in particular 'expectations' and the influence of current and immediate past experiences upon them. But I can't make it precise'. (Shove in Keynes 1973; *CW*, vol. XIV, 1973, 1).

short period when overall capacity is taken as given, the higher is the marginal cost of production, because of diminishing returns to the variable factors in the short period and because of a tendency at high levels of utilisation for money-wages to be higher. (Keynes 'always regarded decreasing physical returns in the short period as one of the very few incontrovertible propositions of our miserable subject!', Keynes to Ohlin, 29 April 1937 (1973; *CW*, vol. XIV, 1973, 190)). As Keynes in *The General Theory* usually assumed free competition and so marginal cost pricing in all industries, the higher is the rate of production, the higher would be the value of S, reflecting the higher marginal costs of production of capital goods. The only way the equality between the LHS and the RHS of (4.1) may be preserved is for ρ to have a lower value. Total investment expenditure would be pushed, Keynes argued, to the point where $\rho = r$, where r is the money rate of interest.

The second reason which reinforced this tendency was, Keynes argued, more long-term. The greater is the rate of investment undertaken now, the greater will be the amount of capacity available in future periods. This meant that the short-period supply curves of the capital and other goods industries would be further and further to the right, the greater is the rate of investment occurring now. Keynes also assumed that the longer-term demand schedules for the products of all industries using these capital stocks could be taken as given. Together, this implied lower values of the q_is, the higher is the rate of investment now (because the expected prices of products would be lower, the more to the right were the intersections of the supply curves with the given downward-sloping demand curves). So, again, the equality between the LHS and RHS of (4.1) could be only maintained by lower values of ρ. This in stark outline is Keynes' theory in chapter 11.

Lerner's internal critique

Abba Lerner in a number of places (for example, Lerner 1944), pointed out that Keynes had failed to distinguish between the *mei* and the *mec*. Properly stated *within Keynes' own framework*, Lerner argued, Keynes' theory consisted of two propositions:

(1) In full stock-flow equilibrium,

$$mec = mei = r$$

(2) In short-period flow equilibrium (in which Keynes was primarily interested)

$$mei = r, \text{ with both } < mec$$

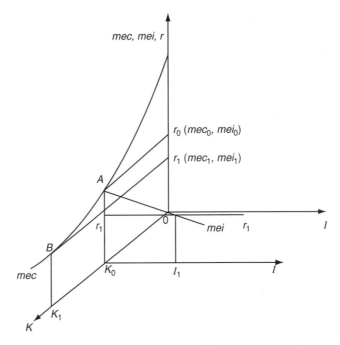

Figure 4.1. Lerner's determination of Keynes' theory of investment.

Lerner illustrates these propositions by means of a well-known three-dimensional diagram (see figure 4.1). On the vertical axis, we measure *mec*, *mei* and *r*. On one horizontal axis, we measure the optimal stocks of capital goods (K) implied by different values of *r* in a given situation. They are the stocks that will give the optimum combinations of the services of the capital goods combined with the services of labour to produce output in the existing conditions at each value of *r*. For example, with an (exogenously given) value of r_0, the optimal stock is $0K_0$, and $mec = mei = r_0$, as only replacement investment is needed to maintain $0K_0$: proposition (1).

Now consider a lower value of *r*, r_1. The optimum stock of capital goods becomes $0K_1$. (Keynes and Lerner took it for granted that a lower value of *r* implies a higher capital–output and capital–labour ratio for 'good' neoclassical reasons. Needless to say, this proposition came under attack during the capital theory debates of the 1950s–1970s, see appendix 2, pp. 181–4.) A gap has now opened up between *r* and the expected profitability of investment expenditure, *mec* and $mei = \rho$. But investment is a *flow* and so we must ask how fast, other things being equal, may the economy move from $0K_0$ to $0K_1$. Only if capacity was infinite and marginal costs of production of capital goods constant could the gap be closed instantaneously by implementing an infinite rate of investment. But on Keynes' and Lerner's reasoning, the higher is the flow rate of investment at any moment of time, the lower is the *mei* – see the curve starting out from where $mec_0 = mei_0 = r_0$ and then taking on lower and lower values of the *mei* as higher and higher values of investment expenditure are considered. At a rate of investment $K_0 I_1$, $mei_1 = r_1$ and both are less than mec_0: proposition (2).

In the next period, this amount of accumulation will have been added to the stock of capital goods and a new *mei* investment schedule, starting at a lower value of *mec* (but one still greater than r_1, so that investment opportunities remain) becomes relevant. Period by period, the economy 'converges' on $0K_1$, with lower and lower rates of investment per period. At $0K_1$ full stock-flow equilibrium is attained again with lower values of *mec, mei* and r.[2]

This, 'tidied up' by Lerner, is Keynes' theory of investment in chapter 11.[3]

In chapter 12, 'animal spirits' take over:

Even apart from the instability due to speculation, there is instability due to the characteristic of human nature that a large proportion of our positive activities depend upon spontaneous optimism rather than a mathematical expectation, whether moral or hedonistic or economic. Most, probably, of our decisions to do something positive, the full consequences of which will be drawn out over many days to come, can only be taken as a result of animal spirits – of a spontaneous urge to action rather than inaction, and not as the outcome of a weighted average of quantitative benefits multiplied by quantitative probabilities. Enterprise only pretends to itself to be mainly activated by the statements of its own prospectus, however candid and sincere. Only a little more than an expedition to the South Pole, is it based upon an exact calculation of benefits to come. Thus if animal spirits are dimmed and the spontaneous optimism falters, leaving us to depend on nothing but a mathematical expectation, enterprise will fade and die; – though fears of a loss may have a basis no more reasonable than hopes of profit had before.   Keynes (1936; *CW*, vol. VII, 1973, 161–2)

---

[2] Strictly speaking, the approach is only asymptotic.
[3] Pasinetti (1997) argues that at any moment of time there is a certain stock of investment opportunities available, which may be ordered by the values of their respective ρs. If lower values of r are considered, more items in the stock will be deemed to be profitable and investment expenditure will be greater, regardless of the respective capital–output and respective capital–labour ratios of the projects.

Kalecki's, Joan Robinson's and Asimakopulos' Keynesian critique

At first sight Keynes' and Lerner's set of arguments may seem convincing. Let us examine the first. Implicit in the argument is a sort of rational expectations argument. Individual decision-makers[4] must be supposed to use in their calculations of the expected rates of profit on their investment projects (i.e. their *mei*s or ρs) *not* the *existing* prices of capital goods but instead the ultimately-to-be-established equilibrium prices associated with the economy-wide equilibrium position. Only then will the values of ρ be such that *mei = r*. Otherwise, the collective decisions of the decision-makers (in the sense of *our* putting together of *their* individual decisions) will not establish the economy-wide rate of investment that establishes the values of ρ that imply that $\rho = r$. Now it may appear possible in some circumstances at least to postulate businesspeople with such firm and correct expectations of the prices of their capital goods as to bring this overall result about. But surely it is more reasonable to suppose that, in making investment decisions, they use the existing values of S, existing values which are non-equilibrium prices in the sense above, in which case, overall investment will not then be such as to make $\rho = r$. This is especially so if we suppose that investment goods are made and priced to order. So we may conclude that Keynes' first argument is logical, given special assumptions, but not really plausible as an explanation of what actually happens.

What of his second argument? Here the weakest link is the reasoning in the assumption that while future short-period supply curves would be further and further to the right, the greater is the rate of investment undertaken now, the long-term demand curves will be stable so that we get lower and lower expected prices of products and therefore lower and lower values of q_i, the greater is the rate of investment now (see figure 4.2).

But in making such an assumption, Keynes is not being true to his own reasoning in the same chapter – that in the face of an uncertain, unknowable future what is happening in the present is the most important determinant, often too much so, of what businesspeople expect to happen in the future. Thus, on p. 148, he wrote:

It would be foolish, in forming . . . expectations, to attach great weight to matters which are very uncertain. It is reasonable . . . to be guided to a considerable degree by the facts about which we feel somewhat confident, even though they

---

[4] These days, even more so than when Keynes was writing, there is 'a cadre of professional managers trained to use sophisticated techniques of project evaluation based to be sure on Keynes' chapter 11', as Tom Russell (personal communication, May 2005) reminds me.

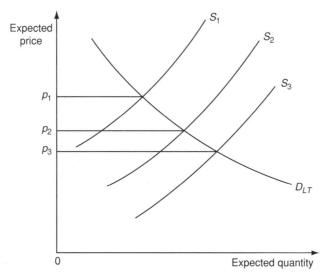

Figure 4.2. Keynes' second argument as to why ρ is lower, the greater is investment now.

may be less decisively relevant to the issue than other facts about which our knowledge is vague and scanty. For this reason the facts of the *existing* situation enter, *in a sense disproportionately*, into the formation of our long-term expectations; our usual practice being to take the existing situation and project it into the future, modified only to the extent that we have more or less definite reasons for expecting a change. (emphasis added)

Thus Keynes' own arguments lead to the conclusion that the higher is the level of investment now, the higher will be levels of sales, incomes, prices, profits and so on. These in turn should lead to expectations of long-term demand curves further and further to the right as well. In that case, it is not certain that expected prices will be at lower levels, the higher is the level of investment now, so that ρ will inevitably be smaller and converge on r: it all depends on the respective relative movements outwards of the supply and demand curves for given levels of investment now.

Keynes' reasoning therefore implies a sort of rational expectations argument for the first reason and indeterminate results for the second as to why the values of ρ should be lower.

Joan Robinson's banana diagram

The previous section was a summary, not necessarily in their words, of the criticism of Keynes' chapter 11. It was made, first, by Kalecki in his 1936 review of *The General Theory* and, then, by Joan Robinson and Asimakopulos. Kalecki wrote that:

it is difficult to consider Keynes' solution to the investment problem to be satisfactory. The reason for this failure lies in an approach which is basically static to a matter which is by its nature dynamic. Keynes takes as given the state of expectations of returns, and from this he deduces a certain determined level of investment, overlooking the effects that investment will have in turn on expectations.   (Targetti and Kinda-Hass 1982, 252)

Kalecki's reaction was to build up over his lifetime a more comprehensive explanation of the determination of the rate of investment in terms of the existing stock of capital goods, expected profitability, availability of finance and so on. His final paper on this topic contains one of his most important methodological statements:

In fact, the long-run trend is only a slowly changing component of a chain of short-period situations; it has no independent entity.[5]

(Kalecki 1968; *CW*, vol. II, 1991, 435)

Kalecki's statement reflects the view that in historical-time process analysis, actions must always be by definition in the short period,[6] though the importance of relative long-period and short-period factors will vary according to the economic decisions being considered. Thus long-term considerations will dominate investment decisions, short-term factors, the determination of current rates of output and, sometimes to a lesser extent, employment. In considering price-setting (as opposed to price-taking, where short-term considerations rule) medium-term factors are likely to dominate (as we noted in chapter 3). Movements over time in the economy are thus the result of one short period giving way to another, handing over in the process inherited stocks of capital goods and the ingredients on which to build new sets of expectations, both short-term and long-term. This method underlies

---

[5] This is prefaced by his criticism of the procedure in what was then contemporary growth theory of considering the 'problem of trend and . . . cycle in terms of a moving equilibrium rather than adopting an approach similar to that applied in the theory of business cycles [i.e.] establishing two relations: one based on the impact of effective demand generated by investment upon profits and national income and the other showing the determination of investment decisions by . . . the level and rate of change of economic activity. [The latter was, for Kalecki] the *pièce de résistance* of economics' (Kalecki 1968; *CW*, vol. II, 1991, 435, emphasis in original).

[6] I have a 'bee in my bonnet' that 'period' is an analytical concept where the economist is in control of what may vary and what is locked up, at least provisionally, in the *ceteris paribus* pound; 'run' by contrast, is an historical concept where whatever is either changing or constant in a given situation is an historical outcome. I know that neither Marshall nor Keynes were entirely consistent in their usage of 'period' and 'run,' but I would argue that nevertheless such a distinction may be discerned in their writings.

both Kalecki's own contributions and the parallel (but independent) contributions of Richard Goodwin.

As for Joan Robinson, and Asimakopulos after her, her response was to develop from Keynes and Kalecki's own contributions, and from Kalecki's criticisms of Keynes' theory, a two-sided relationship between accumulation and distribution which resulted in her famous banana diagram (see Robinson 1962a, 48).

One of the relationships between accumulation and profitability builds on Kalecki's original macroeconomic theory of distribution whereby the actual rate of accumulation determines actual profitability. The exact nature of the relationship depends on the different saving behaviour of wage-earners and profit-receivers. For, as we saw in chapter 2, this will ultimately determine what the level of activity *and* the distribution of income must be in order that planned accumulation becomes actual accumulation and equals planned and actual saving. If we assume that $s_w = 0$ and $s_\pi \leqslant 1$, the actual rate of accumulation, g_a, will equal the rate of saving out of profits, $s_\pi r_a$, where r_a is the actual received rate of profits, and $r_a = \frac{g_a}{s_\pi}$.

In order to avoid the unholy mass of *ex ante* and *ex post* factors in Keynes' theory of investment determination, Joan Robinson posits a simple relationship between the expected rate of profits, r_e, and the planned rate of accumulation, g_e: with given long-term expectations and conditions of finance, g_e is greater, the higher is the value of r_e. r_e, in turn, is taken to be a function of r_a. This uses Keynes' argument that in situations of inescapable uncertainty, the convention that what is happening in the present is the major determinant of what is expected to happen in the future is adopted.

These considerations determine the position, shape and slope of the function, named by Joan Robinson, the 'animal spirits' function (see p. 64). Its position relative to the vertical axis (on which are measured r_a and r_e) is determined by the state of 'animal spirits' themselves. If they are sluggish, the curve will be close to the vertical axis; if they are optimistic and dynamically confident, it will be much further away. Both relationships are defined for a given situation (see figure 4.3). Where (if [7]) the two relationships intersect we get a figure which looks like a banana, albeit one that has been sat on. At the point $(r_a)_e$, $(g_a)_e$, we have a (sort of) stable equilibrium position, for the expected rate of

---

[7] It is not inevitable that a 'banana' be formed, as Joan Robinson commented: 'If accumulation were more sensitive to [expected profitability] than [actual profitability] is to the rate of accumalation, there would exist no path capable of being steadily maintained' (Robinson 1965a; *CEP*, vol. III, 1965, 54) – even in a *ceteris paribus* situation.

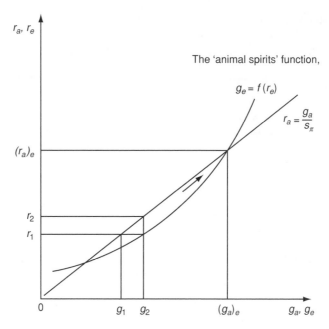

Figure 4.3. Joan Robinson's banana diagram.

profits has called forth an actual rate of the same value, thus justifying businesspeople continuing at the same rate of accumulation. As we shall see, this is Joan Robinson's version of Harrod's warranted rate of growth, g_w.

If the economy is not at this intersection of the two curves (the bottom intersection is an unstable equilibrium position), it is easy to show that an iterative procedure will take the economy to the top intersection. Suppose that the initial rate of accumulation is g_1. This establishes a rate of profits of r_1. Assuming for simplicity that $r_e = r_a$, this calls forth a rate of accumulation of g_2 and establishes an actual rate of profits of r_2; and so on until the economy 'arrives' at the top intersection.

But, of course, all this is on the assumption that neither of the two relationships changes during the approach, either because of exogenous shocks to, say, confidence or because the very achievement of the g/r combinations alters over historical time the fundamental determinants of the two relationships themselves through endogenous feedback on them – e.g. by changing the structure of production and the distribution of income. So we have an example of Keynes' shifting equilibrium analysis, not in terms of levels but in terms of rates of growth. (Keynes defined the theory of shifting equilibrium as 'the theory of a system in which changing views about the future are capable of influencing the present situation . . . [a system which reflects] problems of the real world in which our previous expectations are liable to disappointment and expectations about the future affect what we do to-day' (Keynes 1936; *CW*, vol. VII, 1973, 293–4).) In modern terms we have a path-dependent process whereby where the economy ends up, *if it ever does*, depends upon the characteristics of the path it takes along the way.

Joan Robinson's theory therefore predicts that accumulation and profitability will follow a *qualitatively* cyclical pattern over time, a re-assuring conclusion. But it is much harder to translate all this into a usable quantitative set of relationships describing and explaining the movements in rates of accumulation over time; that is still the Holy Grail of modern economics, and of policy-makers. Indeed, the late Trevor Swan, when commenting on the failure of the investment function in the Reserve Bank of Australia's macroeconomic model to predict turning points in investment expenditure, remarked 'it all depends on those animal spirits which cannot be bottled', an astute and ironical remark (in equal proportions) when it is remembered how fond Trevor was of spirits which could be bottled.

5   Money and finance: exogenous or endogenous?

In 1974, Jim Cairns, my former teacher at the University of Melbourne who at the time was Treasurer in the Whitlam ALP government, asked me to be Governor of Australia's central bank (the Reserve Bank of Australia). I replied: 'You know me, Jim, I'm a real man not a money man, so thanks but no thanks.'

So in my lectures I usually mentioned money and finance only in passing. Hence this is a short chapter; it concentrates on whether the money supply may or should be regarded as exogenous or endogenous.

My own view is that it is mainly, but certainly not completely, endogenous. I take as my authority Keynes himself, who for virtually all of his professional life was overwhelmingly an endogenous money person. As a follower of Marshall, he understood the role of mutual determination; but also, as Luigi Pasinetti has pointed out (see Pasinetti 1974, 44), Keynes also argued most strongly (and led by example):

that it is one of the tasks of the economic theorist . . . to specify which variables are sufficiently interdependent as to be best represented by simultaneous relations, and which variables exhibit such an overwhelming dependence in one direction (and such a small dependence in the opposite direction) as to be best represented by one–way–direction relations.

Immediately, the apparent exception of *The General Theory* surely comes to mind. Sheila Dow (1997) has provided a convincing explanation of why this is not so. She points out that Keynes' method was to classify variables as either exogenous (given, determinant) and endogenous (to be determined), according to the purpose and issues to be analysed – i.e. to classify variables in a relative not an absolute sense. For his central – indeed, fundamental – purposes in *The General Theory*, the analysis could usually start at a point at which money could conveniently and legitimately be taken as *given* (not exogenous in any absolute sense). Dow cites evidence from both Keynes' general method and associated with this particular assumption (see Dow 1997, 63); the evidence squares well with Pasinetti's interpretation. Thus: '[t]he division of the determinants of an economic system into two groups of given factors and independent variables is, of course, quite arbitrary from any absolute standpoint (Keynes 1936; *CW*, vol. VII, 1973, 247). Dow further cites a passage on pp. 200–1 of *The General Theory*, commenting that 'the passage makes clear that Keynes was very conscious that the money supply was not exogenous in the sense of helicopter money; it only changes as part of a larger process' (Dow 1997, 63).

Of course, Keynes has not generally been so interpreted. Indeed, perhaps his most important successor in the post–war period, the person who most resembled Keynes in his interests and activities as well as his intelligence and fertility of mind, Nicky Kaldor, chided Keynes for making the money supply exogenous. For after Keynes' death and when the time was ripe Kaldor thought Keynes' apparent stance allowed the rise of Monetarism, principally in the dominant personality of Milton Friedman. Friedman patiently and skilfully developed his cumulative attacks on the key relationships of Keynes' system – the consumption function, the investment function, the demand for money, the determination of the general price level. His aim was not only to destroy the theoretical constructions but also to negate the interventionist policies rationalised by Keynes' theory in the war and post–war years. (Kaldor thought that Keynes made a number of tactical errors in the presentation of his theory, this one especially, but also his assumption of free competition in the product and labour markets as well.) Be that as it may, I think Kaldor was wrong on both counts, certainly as an interpretation of Keynes' stance in *The General Theory* and after.[1]

One point where Keynes himself admitted that his analysis was wrong, or at least incomplete, was where he took it for granted that readers of *The General Theory* would be familiar with the rich institutional and detailed analysis of money and credit in *A Treatise on Money* (Keynes 1930), when he truncated this to a mere summary in *The General Theory*. There, he concentrated on *the* rate of interest and ignored almost completely the fundamental role of the banking system in the processes of modern capitalism. Keynes partially redressed this omission in his 1937 articles on the finance motive as an additional reason for demanding money (read: credit) from the banks in this context (see Keynes 1937a, 1937b; *CW*, vol. XIV, 1973, 201–23).

---

[1] I must not be taken to mean that Kaldor's own arguments that, *in a credit money economy*, the money supply is endogenous, overwhelmingly determined by the demand for, principally, credit, are wrong. The sophisticated and persuasive accounts of his views in, for example, Kaldor (1983) is, I hope, faithfully reflected in this chapter. I am indebted as ever to Jim Trevithick for explaining the essence of Kaldor's arguments to me.

As Keynes saw it at the time of the writing of *The General Theory*, the typical stages in the accumulation process of an individual firm – say, a joint stock company – was as follows. An investment project is evaluated much as Keynes described it in chapter 11 – that is to say, a comparison of expected profitability over its expected lifetime with the rate of interest. If it is decided that the project is worthwhile, the decision–maker would approach the trading bank system for a short–term loan with which to finance the project. If the subsequent (net) cash flows start to be realised as expected, the firm could then issue shares or bonds without adversely affecting their existing values on the stock exchange, and use the proceeds to repay the bank loan. The balance sheet of the firm will then be adjusted, with the new long–term liabilities replacing the short–term liabilities reflecting the bank loan, on the liabilities side, while the new assets associated with the project will be found – in fact, are already there – on the assets side of the balance sheet.

We now generalise this to the economy as a whole. Suppose that there is a rise in planned investment expenditure over and above what it has been in the recent past. We suppose that it is financed by additional bank credit, either newly granted and/or by activating previously unused overdraft facilities. If again the extra net cash flows associated with operating the newly installed capital goods are such as to fulfil expectations, the bank loans may be repaid from the proceeds associated with the issues of new shares or bonds. The corresponding extra demand for these new issues comes from the placement of the increase in total saving associated with the rise in total income induced by the higher level of investment expenditure and the consequent multiplier process working itself out.

One of Kaldor's most important theoretical contributions (Kaldor 1939), was to show what actions a particular class of speculators would need to take so that the multiplier could work itself out completely and planned investment become actual investment, by ensuring that the rate of interest remained unchanged over the entire process. Otherwise, the rise in planned investment demand could so affect the overall demand for money as to lead to a rise in the rate of interest which would choke off some of the initial rise in planned investment expenditure.

Keynes also associated this analysis of the finance motive with the concept of a revolving fund of finance which continually refurbished itself over time if it is assumed that aggregate investment expenditure flows at a constant rate, but which needed to be added to if planned investment rose to a higher level. Hence Keynes' 'most fundamental of . . . conclusions within this field': 'The investment market can become congested through shortage of cash [read: credit]. It can never become congested through shortage of saving' (Keynes 1937b; *CW*, vol. XIV, 1973, 222).[2]

It should also be pointed out (see Dow 1997), that Keynes was careful to distinguish whether it was the monetary authorities – i.e. the central bank – or the banking system itself which was an originating actor in the process of credit creation and control – a feature that was more explicit in *A Treatise on Money* than in *The General Theory* but, nevertheless, was there.

Keynes' 1937 articles (1937a, 1937b)are one of the most important bases from which the post–Keynesian debates on the demand for and supply of money and credit arise. One extreme version is the claim that the money supply (defined widely enough to include bank credit) is essentially demand–determined, as opposed to supply–determined, summarised in Basil Moore's 1988 pithy phrase, 'horizontalists versus verticalists'. Moore takes the view that whatever people and firms want to have in the way of credit, they may obtain, so that advances by the trading banks determine deposits by this process, rather than deposits through institutional rules determining what the amount of advances may be. This is an extreme view, because it neglects any discussion of credit rationing, the use of different rates for different potential borrowers and different responses to would–be borrowers at given rates of interest, according to the suppliers' assessments of the would–be borrowers' creditworthiness.[3] It also represents a reaction to institutional changes whereby, from the 1970s on, the monetary authorities in many advanced capitalist economies ceased to insist on certain reserve requirements.[4] This is partly because entities other than trading banks have increasingly come to supply credit in more and more unregulated markets, so that the rate of interest increasingly came to be the instrument used to try to implement monetary policy.

Again, the extreme version is the notion that a rate of interest is imposed on the system by the monetary authorities. The borrowers and lenders respond to its direct and indirect effects in the market

---

[2] Keynes' analysis and conclusion precipitated a large debate starting with an article by Asimakopulos in the 1983 Joan Robinson Memorial Issue of the *Cambridge Journal of Economics* (Asimakopulos 1983). It only came to an end and, I think, a just conclusion in the chapters by Paul Davidson and Jan Kregel in the volume in honour of Tom after his death in 1990 (see Davidson 1995 and Kregel 1995, in Harcourt, Roncaglia and Rowley 1995; see also Harcourt 1995b, 10). Another major strand that comes from Keynes' writings at this time is Hyman Minsky's insights on how the non-realisation of expected (net) cash flows from investment projects leads to an endogenous cycle in activity in which real and monetary factors are indissolubly mixed.

[3] These provisos are explicit in Kaldor's arguments.

[4] Tom Russell (personal communication, May 2005) assures me that this is not so in the USA.

for credit. For the extreme horizontalist, demand always is determined at the given rate of interest and the money supply responds but has no independent role. Keynes' theory of liquidity preference, whereby the rate of interest is determined in the money market as a result of various sources of demand for money, including the speculative motive, and given the money supply, ceases to be relevant – we have in effect 100 per cent endogeneity.

A less extreme, more balanced view, which includes not only Keynes' own insights but also takes into account historical and institutional changes, is to be found in the writings of, for example, Victoria Chick, Sheila Dow and Giuseppe Fontana. In this approach, mutual determination is involved, both the monetary authorities and the banking system have large but not a dominant or necessarily completely deterministic role to play, in the sense of complete control. As well as historical and institutional changes having roles, a role is also preserved for liquidity preference. The latter is associated, of course, with reactions to uncertainty, especially about the future levels of interest rates with regard to their present and conventional levels. This is reflected in the compositions of the portfolio holdings of persons and firms. The approach allows a place for rates of interest charged by trading banks to be prices set by competing oligopolists once a floor has been established by the monetary authorities' control over the setting of key interest rates. The latter are associated with the authorities' inescapable role, if financial systems are to be viable, of lenders of last resort.

The analysis proceeds by distinguishing between the market for credit and the market for money. Keynes' distinction between lender's risk and borrower's risk – their respective assessments of the extra compensation needed in order to enable individual investment projects to be undertaken – plays a key part. Both the supply of credit (from the banking system and other sources) and the demand for it are captured in supply and demand schedules of less than perfect elasticity at most points on them. How elastic and at what volumes they become less than perfectly elastic at any instant of time are very much functions of confidence and expectations, expressing the liquidity preference of the suppliers of credit. This in turn is reflected in the composition of both sides of their balance sheets.

The positions and elasticities at each point of the demand schedules are also functions of confidence and expectations. That, as curves, they always slope downwards reflects the argument that, *in a given situation*, the lower is the value of the rate of interest, the more credit will be demanded to finance expenditure on capital goods (and, in these days of 'credit for all', on consumer durables as well). The resulting prices are therefore mutually determined, as are equilibrium flows of credit. This is then included in the supply of money that is 'given' at any moment of time – this is Dow's interpretation of Keynes' procedure (see Dow 1997) – and the rate of interest which 'clears the market' is the one which reflects the rate that induces agents (ugh!) not to hold more money than is available at a moment of time.

So we started from Keynes' 'most fundamental of . . . conclusions'. It linked onto the view also arrived at by Kaleckians and other post–Keynesians – namely, that finance of one form or another is the ultimate binding macroeconomic constraint on the economy, a central finding that lies behind specific analyses which respond to changing market features and developments in mature capitalism. It also reflects the revolutionary change in outlook that James Meade attributed to Keynes:

Keynes' intellectual revolution was to shift economists from thinking normally in terms of a model of reality in which a dog called *savings* wagged his tail labelled *investment* to thinking in terms of a model in which a dog called *investment* wagged his tail labelled *savings*.   (Meade 1975, 82, emphasis in original)

Meade maintained this stance to the end of his life, both with regard to the domestic economy and the international economy.[5]

Within this particular set of discussions, some have stressed the stock aspects of money and financial assets generally, others the flow aspects of credit as a source of finance for important flow expenditures. Associated with this distinction is a group of post–Keynesian economists who have concentrated on one period only in their analysis of money – the 'accommodationists'. They have been contrasted with another group, the 'structuralists', who emphasise a period–by–period analysis in the manner of Kalecki's later views, and also those of John Hicks (see Fontana 2003, 2004a, 2004b). The upshot has been the preservation of the significance of Keynes' theory of liquidity preference in an explanation of the demand for money and other financial assets, and of banks extending credit guided by their own states of liquidity preference, so that not all demand is necessarily accommodated (see Cottrell 1994).

---

[5] Would that the bulk of the profession had stayed with him! For possibly his last statement of this view, see Harcourt (2001a, 82). James was commenting on a critique by Paul Dalziel and myself of the influential, but in our view, pre-Keynesian and misguided, article by Feldstein and Horioka (1980).

6 The complete model: its role in an explanation of post-war inflationary episodes

The post-war period in advanced capitalist economies may be subdivided broadly into three: first, the so-called 'Golden Age' of Capitalism (or the Long Boom) up to the early 1970s, marked by strong growth but also tendencies for long-term price and wage inflation to accelerate; secondly, the stagflation period of the 1970s and much of the 1980s when long-term inflation, lower rates of growth and rising unemployment went hand in hand; and, thirdly, a stagnant but less inflationary period when the rates of growth of the 'Golden Age' period on the whole were not regained (though there were important exceptions in, for example, the USA) but rates of price and wage inflation were much lower.

Two seminal articles and one book – Rowthorn (1977; 1980), Marglin (1984a, 1984b) – attempted to provide a framework within which to discuss these episodes, bringing together theories of distribution and growth and developing the concept of conflict inflation. The latter concentrates on the power and/or class struggle between capital and labour. It suggests that sustained inflation may often be the means by which an uneasy truce is brought about between the two contenders, so that while neither attains their full aspirations yet the amounts by which they fall short of them do not tend to worsen over time. While Bob Rowthorn's elegant and influential (1977) paper clearly has priority over Marglin's contributions in this literature, we nevertheless follow Stephen Marglin's exposition and use his apparatus because it more obviously builds on important aspects of the framework that we have developed in earlier chapters. In particular, we concentrate on Marglin's 1983 Alfred Marshall Lectures as they were subsequently published in the *Cambridge Journal of Economics* in 1984 (1984a). Marglin's approach is a mixture of two traditions: his 'vision' of the workings of modern capitalism is most consistent with those of the economists whose theories we discussed above. His method, though, is far too Marshallian in origin and mainstream in practice to be acceptable to, say, Goodwin, Kaldor, Kalecki and Joan Robinson. By this,

I mean that he uses the concepts of long-period equilibrium relationships and positions as magnets to which short-period equilibrium positions are attracted, stations on the way to dominating long-period crosses. Marglin argues that the latter's characteristics are those which most illuminate the broad characteristics of the three historical periods identified above.

This method would be more acceptable to, say, Pierangelo Garegnani and perhaps Luigi Pasinetti. Garegnani, for example, sees the method as underlying, in its guise as long-period positions and the relationships responsible for them, economic theory since its earliest inception in, for example, the physiocrats, Adam Smith and Ricardo. Moreover, it could be argued that it is the basic economic theory that also underlies modern econometric procedures associated with the concept of cointegration (see Granger 1993). But it certainly is at odds with those who stress the need for analysis of processes in historical time that we illustrated in earlier chapters.

Marglin himself says that he is addressing himself to the longer-run issues of growth and distribution. From his vantage point of the early 1980s, Marglin poses four basic questions (some of which are obviously out of date from our later vantage point):

- First, how (or why) have capitalist economies as different from one another as Japan, Italy, Germany and France grown so much more rapidly since the end of the Second World War than the USA and the UK?
- Secondly, why was the rate of profits near 30 per cent in Japan and only 10 per cent in the UK?
- Thirdly, what determines the distribution of income between wages and profits?
- Fourthly, a related question, how are distribution and growth related?

Marglin thought he was no nearer than asking the right questions rather than providing definitive answers. For example, does the mainspring of the development of capitalism lie within the household, the sovereign consumer of neoclassical theory, or with the entrepreneur, the central focus of Keynes and post-Keynesianism (Marglin calls it neo-Keynesianism), and Marx and neo-Marxian theory?[1] The first approach is Fisherian whereby the lifetime utility maximising consumer, allocating lifetime incomes between consumption and saving, drives the economy

---

[1] Obviously Joseph Schumpeter should also be mentioned – though, as Joan Robinson often remarked, he was but Marx with the adjectives changed.

along and all other capitalist institutions – the firm, the stock exchange, the financial system generally – are but their agents in this dominating process. In the second approach, the ruthless and swashbuckling entrepreneur/capitalist rules the roost, with accumulation and profit-making ends in themselves and all other classes are their agents/the means to enable them to achieve, for better or for worse, sometimes fully, more often not, their ends.

Secondly, what is the role of the class struggle between capital and labour in shaping the development over time of a typical modern capitalist economy?

To bring out the underlying essentials of his approach, Marglin uses a simple, one-commodity ('corn') model in which production is carried out using fixed coefficients of production. The choice of technique is abstracted from, just as it was in the basic model of Joan Robinson's 1956 volume, and technical progress is ignored. Corn can therefore be used either for consumption or for investment. (It lasts only one period in either use.)

The separate ingredients of Marglin's model are mostly already familiar to us. Periodic production and expenditure are divided between consumption and investment, the income so created is distributed between wages and profits, wage-earners do not save, profit-receivers save s_c of their profits.

Marglin writes $g = s_c r$, where g is the rate of growth of income and capital r is the rate of profits and $s_c \leq 1$. The relationship, Marglin argues, is neither a theory of growth nor a theory of profits (distribution); it merely defines a line on each point of which the relationship $g = s_c r$ is satisfied (see figure 6.1). Marglin next introduces a key concept, the *conventional real wage*, $w^\star$, a modern updating of the subsistence wage of Ricardo and Malthus (also Marx, but for different reasons), in order to take into account the more modern roles of trade unions, class struggle and so on. Then, because periodic income breaks down into wages and profits and there are fixed coefficients of production, at any moment there corresponds a definite value of the rate of profits, $r^\star$, to any given value of $w^\star$. (As we shall see in chapter 7, p. 119, Donald Harris 1975, 1978 preceded Marglin with this argument.)

Corresponding to the given values of $w^\star$ and $r^\star$ is a given value of g, $g^\star$, for Marglin, like Kaldor before him (but Kaldor had *wages*, not profits as the residual share of income), abstracts from effective demand problems. He uses a Say's Law world in which what is not wages is potential profits which are always realised (see figure 6.2).

Marglin draws attention to which variables are regarded as endogenous (determining) and which are exogenous (determined) in the rival

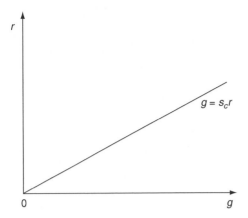

Figure 6.1. The relationship between growth and profitability.

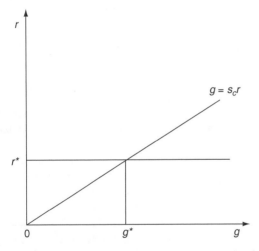

Figure 6.2. Distribution and growth determined in Marglin's model.

views of what are the driving forces at work in modern capitalism.[2] The orthodox mainstream theory appeals to utility-maximising and market-clearing prices to 'close' the model. Thus the role of the real wage is to clear the labour market and the growth rate then adjusts to the growth

---

[2] A fuller account of the literature to which Marglin is referring can be found in chapter 7.

rate of the labour force, with distribution being such as to provide the saving (equals investment) needed to achieve that rate of growth. This is to say that the growth of labour and consumption through lifetime patterns of consumption are *logically* prior to distribution, which then has to adjust to the exogenously given rate of growth. If the last were to change, everything else in the economy would have to change, too.

In the neo-Marxian/Keynesian model distribution is logically prior to resource allocation. If the conventional wage were to change, both distribution and growth would change, too.

In the neo-Marxian/Keynesian model there is no role for the rate of growth of the labour supply (Harrod's natural rate of growth, g_n). The model concentrates on the growth of the capitalist sector of the economy, so that if g_n grows at a different rate to that of the economy the Marxian reserve army of labour takes up the slack – is a buffer stock as it were, either receiving the rising unemployed or providing the needed extra labour over time. Marglin's model is meant to illuminate broad trends over periods of fifteen–twenty years. Non-capitalist and foreign sectors may also be sources of labour, either as in the Arthur Lewis model of unlimited supplies of labour from other sectors (but at the 'conventional' not a 'subsistence' wage) or, as we have seen, a repository for sacked labour.

In the neo-Keynesian model there is the usual long-period investment function, the relationship between the expected rate of profits and investment demand per unit of capital, $g_e = f(r_e)$. Financial conditions, summed up in a given value of the rate of interest, are assumed to be given, as in Joan Robinson's banana diagram.[3] Then accumulation and distribution are simultaneously determined (see figure 6.3, where $g^\star \leq g_n$). This inequality is claimed to hold by Marglin but, as we shall see in chapter 7, this is not necessarily so.

Marglin develops a short-period accumulation and distribution mechanism akin to that of Keynes/Kaldor to show how the short-period behaviour of accumulation and distribution is such as to allow them to converge on the long-period point, $g^\star$, $r^{\star\star}$. We need not concern ourselves with the details of this; suffice it to note that Marglin postulates a process whereby the reactions of decision-makers to the non-fulfilment of expectations in any short period nevertheless implies values of r and g that converge on a long-period position. At $g^\star$, $r^{\star\star}$, capitalists' aspirations are fulfilled (this is not necessarily so in the short-period

---

[3] In the short-period version of, for example, Keynes' *The General Theory*, it is the array of prospective rates of profit on different investment projects that are given and the rate of interest is the determining or exogenous variable.

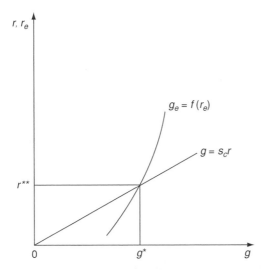

Figure 6.3. Neo-Keynesian model of growth and distribution.

approaches to the long-period position) and the frustration of aspirations is entirely transferred to the wage-earners. Their share of income
is entirely the residual remaining after desired accumulation has become
actual accumulation.

The point is that the capitalists have the ability to borrow or raise
finance, which allows them to achieve their desired rate of accumulation,
whereas wage-earners are much more constrained by their disposable
incomes, though they can borrow on the basis of the size of their assets.
(In Marglin's model, it is difficult to see how they could ever have
acquired assets.) Capitalists, though, borrow or raise funds on the
strength of their prospects, the assessment of which is subject to the
same influences, psychologically, as those that determine investment
demands. Marglin uses this factor as the entry point for finance capital
to play a role in determining the different stories about different capitalist economies–for example, why the conventional wisdom (which may
be actual foolishness) is that British banks, unlike Japanese banks, leave
financing of basic accumulation very much alone.

Implicit in this Keynesian/Kaldorian analysis is an assumption of
given money-wages – an assumption which Marglin criticises as he
does the absence of demand (for investment) in the neo-Marxian version
above.

To overcome this limitation, we need to take in all these considerations.
As it stands, though, this results in an overdetermined system – three

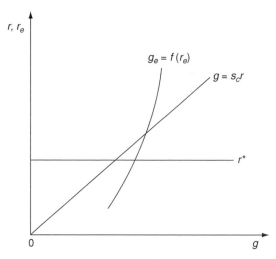

Figure 6.4. Overdetermination of g and r.

equations, but only two unknowns (see figure 6.4). So it would be only a fluke if the three relationships all intersected at the same point.

What is to be done?

The first point to make is that while wage-bargaining of necessity in a monetary production economy must be made in money terms, in the long term bargaining takes place in real terms, in the sense that the money–wage bargain is meant to procure a given level (and rate of increase) of real wages.[4] Secondly, Marglin argues for a move from a static characterisation of disequilibrium (levels) to a dynamic one whereby, by using the elements contained in the insights of Marx and Keynes, equilibrium rates of growth and rates of profits are brought about by equality between the rate of *money-wage* inflation and the rate of *price* inflation.

To derive this equilibrium we note, first, that changes in money-wages are likely to be greater – the wage-earners will be more stroppy, less grudgingly acceptable of their residual share of national income at any moment of time – the higher is the actual rate of profits above the rate associated with the value of the conventional real wage ruling at the same time – that is to say, the extent of the squeeze of the real wage in the current short period (see the $\underline{w}$ line in the left-hand quadrant of

---

[4] This point was made by David Champernowne in his (1936) *Review of Economic Studies* article on these and other aspects of *The General Theory*.

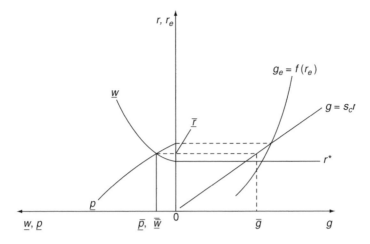

Figure 6.5. The uneasy truce engineered by sustained inflation.

figure 6.5 Rates of change of money-wages ($\underline{w}$) and of prices ($\underline{p}$) are measured on the horizontal axis.

Secondly, the rate of change of prices will be greater, the greater is the gap between planned investment and planned saving – that is to say, the greater is the inflationary gap (see the $\underline{p}$ line in the left-hand quadrant of figure 6.5). The $\underline{w}$ line starts on the vertical axis at the value of the rate of profits, $r^\star$, corresponding to the conventional wage, $w^\star$, and fans out in an upward-sloping manner, showing the higher and higher values of the increases in money-wages associated with the higher and higher non-fulfilment of the wage-earners' aspirations, the realisation of their conventional wage.

The $\underline{p}$ line starts on the vertical axis at the level of r corresponding to the intersection of the investment and saving relationships at which accumulation flows are being realised. It fans out in a downward-sloping manner, reflecting the greater and greater inflationary gap associated with planned investment exceeding planned saving more and more. Where the two lines $\underline{p}$ and $\underline{w}$ intersect, prices and wages are changing at the same rate and the real wage, though less than the conventional wage, is nevertheless constant over time, as is the rate of profits. (It should be remembered that there is no technical progress occurring.) If the economy is on the saving line so that saving intentions are realised, we have long-period equilibrium values of $\bar{p}$ $\bar{w}$, $\bar{r}$ and $\bar{g}$ established. Neither class achieves their full aspirations but then neither class's disappointments are increasing (or decreasing). The reserve army of labour adjusts labour supply to labour demand by absorbing numbers arising from the appearance of discouraged workers, the reversal of more women entering the workforce, guest workers 'going home' and so on. The inequality between investment demand and the supply of saving is a *permanent* feature, as are the departure of the real wage from the conventional real wage and the existence of permanent inflation of $\underline{p}$ and $\underline{\bar{w}}$. The dynamic equilibrium may be described in terms of a balance, an uneasy truce, between the pressure of aggregate demand on aggregate supply and the pressure of wage-earners on money-wages, so that the sustained rate of inflation measures – is an index of – both the frustration of the wage-earners trying to maintain a conventional real wage and the frustration of the capitalists trying to carry out their investment (accumulation) intentions.

Finally, we may use this apparatus to suggest – no more than suggest – why we have had some modern post-war problems, for example, the Phillips Curve going 'mad', the experience of stagflation and, more recently, the emergence of relative stagnation accompanied by lower rates of price and wage inflation.

First, consider what happens if there is a long-term increase in investment demand so that the investment demand function, $g_e = f(r_e)$ moves to the right, say from $\underline{f}\,(\underline{r_e})$ to $\underline{f_1}\,(\underline{r_e})$ (see figure 6.6).

The real effect is both a rise in the rate of growth (from $\bar{g}_0$ to $\bar{g}_1$) and the rate of price and wage inflation (from $\bar{p}_0$ to $\bar{p}_1$ and from $\bar{\underline{w}}_0$ to $\bar{\underline{w}}_1$). The capitalists are better off in the sense that they achieve a higher rate of accumulation (but not as high as their aspirations) and a higher rate of profits. The wage-earners are relatively worse off in that, in the new position, they are even further away from attaining their conventional wage. Higher real growth and higher rates of price and wage inflation are found to go together – the 'old' Phillips curve pattern, Marglin tells us.

Now suppose that the conventional wage increases (and $r^\star$ is reduced correspondingly) because wage-earners' aspirations have risen. This leads to a *rise* in the sustained rate of price and wage inflation and a fall in the sustained rate of growth – a dynamic form of stagflation (see figure 6.7, where the $\underline{w}$ curve shifts downward to $\underline{w}_1$, implying a higher rate of sustained price and wage inflation and a lower rate of growth).

In the early post-war years we had a Phillips Curve phenomenon which in turn brought about the rise in the conventional wage as prolonged full employment in many economies associated with the Long Boom or 'Golden Age' of Capitalism brought about a cumulative shift in economic, social and political power from capital to labour. This produced the inevitable response through Monetarism – 'the incomes

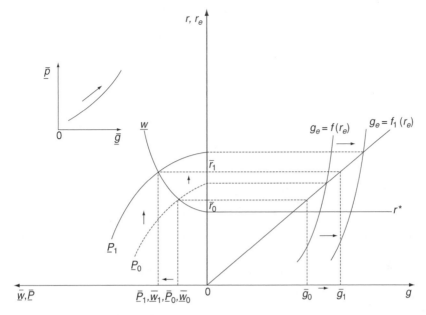

Figure 6.6. Episode 1: higher growth, higher price inflation.

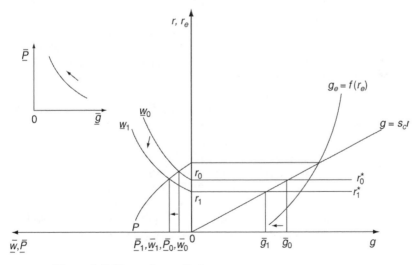

Figure 6.7. Dynamic stagflation.

82   The Structure of Post-Keynesian Economics

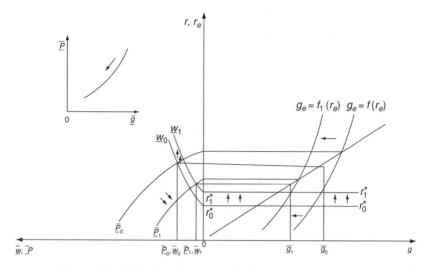

Figure 6.8. Episode 3: lower growth, lower inflation.

policy of Karl Marx' as Thomas Balogh (1982, 77) had it – whereby
under the guise of controlling inflation unemployment was deliberately
increased and the shift in power reversed. This is a dynamic version of
what Kalecki predicted in his classic (1943)(!) article 'Political aspects
of full employment'.[5]

In all probability these changes resulted in the next episode – a lower
rate of growth but also a lower rate of price and wage inflation. By
attempting to control inflation by increasing unemployment and
lowering money-wage demands, and the level of the conventional wage,
the 'animal spirits' of business people may be adversely affected as well.
So not only does r^* rise (see figure 6.8), creating a $\underline{w}$ curve closer to the
vertical axis in the left-hand quadrant but also the investment function
moves to the left in the right-hand quadrant, causing the $\underline{p}$ line in the
left-hand quadrant to move down. The new dynamic equilibrium that
results has a lower rate of price and wage inflation and a lower rate of
growth (see $\underline{p}_1$, $\bar{w}_1$, $\bar{g}_1$ in figure 6.8). We thus have a similar (qualitative)
relationship between inflation and growth to that of the first episode but
it is now a move *down* the relationship, not up, as in the 'Golden Age'
episode. I submit, therefore, that by putting the Marglin model through

---

[5] These developments, and possible policy approaches to deal with their consequences, are
discussed in chapter 8.

its paces we have been able to get a useful if broad grip on the factors behind the economic history of advanced capitalist economies in the post-war period.[6]

---

[6] Tom Russell (personal communication, May 2005) commented: '[T]he Marglin model was developed to explain the circumstances of its time, inflation, the rise of Japan, etc. Today we have no inflation and Japan is a decade old basket-case. Did the Marglin model see any of this coming? If not, what good is it?' In the text, I used Marglin's construction to go outside the periods on which he was commenting to try to make sense of what followed. His model is not designed to predict, but to explain. This in my view (and, of course, in that of many others, for example, Frank Hahn) is generally the most that can be required of theory in economics.

7   Theories of growth: from Adam Smith to 'modern' endogenous growth theory

Introduction

From Adam Smith to endogenous growth theory (the 'new' growth theory) via Ricardo, Marx, Harrod and the early reactions – neoclassical and post-Keynesian – to Harrod (the 'old' growth theory): this is the theme of the present chapter. Are we then only now back from where we started–that is to say, with Adam Smith? Arthur Smithies (1962) certainly thought so, indeed he thought that we had not even left Smith's insights!

> Perhaps the whole problem is too complicated for adequate reflection in a formal model. In that event, we could do worse than re-read Adam Smith (or possibly read him for the first time). In Book I, he said that the division of labour was the mainspring of economic progress; and in Book II, that accumulation was a necessary condition for increasing division of labour. How far have we got beyond this? (1962, 92)

Luigi Pasinetti (1981, 1993) thought that his writings in many ways served to fulfil the suggestions and conjectures to be found in Smith. Heinz Kurz (1997) argued that the 'new' growth theory would have had nothing of substance to tell Smith and Ricardo that they did not already know from their own contributions: all very sobering and modesty-making! Prue Kerr (1993)[1] has argued – and I certainly agree with her – that Smith did provide both the concepts and the wherewithal for a richly satisfying theory of distribution and growth in which was incorporated a theory of endogenous technical change based on the two propositions of which Smithies 1962 reminded us.

The chapter proceeds by examining Smith's contributions, how Ricardo and Marx reacted to them, Marx's singular take on his predecessors in his account and analysis of the 'laws of motion' of capitalist society, Harrod's (unconscious) rediscovery of aspects of Marx's theory

---

[1] Her article is one of the most illuminating articles on Smith I have ever read.

as he developed 'old' modern growth theory in the aftermath of the Keynesian revolution, Solow's and Swan's reactions to the puzzles raised by Harrod's contributions, the post-Keynesian developments associated with Kaldor, Joan Robinson, Richard Goodwin and Pasinetti, and finally the rise of the 'new' neoclassical endogenous growth theory following the seminal contributions of Paul Romer (1986) and Robert Lucas (1988), a literature that incorporates (not necessarily consciously) insights from Kaldor's later writings on cumulative causation and increasing returns, and attempts to provide a neoclassical analysis of issues first raised in Smith's writings.

Smith and Ricardo

We start by pointing out that Smith, despite the destruction of many of his papers after his death (on his instructions), nevertheless bequeathed to us, his successors, not only *An Inquiry into the Nature and Causes of the Wealth of Nations* (*WN*) (1776) but also his first major treatise, *The Theory of Moral Sentiments* (*MS*) (1759a), *Lectures on Jurisprudence* (1759b) and *Essays on Philosophical Subjects* (n.d.), all of which are complementary to the development of Smith's theories of distribution and growth. He also provided later political economists with the central concepts of their trade: the notion of the surplus – how it is created, extracted, distributed and used; the distinction between (short-term) market prices and (long-term or long-period) natural prices of commodities and the services of labour, capital and land, the centres of gravitation of the economic system; the classification of historical development into idealised stages, each containing factors that led on inexorably to the succeeding stage. These stages also served as reference points against which to judge the performances of actual economies' political and social processes, and to create and discuss institutions and roles of governments through and by which reality might be brought closer to the ideal.

Embedded in Smith's writings may be found the concepts of increasing returns and processes of cumulative causation – interrelated feedbacks between different sectors of the economy and society, both internally and externally, that lead to cumulative expansions (or contractions) for long periods of time, especially within what he dubbed 'commercial society', the fourth of his idealised stages.[2] The dynamic

---

[2] Smith's concepts correspond to the second wolf pack analogy discussed in chapter 8 (pp. 145–6).

processes of freely competitive capitalism, whereby there is a tendency to equality in all activities of rates of profit on capital, entails that, with freedom of entry and exit, the search for profitable opportunities initiates the productivity-enhancing forces of the division of labour and the expansion of the market. To establish such an economy also needs analysis of the role of government in creating institutions, raising revenues and undertaking expenditures. This is an early example of the insight that the competitive market could not be relied upon to do all these functions properly, or at all, and of the need for a system of laws which protects and encourages the productive activity of the capitalist class.

In all these developments Smith was not necessarily the first to introduce them into the literature. But his developments of them and his sophisticated analysis of how they were interrelated take his contributions on to a new plane, as far as laying the foundations of our discipline is concerned (not that this would have secured him tenure, or even a post on tenure track today – after all, he wrote books).

Smith inherited the concept of the surplus from the Physiocrats who identified it with the surplus of produce over what was needed at the beginning of the production period in agriculture to create total agricultural output. Activities, including labour, in the agricultural sector, were identified by the Physiocrats as the only productive activities in the economy, giving rise to the concepts of productive and unproductive labour. All other sectors and activities were unproductive, depending on the size of the agricultural surplus and their share and use of it for the extent of their own activities.

Smith generalised the concept to all sectors of society, defining productive labour (at least in one of his definitions of it) as that associated with the production of surpluses at the end of their respective production periods. Not that Smith gave agriculture a back seat, or even reduced it to equality with the activities of other sectors. In his view, the development of other sectors – manufacturing, commercial, services – was seen as crucially dependent upon a rapidly growing and productivity-improving agricultural sector. Only through these means would the overall surplus be maintained and increased each period. For the agricultural surplus allowed wage goods to be paid to those making capital goods that served in turn to enhance the productivity of labour in agriculture and the other sectors.

Smith linked the determination of the size of the surplus to the increase in the division of labour, technical advances in the methods of production in each sector that in turn depended upon the size of the markets for the final products of each sector. He saw clearly how each sector constituted demand and supply for each others' products in an interrelated process more akin to what Sraffa was later to call 'production of commodities by means of commodities' than to the Keynesian national accounting system of expenditure, production and income-creation. Nevertheless, the latter was also present, at least in embryo, and contributed an essential part to Smith's narrative of development as well as to modern macroeconomic analysis.[3] For Smith also linked the creation of the surplus to its distribution as different incomes to different classes, and their subsequent uses of their shares. Indeed, the progress of the nation depended upon who received these incomes and on their spending and saving behaviour, insights that surfaced again, as we have seen, in Kaldor's post-war writings. Though Smith had delightfully sardonic and even cynical twists to his writings and views, so that he never uncritically admired the capitalist entrepreneur as hero, as did Joseph Schumpeter, nevertheless he recognised that the role of this class and of the profits they received was to permit the latter's reinvestment in capital goods, at the same time embodying new ways of making commodities and contributing to continuous, even accelerating growth overall in ways which would not be forthcoming if the surplus went mainly as rent to landlords. The latter would spend the bulk of their incomes on riotous living and luxury goods, and to the non-creation of productivity-raising accumulation. Wage-earners, though their specialisation due to the division of labour was essential for the rise in productivity, received such low wages as to make their ability to save virtually non-existent. Their wages, therefore, had to be covered as 'necessaries' before the surplus was struck.

Once the surplus and the gross and net products associated with its creation were identified as collections of heterogeneous commodities, the need for a theory of value (and price) became obvious. Smith gave us two theories, not in general consistent with one another, and both of which have been developed in further ways by later economists. The first was a labour-embodied theory in that the major determinant of the long-period, natural price of the commodity was the amount of labour required directly and indirectly for its production – that is to say, a measure of the (relative) difficulty of its reproduction. The other was a labour-command theory – the amount of labour which the natural price of a commodity would command when the command concerned

---

[3] I first became really aware of these links when I was working with Vincent Massaro on Sraffa's concept of subsystems (see Harcourt and Massaro 1964), at the same time as I was writing the first draft of the chapter on the national accounts in *Economic Activity* (Harcourt, Karmel and Wallace 1967).

was related to the natural rate of wages. Smith distinguished between *observed* market prices subject at any moment of time to temporary whims, gluts, shortages and so on, and *natural* prices, the prices needed in order to justify the continuing production of commodities or provision of services from labour, capital and land, given what he called the effectual (long-period) demand for the commodities and services concerned.

The natural prices were seen as centres of gravitation around which the market prices fluctuated over time, or in certain circumstances, perhaps more theoretical than historical, tended to converge on. All these concepts were set in freely competitive situations, often more ideal than actual, characterised by diffusion of power on both sides of the markets for the exchanges of commodities and services between transactors. No one transactor *as an individual* had, in effect, any power. Of course, Smith was well aware of monopoly groups and collusion among businesspeople and between them and governments. He had no illusions as to which was the stronger group in labour markets, or *vis-à-vis* the general public in the provision of consumption goods.

The *Wealth of Nations* was written partly as a critique of the mercantilist system of government and was especially an attack on Sir James Steuart's defence of government and monopoly intervention, though Smith never mentioned him by name (see King 1988, 35).

Smith also used his development of the roles of the division of labour and the market to argue for the emergence of free trade, both between regions and internationally, in order to enable the benefits of these interrelated processes to be spread within countries and world-wide. Indeed, the potential contributions of the division of labour depended upon the widening and larger markets associated with the spread of free trade.

Smith bequeathed to his successors, therefore, the concept of the surplus in the economy as a whole; a threefold division of activity into agriculture, manufacturing and services including the government sector; a choice of value theories in order to understand the structure of relative (natural) prices and to measure the size of the surplus at a moment in time and over time; the 'vision' of an ongoing process of development and growth interrelated with the distribution of the product between three different classes with different saving, spending and employment functions – wage-earners, capitalists (agricultural, industrial and commercial) and land owners. While he analysed the impact on development of population changes, it was left to Thomas Robert Malthus to develop the theory of population growth (or lack of it) which characterised later developments of classical political economy, and which played an essential role in David Ricardo's contributions, to which we now turn. (Our exposition is an adaptation of Pasinetti's (1960) article on the Ricardian system.)

As well as Malthus' theory of population and Robert Torrens/ Malthus/Edward West's theory of rent, Ricardo took from Smith the concept of the surplus, the (labour-embodied) theory of value, including the distinction between the determinants of market prices and natural prices, with an overwhelming emphasis on the latter,[4] and the concept of competition as a dynamic process tending to bring equality of rates of profit in all sectors of the economy through movements of capital and labour and changes in levels of production in different activities.

Ricardo is famous, even infamous, for his dictum that 'To determine the laws which regulate [the proportions in which 'the produce of the earth is divided among the three classes of the community'] is the principal problem in Political Economy' (Sraffa with Dobb 1951–73, 5). The dictum, though, had wide-ranging application and it is the core part of his theory of value, distribution and growth. Even more than Smith, Ricardo concentrated on long-period persistent tendencies in the emerging industrialised capitalist world of his time, and on the relationships between them. As he told his great friend and protagonist on political economy, Malthus, one of the reasons that they so often disagreed, or at least, were at cross-purposes, was that he (Ricardo) was concerned with the permanent effects of a change in an important determining factor, a long-period perspective, while Malthus was much more concerned with the immediate, short-term impacts.[5]

This distinction was later to put Keynes on the side of Malthus in Malthus' arguments with Ricardo, seeing him as a forerunner of Keynes, as the 'first of the Cambridge economists' (Keynes 1933; *CW*, vol. X, 1972, 71). Sraffa, though, was on the side of his 'dear David', whose work, along with Marx's, were the principal influences on his revival of the 'standpoint [of] the old classical economists from Adam Smith to Ricardo, [which had] been submerged and forgotten' (Sraffa 1960, v),

---

[4] In Ricardo's *Principles* the chapter on supply and demand is near the end of the book of thirty-two chapters (chapter XXX, 'On the influence of demand and supply on prices') and takes up only a few pages (pp. 382–85 of the Sraffa with Dobb edition 1951); whereas the first chapter, 'On value', is concerned with natural prices, is many pages long (pp. 12–66 in the Sraffa with Dobb edition 1951) and was considerably revised by Ricardo in the three editions published in his lifetime.

[5] '[O]ne great cause of our difference in opinion . . . is that you have in your mind the immediate and temporary effects of particular changes, whereas I put these . . . effects quite aside, and fix my whole attention on the permanent state of things that will result from them.' Ricardo to Malthus, 24 January 1817, quoted by Keynes, 1933; *CW*, vol. X, 1972, 97.

following the rise to dominance of the supply and demand theories (Bharadwaj 1978) since 'the advent of the 'marginal' method' (Sraffa, 1960, v). For, as Sraffa pointed out in his Introduction to the Sraffa with Dobb edition of Ricardo's works and correspondence (1951–73), the corn model of the economy permits the determination of the rate of profits in terms of a ratio of corn as surplus to corn as capital, a procedure that is logically prior to any discussion of value and prices. Moreover, if such an independence could be established, the knowledge of the resulting value of the rate of profits (or, initially, the rate of wages), together with the conditions of production in all industries, would permit the determination of the pattern of natural prices of commodities in all sectors. They would have to be such as to allow the receipt of the overall, economy-wide rate of profits on capitals in all activities and uses.

One interpretation of Ricardo's argument (see Pasinetti 1960; 1974), is that we concentrate on situations in which the long-period natural rate of real wages is at the subsistence level determined by Malthus' theory of population: if the market rate of wages were to be greater than the natural rate, population would so increase as to bring the real wage down to the subsistence level due to the operation of long-term historical diminishing returns in agriculture (if the market rate were to be less than the natural rate, population would so decline as to restore the natural rate). If we abstract from the impact of technical progress, a larger population lowers the yield at the extensive margin – less fertile plots and/or plots further from the market for 'corn' have to be brought into cultivation. Moreover, production on these less fertile lands would be taken up to the point where the intensive margins of cultivation would result in yields that coincided with those at the intensive margins on more fertile plots.

Ricardo argued that the long-term natural price of 'corn' is determined at the intersection of these two margins on *no-rent* land. There, fertility is such that only the natural wage and the natural rate of profits on advanced wages and seed corn may be received. This was the basis for Ricardo's theory of rent. Ricardo, it was argued, concentrated on various long-period positions associated with higher and higher levels of the population and workforce and played down the accumulation and transition processes through which the economy moved from one long-period position to another.

Nevertheless, as Ricardo was interested in the processes of distribution and growth over time, and as he was possibly the first of the modern economists because of his rigorously precise analysis and use of 'strong' cases to bring out starkly the essential relationships at work, he increasingly came to see the need for a theory of value which provided an invariable measure of value. For he wanted to be able to say precise things about the size of the surplus at any moment of time (or, rather, at different points of time) without the measure itself being affected by either changes in the distribution of income at any moment of time, or by changes in levels of activity and methods of production over time. Hence we have in his writings musings on the invariable measure of value, so incomprehensible to many modern minds – read Frank Hahn – in the last months before his untimely death in 1823 at the age of fifty-one. (We know now that he was probably chasing a will-o'-the wisp in the sense that Sraffa's Standard commodity solved the first aspect of his problem but showed that the second was not solvable, in that there was a different Standard commodity associated with each level of activity and pattern of methods of production.)

As is well known, Ricardo was a great advocate of free trade, which in his day meant the abolition of the Corn Laws in order to allow free imports of 'corn' from abroad. Partly his argument was based upon his statement of the principle of comparative advantage in the chapter on trade in the *Principles* whereby, applying Smith's analysis of specialisation and the division of labour to the international scene, Ricardo advocated that all economies concentrate the services of their own supplies of land, labour and capital at any moment of time in those activities in which they have a comparative advantage and then swap commodities with other nations through free international trade. In this way, the maximum efficient use would be made of the services of world's supplies of direct and indirect labour. Such was the basis of the arguments Ricardo presented in the House of Commons where he was listened to with great respect (if not comfort, he evidently had a shrill, high-pitched voice) by all sides of the House. By this institutional change, he argued, individual countries and the world alike could stave off for generations the onset of historical diminishing returns associated with the finite limit on the amount of cultivatable lands in the face of growing world population. That is to say, the spectre of the classical stationary state in which the rate of profits would have been reduced below the necessary level to induce capitalists in all sectors to do their things, the entire surplus would go as rent to the landlords and wage-earners would receive only subsistence wages in their share of the national income, would be put off.

To illustrate his argument, consider a freely competitive economy and concentrate on the agricultural sector where tenant farmers operate as capitalists, employing labour and 'corn' capital in given proportions – doses – to produce 'corn' on farms rented from landlords. Because there is freedom of entry (and exit), whether they are on very fertile or

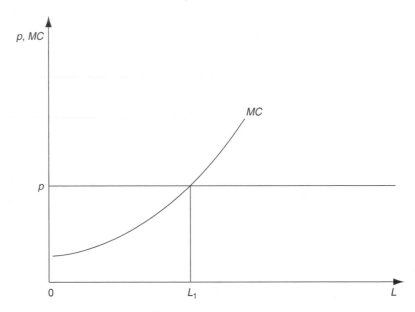

Figure 7.1. The individual capitalist tenant farmer.

marginal lands they cannot keep for themselves any more of their annual produce (or, rather, the revenues from its sale) than is enough to advance the subsistence wages of their workers each period, provide seed corn for the next period and receive the ruling rate of profits in the economy on their own 'corn' capital (the ruling rate must be equal to 'corn' as surplus divided by 'corn' as advanced wages and seed corn). If the tenant farmers tried to keep more than this, other potential tenants would enter agriculture by offering to pay (more) rent to the landlords.

Consider a typical tenant farmer's position. The more intensely he/she works his/her plot by increasing the application of doses of labour and capital, the less is the size of the ensuing marginal product. As he/she is a competitor, he/she takes the price of 'corn' (p) as is given (or as unity if we measure it in terms of 'corn'), and produces up to the point where the marginal cost of production (MC) equals the price of corn (see figure 7.1, where L is application of 'doses' of labour and capital to a given plot).[6] The height of the MC curve reflects the specific fertility of the plot, its upward slope reflects diminishing returns to increased

---

[6] I am indebted to Tom Asimakopulos for the diagram and the analysis associated with it.

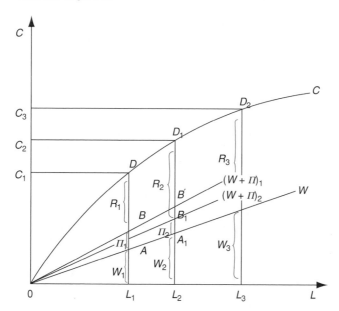

Figure 7.2. Total 'corn' production in the agricultural sector.

application of doses of labour and capital. Because the real wage must
be advanced

$$MC(\text{in money terms}) = \frac{mw(1+r)}{MP_L}$$

$$\text{or } 1 = \frac{mw(1+r)}{pMP_L} = \frac{w(1+r)}{MP_L}$$

in real ('corn') terms, where mw = the money wage.

This shows that the MP_L is just sufficient to cover the real wage and
the profits on advanced capital (the real wage, if we ignore seed 'corn' for
simplicity) – there is nothing left for rent at the margin. Therefore the
area under the MC curve is $MP_L L_1$ (the wage bill plus profits on capital)
and the area created above it, bounded by the price line, is rent.

Now look at the agricultural sector of the economy as a whole (see
figure 7.2). Suppose past accumulation has allowed the sector to employ
a workforce of $0L_1$ (with the accompanying required amount of capital)
and produce a total output of $0C_1(= L_1D)$. L_1A is the wage bill (the
slope of $0W$ is determined by the natural rate of subsistence wages and
$L_1A = w.0L_1$). The slope of the total product curve (MP_L) is equal to

$w(1+r)$, shown by the tangent to point D. Drop a straight line parallel to this tangent until it goes through the origin (see $0(W+\Pi)_1$ in figure 7.2). Then AB is total profits, AB/L_1A is the rate of profits and BD is rent, where rent is the difference between the AP_L and MP_L multiplied by $0L_1$.

We now show that as accumulation occurs (offstage) and population grows, the total product will increase but at a decreasing rate and the absolute amount of rent and its share in total product will increase, the rate of profits and eventually total profits themselves will fall towards zero and the classical stationary state will be reached.

Suppose accumulation temporarily raises the market rate of wages above the natural rate. This allows population, the workforce and accumulation to increase until new higher levels are reached, say $0L_2$. The wage will now be L_2A_1. For the rate of profits to remain unchanged, the new amount of profits would have to be A_1B'. But MP_L is less – the total product curve is flatter – and so when we draw the new line parallel to the slope we see that profits are in fact A_1B_1, implying a lower *rate* of profits, and rent is now B_1D_1. Eventually accumulation and population growth will take the sector to the position where the slope of the total product curve is parallel to the wage line $0W$, so that our parallel line will *coincide* with $0W$ and the whole of the total product will be absorbed by rent (R_3) and wages (W_3), the classical stationary state will have arrived. (For simplicity, we have ignored the minimum rate of profits which keeps capitalists at it.)

So far, we have abstracted from the effects of technical advances in agriculture. Allowing for them means that the total product curve rises over 'time' but keeps its essential qualitative shape (depending on the nature of technical progress) so that, other things being equal, the stationary state must eventually be approached depending upon the relative offsetting effects of technical advances on the one hand and historical diminishing returns to the fixed supply of land on the other. Ricardo's argument for free trade was, in effect, that it had effects akin to technical progress, raising the total product curve above what it would have been in the absence of free trade as the world's supply of labour was used in the most efficient way according to the principles of Adam Smith. That Ricardo as a landlord would suffer, in that the share of rent would be less, shows that he had a level of integrity that would be surprising at any moment of time, not only his own!

These in starkest outline are the narratives and accompanying concepts that Karl Marx inherited when, in spite of his carbuncles (or perhaps because of them), he started his mammoth task of absorbing classical political economy in his days at the British Museum.

Marx[7]

Marx was the most profound interpreter of the capitalism of his age, arguably of any age. Because some of the tendencies which Marx identified (and his critics mistakenly interpreted as predictions) have not in fact occurred, he must rest content instead, as Ronald Meek told us (1967, 128), with being 'just another genius'. He bequeathed to us a set of methods with which to approach issues of high theory, historical and philosophical analysis and practical policies in the social sciences.[8] The principle that he evolved, of soaking himself in historical facts and figures and in the writings of those who came before him, initially criticising them from within their own texts and then developing his own alternative theory and approach, incorporating and expanding and often changing profoundly what he had criticised and discarding what was misleading, incoherent, or just plain wrong, is surely the right way to do original work in social science.

Marx came to political economy from philosophy, trained especially in German philosophy and crucially influenced by the philosophical views of Hegel and the principle of dialectical change. The use of a dialectic led him always to look for internal contradictions in both systems of thought and in the working out of social processes. His organising concept when he came to political economy was, as is to be expected, the notion of *Surplus* – its creation, extraction, distribution and use – in different societies. Marx looked at human history as succeeding epochs of different ways of surplus creation *et al.*; he was determined to find by analysis of the power patterns of each the seeds of both their achievements and their internal contradictions and eventual destruction and transformation as, through the endogenous processes thus discovered, one form gave way to the next. The jewel in his crown was his analysis of capitalism.

Marx's method of analysis may be likened to an onion. At the central core which underlies the overlapping outer layers of skin is the pure, most abstract yet fundamental model of the mode of production (Marx's phrase) being analysed. All fossils from the past, all embryos of what is to come, are abstracted from. The system is revealed in its purest form.

---

[7] This section is based on a joint paper written with Prue Kerr (Harcourt and Kerr 1996), reprinted in Harcourt (2001a).

[8] His views on the operation of socialism and of its transformation to communism are on a different plane, often approaching in naivety those of Utopian Christian Socialists – hence the *non sequitur* involved in supposing that the overthrow of the USSR and Eastern European regimes discredits Marx's most enduring contributions, Baroness Thatcher notwithstanding.

The aim is to show that the fundamental characteristics and relationships thus revealed are robust – that they survive the complications provided intact by adding back (in analysis) the inner and outer layers of skin of the onion, that they still remain the ultimate, deepest determinants of what is observed on the surface. We may illustrate this by the transition from vol. I to vol. III of *Capital* (the latter was written before vol. 1 but published only after Marx's death, edited by Engels). Though there is little explicit mention in vol. I of the (near) surface phenomenon of prices of production of vol. III, yet the links from the underlying labour values of vol. I are always at the forefront of Marx's intention – not in the mainstream sense of providing a theory of relative prices (the usual interpretation of what the labour theory of value (LTV) is about) but in making explicit the link as a necessary part of the story of production, distribution and accumulation in capitalism.

Having mentioned the dreaded phrase 'LTV', let us say what we understand by it. As we said, the principal task Marx set himself was to explain the creation *et al.* of the surplus in capitalism. Naturally, he linked this in capitalism with an explanation of the origin of profits and the determination of the system-wide rate of profits in this mode of production. He identified in previous modes the role of classes in each – one dominant, one subservient – with reference to the creation of wealth and so social and economic power, and the connection of their relationship to the creation *et al.* of the surplus by a process of explicit exploitation of one class by another. For example, in feudalism the process was obvious: its institutions and laws ensured that the lords of the manor could physically extract from the serfs part of the annual product, either by making serfs work for set periods on the lords' lands or because the serfs were tenants, requiring them to 'hand over' part of the product of the land which their labour had brought forth.

When we get to pure *competitive* capitalism, such a process seems impossible. For one aspect of capitalism, purified in modern theory to become price-taking behaviour by all agents with prices set by the impersonal forces of the market, in classical and Marx's times more robustly specified as a wide diffusion of power among *individual* capitalists and *individual* wage-earners, seems to make it impossible for individual capitalists to coerce free wage-earners into doing what they do not wish to do. They could always leave one and work for another, just as any one capitalist and his/her capitals could leave or enter any activity – hence the *tendency* for rates of profit to be equalised in all activities and the need to explain what determined the origin and size of the systemic rate of profits to which their individual values tended. Moreover, each free wage-labourer was paid a definite money wage for all the hours he or she worked. Under these conditions, how could exploitation occur, a surplus arise, and so where *did* profits come from?

Marx answered this in terms of the distinction between the necessary and surplus labour time associated with the class relations of capitalist society. Capitalists *as a class* (subdivided into industrial, commercial and finance capital) had a monopoly of the means of production and finance. Workers *as a class*, having only their labour power to sell, had to do as they were told in the workplace. As propertyless, landless but free wage-labourers, the proletariat whose creation was the by-product of feudalism giving way to capitalism, they had but one choice – *either* to work under the conditions established by the capitalist class, *or* to withdraw from the system entirely, and starve. Therefore the working day could conceptually be split into two parts: the hours needed with the existing stock of capital goods, methods and conditions of production to produce wage goods – necessary labour; and the rest – surplus labour – which was the source of surplus value in the sphere of production, and of profits in the sphere of distribution and exchange. Marx adopted Ricardo's idea that all commodities had an embodied labour value to explain how labour services, a commodity saleable just like any other in capitalism, would tend to sell at their values. But human labour had the unique property that it could create more value – produce more commodities – than was needed for its own reproduction, and this was embodied in the commodities corresponding to this surplus labour time.

A subsidiary part of the story was that the actual operations of capitalism resulted in the waxing and waning of the reserve army of labour (RAL) – a much more suitable euphemism for the unemployed than the modern description of the same phenomenon as flexible labour markets – causing actual wages to tend towards (or fluctuate around?) their natural values (a purely classical story). But the main story was that while the surface phenomenon seemingly reflected fairness and efficiency – people paid fully for what they did and all the hours they worked – this masked the underlying exploitation process arising from the situation of class monopoly. In the sphere of production there was a tendency to equality in length of the working day (week, year) and intensity of work, too. In the sphere of distribution and exchange, abstracting from actual (market) prices, there was a tendency for the prices of production to be such that a uniform rate of profits was created (the first great empirical generalisation of classical political economy) and for the profit components of the prices of production to be such as to constitute uniform rates of return on total capitals, similarly measured, in all activities.

The total capitals consisted of two parts – advances of wages to the wage-earners, variable capital (v) (variable because this component *alone* created more value than it started off with); and constant capital (c), 'dead' labour embodied in durable assets from previous rounds – circuits – of surplus labour, surplus value and profit-creation and re-investment. Marx famously pictured the capitalist process as the circuit of capitals: $M \to C \to C' \to M'$, where M and M' were money quantities with M' hopefully $> M$, and C and C' were commodities encompassing wage goods and services of constant capital which were transformed, again, hopefully, through the production process into commodities (C') saleable at a profit $M' - M$.[9]

Many have come to see the 'transformation problem' relating the underlying embodied labour values of commodities to their prices of production as a sterile exercise and debate. Yet viewed in this way it makes sense, both in explaining a fundamental characteristic of capitalism and in illustrating the power of Marx's method and approach. In order to show that anything classical political economy could do Marx could do as well and better, it was necessary to reconcile the pure theory of the origin of profits in the capitalist mode of production with the other major 'finding' of political economy – the tendency to a uniform rate of profit in all activities – and also to 'explain' what determined the size of the system-wide rate of profits. (Sraffa, who had a deep knowledge of and admiration for Marx's work, always spoke of the rate of profits, indicating that it *was* the system-wide concept which needed to be explained within the classical and Marxist system. As Pasinetti said of his own modern variant of the theory of the rate of profits: 'It is macro-economic because it could not be otherwise', Pasinetti. 1974, 118.)

The various conundrums arise because, while competition would ensure a uniform rate of exploitation (s/v, where $s =$ surplus labour and $v =$ necessary labour) in all industries because, as we have seen, free wage-labourers can always move from one occupation to another, there is nothing obvious or even not obvious in the forces of competition and their impact on technical progress to ensure that the corresponding organic compositions of capital (c/v) (with some licence, the capital–labour ratios) should also tend to equality. But since a well-known Marxist result is that $r = s/v/(1 + c/v)$, when all variables are measured in terms of abstract socially necessary labour time, *if* the LTV meant that commodities exchanged in proportion to their embodied labour amounts, there would not be a tendency, not even a long-run

---

[9] On the way to creating *The General Theory*, Keynes applauded Marx for this insight.

one, to equality of rates of profit (so measured) in all activities. Therefore it became necessary to explain the deviations of the prices of production with their uniform profit components around the underlying labour values, at the same time requiring the explanation to embrace the magnitudes of surplus value *et al.* in the sphere of production.

This step is what the various proposed 'solutions' of the transformation problem were meant to establish.[10] The fact that Marx's own solution was wrong and that Engels would not part with the promised prize to those who got it right (even when they did) is beside the point, Böhm-Bawerk and *Karl Marx and the Close of his System* (1889) notwithstanding. It also allows us to comment on another modern controversy arising from consideration of the transformation problem – Ian Steedman's argument (1975, 1977) that including joint production techniques in a model of value, distribution and accumulation stopped the Fundamental Marxist Theorem (FMT, as Michio Morishima dubbed it) going through. The FMT is the proposition that the necessary and sufficient condition to observe a positive rate of profits in the sphere of distribution and exchange is to have positive surplus labour (and value) in the sphere of production. Steedman argued that it was possible in a joint production system to have *negative* surplus labour and value in the sphere of production associated with *positive* profits in the sphere of distribution and exchange.

But, as a number of economists soon showed (for example, Morishima 1976), this is not so if Marx's sturdy intuition is specified appropriately in the model. Again, this is not just esoteric game-playing in order to fill out (or up) CVs, but an excellent example of making precise sense of a major insight which still has relevance today. For while the RAL no longer pushes *all* wage-earners' incomes down to subsistence levels, nevertheless recent macroeconomic policy has unwittingly been drawing on Marx's insights to create a potential surplus for greater profits and accumulation by creating cowed and acquiescent workforces whose necessary labour time has been much reduced. Of course, the policy-makers have forgotten another Marxist insight, that there are internal contradictions present in each mode of production. In modern capitalism, as in the capitalism of Marx's time, the policies used to create a potential surplus may simultaneously so dampen and depress the 'animal spirits' of the decision-making and accumulating class that the potential surplus may remain largely unrealised by actual accumulation

---

[10] Sraffa's is the most satisfying, as Meek pointed out in his (1961) review article of *Production of Commodities*.

and actual investment expenditure – the initial $C \rightarrow C'$ in the circuit above. Marx also recognised that industrial, commercial and finance capital must advance in tandem and that, when they do not, crises occur.[11] The dominance of industrial and commercial capital by financial capital has been a major cause of the instabilities in world capitalism of the past twenty years or more.[12]

We now move on to lessons from *Capital*, vols. II and III, especially the role of the Schemes of Reproduction which played such an important part, often unrealised by the people employing them, in both the Keynesian/Kaleckian revolution and the immediate pre-war and post-war theories of growth. As Claudio Sardoni (1981) has made clear, to interpret the schemes of reproduction as precursors of steady-state growth models is to misunderstand what Marx was doing. What Marx's three departmental schemas – wage goods, luxury goods, capital goods – were meant to make explicit were the consistency conditions needed to ensure, period by period, that total demands and total supplies, as well as their compositions, matched. Satisfying the conditions period by period did not imply steady growth over 'time' though it was, of course, a possibility. There is no suggestion in Marx, just as there was not in Joan Robinson's (1956) 'Golden Ages' (nor, to be fair, in Solow's original (1956) neoclassical growth model), that this was descriptive economics. Indeed, in the first two instances, the principal objective was to show just how very special the conditions of the various inter- and intra-departmental purchases and sales had to be, so as to make it a complete fluke if capitalism left to itself with its myriad of decision-makers doing their own thing collectively brought such conditions about. Moreover, if they were not satisfied in fact, these authors went on to show how this could precipitate possibly a crisis and certainly serious malfunctioning. As Joan Robinson pointed out, Roy Harrod (her contemporary), in complete ignorance of a predecessor, discovered this all over again when he discussed the unstable nature of the warranted rate of growth. If the economy was on it, well and good, but if it was not, the system gave out signals which took the economy farther and farther away from it – and this, quite regardless of whether or not the warranted and natural rates of growth were coinciding.[13] In a not unrelated manner, Rosa Luxemburg (1913) argued that c/v would tend to increase to a point where the consumption of wage goods would be insufficient to absorb their production – that is, she raised the spectre

[11] Hilferding (1910) was one of the first major writers on this theme.
[12] This argument is expanded in chapter 8 (pp. 101–9).
[13] We expand this argument below (see the section on Harrod).

of underconsumption, to be initially resolved by the courting of external markets through imperialism and sales of armaments.

Finally, in Marx's work we have one of the first systematic attempts to provide a theory of endogenous technical progress. He attempted to show that the capitalist system would experience deeper and deeper crises, principally by changing methods of production in each cycle such that a tendency to a falling rate of profits was produced. (It was common to all political economists up to and including Marx that there was such a tendency, it was over the explanation that they differed.) A falling rate of profits would in the times when Marx was writing stifle both the desire and the ability to accumulate (have things changed that much?). Because real wages tended to rise in the upswing and boom as the RAL shrank, labour-saving innovations would be induced and embodied in the stock of capital goods by current accumulation. It was sensible – indeed, essential – for each individual capitalist to so respond, in order to try to survive in a fiercely competitive environment (just as it was sensible for them always to try to weaken the power of the wage-earners on the workshop floor); but the systemic result was to swell on trend the RAL and reduce the fund of living labour from which surplus labour and surplus value could be extracted for future accumulation. Thus falling realised profits would reduce both the desire and ability to accumulate – the fundamental contradiction of capitalism was to tend to induce just the sort of technical progress which ultimately would tend to destroy the system itself.

We know now that the details of the argument meant that this was only a *possibility*, not an inevitable result as Marx tended(!) to believe. (If we examine $r = s/v/(1 + c/v)$, it is clear that a rise in c/v would reduce r; but if v is reduced by technical advances it is not obvious that s/v will *not* rise.) The point is that looking at events in Marx's way leads us to concentrate on the appropriate variables and processes to be used and analysed respectively.

Marx's writings on economics generated a tradition of study combining economic history with classical political economy. Confrontation or class struggle had occurred in every mode of production both as an economic and a social/political confrontation. The development of successive forms and forces or modes of production is the process of historical materialism. Capitalism is that phase in this history at which labour-power has become a commodity. Starting from the concept of embodied labour Marx explained the exploitation in capitalism of the direct producers through both the relations of production and the appropriation of the surplus by the class which purchased their labour-power. Struggle over the conditions of its sale and the production, distribution and use of the surplus it produced become part of the contradictory conditions which, through a dialectical process, resolved into new forms – or, ultimately, new social relations or forces, and so new modes of production. Marx saw final events as resolutions of already existing but conflicting features of the economic system. Value, therefore, is primarily an historically relative category, specific to capitalism. The measurement difficulty arising from reconciling labour-embodied values with prices of production can be regarded as no longer a problem if the labour theory of value is seen as a conceptual argument about the origins of the surplus and of expanded reproduction and change.

Marx recognised the drive for capital accumulation. He also recognised the contradictory tendencies present in this pursuit, demonstrating some possibilities in the circuits of capital. He was therefore inconclusive about the exact nature of the collapse of capitalism.

Harrod[14]

The issues associated with the 'magnificent dynamics' of the classical political economists and Marx (this evocative phrase is due to Baumol 1951, see Baumol with Turvey 1970, 13) were rather shunted to one side in the subsequent literature. First, the profession concentrated on the rise to dominance of the supply and demand theories associated with Jevons, Walras, Menger, Marshall and their offshoots in the imperfect/monopolistic competition 'revolutions' of the 1930s; and then on the immediate problems of sustained unemployment and the trade cycle in modern capitalist economies, associated especially with the contributions of Keynes but, of course, with many others as well (see Laidler 1999). Modern growth theory, now classified under the rubric of 'old' growth theory in relation to 'new' endogenous growth theory, has its beginnings in the seminal (and now classic) writings of Roy Harrod just before and after the Second World War.

Harrod himself saw his (1939) article, 'An essay in dynamic theory', and his (1948) book, *Towards a Dynamic Economics*, as putting forward a new, exciting way of seeing and doing economics. It would, he wrote, make 'the old static formulation of problems [seem] stale, flat and unprofitable' (Harrod 1939, 15).

Harrod's primary purpose was to set out some fundamental relationships between rates of change of levels of key variables at a moment of time (instead of relationships between levels as in static analysis). He

---

[14] I have drawn heavily on Harcourt (2001a, 2002, forthcoming) in writing this section.

abstracted from lags between variables in key relationships – they could come in later – and from all but the necessary attention to the impact of certain expectations on economic behaviour and decision-making. This led him to distinguish between four concepts of the rate of growth of economies: expected (g_e), actual (g), warranted (g_w) and natural (g_n). The first two are self-explanatory; the last two are very much his innovations. g_w is rather inelegantly defined by Harrod (1939, 16) as 'that rate of growth which, if it occurs, will leave all parties satisfied that they have produced neither more nor less than the right amount'. This would lead decision-makers to wish to repeat the rates of growth they had first planned and then subsequently achieved. The natural rate of growth (g_n) reflected the supply-side characteristics of the economy; it was determined by the rate of growth of the labour force and the rate at which through technical advances the labour force improved its productivity over time. Harrod supposed g_n to be independent of g_e, g and g_w – on reflection, an unacceptable simplification once the embodiment of technical advances in the stock of capital goods by investment and the accompanying impact on productivity of the labour force are recognised.

Two questions then arose. First, if the economy does not immediately grow at g_w as an aggregate outcome of the activities of individual businesspeople, could the signals given out by the economy – in particular, the implications of the revealed discrepancies between what was initially expected and what was actually achieved – be such as to induce the decision-makers to take such actions as to move g_e and g towards g_w? That is to say, is g_w a stable or an unstable rate of growth? Secondly, even if g_w were to be achieved, would it also necessarily coincide with g_n, so that both full employment of labour and normal capacity working of the stock of capital goods would be achieved?

In outline, this is how Harrod and his interpreters posed the questions. With hindsight, we may see that his contributions fit into two major strands of the preceding literature. The first relates to Marx's schemes of reproduction, Marx (1885; (1978), a link of which Harrod candidly admitted (to Joan Robinson who pointed it out to him) he was not aware when he wrote his two classics. As we have seen (see pp. 100–1, Marx asked in effect: what conditions must be fulfilled as between the three departments of the economy – wage, capital and luxury goods – in his two schema (simple and expanded reproduction, respectively) in order that, as we would say now, both aggregate demand and aggregate supply, and their respective compositions, would match? That is to say, each department could in effect take in its own washing and the appropriate portions of the other departments' washing as well (see Sardoni 1981). Having established the very special conditions implied, Marx conjectured that it would be a fluke if individual businesspeople operating in a competitive environment and pursuing their own goals brought these conditions into being. He argued that if they did not, instability and even crises would result. Harrod's contribution was to provide a precise set of answers to such fundamental questions concerning the laws of motion of capitalism.

The second strand to which he contributed is, of course, the Keynesian revolution. Keynes had analysed the employment-creating effects of accumulation and argued that it was unlikely that, left to itself, a capitalist economy would even on average bring about a level of accumulation that would offset leakages into full employment saving. He had little systematically to say about the capacity-creating effects of current investment expenditure, especially if it were to be acted upon so as to produce full employment in the short run. Harrod did not explicitly (as did Domar) pose questions about the latter – what were the conditions that would make aggregate demand be such as to ensure that the economy advanced along g_e, g, g_w and g_n? If these equalities were not attained, what factors in the economy would provide signals that would lead decision-makers to act in such a manner as to establish them?

So we have two basic questions: first, what determines g_w and is g_w stable? Secondly, if $g_w \neq g_n$ initially, what forces are present, at least in a long-term sense, to bring them to equality?

First, we derive an expression for g_w. Harrod built on the analysis in his (1936) book on the trade cycle of the relationship between the accelerator which determined planned investment expenditure and the multiplier which determined the equilibrium level of income associated with planned investment expenditure. He concentrated on a point in time, deriving the conditions by which the aggregate level and rate of growth of expected sales in the economy would be achieved by creating through investment the capacity for production to match them and the aggregate demand to match the forthcoming aggregate supply. As Amartya Sen (1970) has shown, the desired expressions may be derived as follows: we write the saving function as $S_t = sY_t$, where S is overall saving, s is the marginal (equals the average) propensity to save, Y is income (also realised sales and output) and t is the current period of time; the investment function is $I_t = q(X_t - Y_{t-1})$, where I is planned investment expenditure, q is the desired incremental capital–output ratio (the accelerator) and X_t is the expected level of sales of time t. Harrod assumed that national income is always the short-period equilibrium level of income, so abstracting from the groping process whereby the stabilising signals given out by any initial gap between planned investment and planned saving tend to take the economy toward the equilibrium point, Keynes' level of effective demand, so that planned and actual investment equal planned and actual saving ($sY_t = I_t$). It follows that:

$$Y_t = \frac{1}{s}I_t = \frac{1}{s}q(X_t - Y_{t-1})$$

What is the condition for $X_t = Y_t$?
    Write

$$\frac{Y_t}{X_t} = \frac{q}{s}\left(\frac{X_t - Y_{t-1}}{X_t}\right) = \frac{q}{s}g_e$$

$\frac{Y_t}{X_t} = 1$ if and only if $g_e = \frac{s}{q}$. This is the expression for Harrod's g_w. Moreover, the actual rate of growth exceeds, equals, or falls short of, g_e if g_e itself exceeds, equals, or falls short of, g_w.

Harrod noted that *unless* the economy is on g_w then, even though accumulation plans are always realised, they would not have been made in the first place, had the actual outcomes been correctly expected. This leads to the analysis of g_w's stability.

We may put it this way: having ruled out by assumption the stabilising signals of a gap between planned investment and planned saving in the short period, Harrod sensed the destabilising signals of such a gap in the long period. Suppose that $g > g_e > g_w$. Then businesspeople would be encouraged to undertake an even greater rate of accumulation in the future, so driving the economy even further away from g_w. This occurs because, if we look at levels, the investment relationship, the slope of which, q, is the accelerator, is both greater than unity and s, the slope of the saving function (constrained to be well less than unity), so that the saving relationship is intersected from below. There is excess demand to the right of the intersection (and excess supply to the left), providing exactly the opposite signals to the short-period signals. Moreover, even if the economy is on g_w there is no guarantee that g_w will correspond to g_n, because they are determined by independent factors.

We illustrate Harrod's insight about the long-period gap between planned investment and planned saving in a simple diagram. (The diagram is the essence of Harrod à la Sen 1970.)

The implications of the discrepancies between planned saving and planned investment are obscured by considering only the employment-creating effects of the relationship between the two, implications relating to both the conditions for steady growth and the instability of the economy if the conditions are not attained.

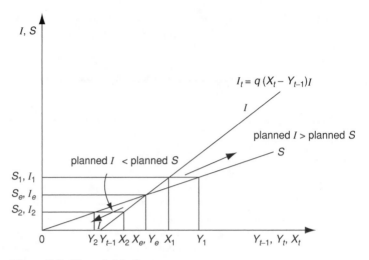

Figure 7.3. Harrod *à la* Sen.

Our diagram (see figure 7.3), shows clearly why the ordering referred to above

$$g_t \gtreqless g_e \text{ if } g_e \gtreqless \frac{s}{q} (= g_w)$$

comes about and makes explicit the sense in which discrepancies between planned S and planned I are the basic cause of them. On the horizontal axis we measure Y_{t-1}, Y_t and X_t; on the vertical axis, S and I. $0S(S_t = sY_t)$ is the saving function and $II(I_t = q(X_t - Y_{t-1}))$, the investment function. When $X_t = Y_{t-1}$, $I_t = 0$. The value of q is greater than the value of s, because it is not constrained to be less than unity and the periods of time that we are dealing with are such as to make q greater than unity.

As we mentioned above, actual income is always the short-period equilibrium level of income – i.e. it is the income associated with the level of saving that equals the level of planned investment, the latter itself given by the II function in conjunction with given values of Y_{t-1} and X_t.

At

$$X_e, Y_e, I_t = q(X_e - Y_{t-1}) = sY_e (= sX_e)$$

and

$$\frac{X_e - Y_{t-1}}{X_e} = \frac{Y_e - Y_{t-1}}{Y_e} = \frac{s}{q}$$

(expected = actual = warranted)

At

$$X_{1,} X_1 \; < \; Y_1$$

$$I_t = q(X_1 - Y_{t-1}) = sY_1(\neq sX_1)$$

$$\frac{Y_1 - Y_{t-1}}{Y_1} > \frac{X_1 - Y_{t-1}}{X_1} > \frac{X_1 - Y_{t-1}}{Y_1} \left(= \frac{s}{q}\right)$$

(actual > expected > warranted).

At

$$X_{2,} X_2 \; > \; Y_2$$

$$I_t = q(X_2 - Y_{t-1}) = sY_2(\neq sX_2) \text{ and}$$

$$\frac{Y_2 - Y_{t-1}}{Y_2} < \frac{X_2 - Y_{t-1}}{X_2} < \frac{X_2 - Y_{t-1}}{Y_2} \left(= \frac{s}{q}\right)$$

(actual < expected < warranted).

Consider, first, the case when expected sales are equal to the value of income associated with the interception of $0S$ and II – i.e. $X_e = Y_e$. Then investment expenditure is I_e and this produces an equilibrium level of Y_e, for at that level $I_e = S_e$. In this case, expected sales and actual sales and income coincide. We then get:

$$I_t = q(X_e - Y_{t-1}) = sY_e(= sX_e)$$

which implies that the expected rate of growth equals the actual rate of growth, which in turn equals the warranted rate of growth.

Now consider the case where expected sales are X_1. At X_1, planned $I >$ planned S, and so the equilibrium level of income, Y_1, is greater than X_1. That is to say, expectations of sales greater than those associated with the warranted rate of growth imply an actual level of income (and rate of growth) which exceed *both* the warranted and the expected level (and rate of growth) – short-period income must settle at that point if S is to equal I. We thus have:

$$I_t = q(X_1 - Y_{t-1}) = sY_1(\neq sX_1)$$

and

$$\frac{Y_1 - Y_{t-1}}{Y_1} > \frac{X_1 - Y_{t-1}}{X_1} > \frac{X_1 - Y_{t-1}}{Y_1} = \frac{s}{q}$$

$$\left(1 - \frac{Y_{t-1}}{Y_1} > 1 - \frac{Y_{t-1}}{X_1} > \frac{X_1}{Y_1} - \frac{Y_{t-1}}{Y_1}\right)$$

i.e. the actual rate of growth is greater than the expected rate of growth because the expected rate of growth is greater than the warranted rate of growth.

Finally, if expected sales were less than X_e, we would get the reverse results: warranted > expected > actual.

All of these follow from the discrepancy between planned S and planned I at the *expected level of demand*, X_t. Expected $I \gtreqless S$ implies actual $Y_t \gtreqless X_t$. It is discrepancies which give rise to Harrod's discussion of stability. For Harrod, as a good Keynesian (without quotes), stresses the link between realisations and expectations. The realisation of a rate of growth of sales greater than the warranted and previously expected rates of growth could lead to an expectation of at least the last period's rate of growth of sales. This, in turn, leads to both the warranted and the expected rate of growth of sales being exceeded again, as a glance at figure 7.3 will show – inflationary instability sets in. By similar reasoning, it is clear that if the expected rate of sales is the warranted rate (and is therefore achieved), and if this expectation is projected, steady growth at the warranted rate will be maintained. If, finally, the achieved rate is *less* than the warranted rate, this will lead, on the same assumption about expectations, to deflationary (contractionary) instability. Moreover, though planned I is always realised, it is not what would have been planned had the businesspeople known the actual Y involved.

Finally, partly as a digression and partly as a generalisation, we note that the derivation of Harrod's simple expression for g_w depends upon dropping the autonomous term from Keynes' consumption (and saving) function. While this is so, it may nevertheless be argued that it does *not* affect the deep insights that Harrod (and Marx before him) offered concerning the basic instability of the motion of unfettered capitalism.

If there is an autonomous term in the consumption function, say A ($-A$ in the corresponding saving function, $S = -A + sY$):

$$Y_t = \frac{q}{s}(X_t - Y_{t-1}) + \frac{A}{s}$$

$$\frac{Y_t}{X_t} = \frac{q}{s}\left(\frac{X_t - Y_{t-1}}{X_t}\right) + \frac{A}{sX_t}$$

and when

$$g_{et} = \frac{s}{q} \cdot \frac{Y_t}{X_t} \neq 1$$

because

$$\frac{A}{sX_t} \neq 0. \left(\frac{Y_t}{X_t} = 1 \text{ when } g_{et} = \frac{s}{q} - \frac{qA}{X_t}\right)$$

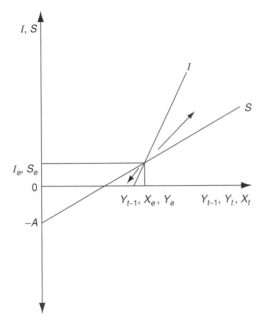

Figure 7.4. Harrod's model with an autonomous term in the saving function.

We draw our diagram again, this time including a (negative) constant term, A, in the saving function (see figure 7.4). A similar story of destabilising signals may be told; the economy will be on and remain on g_w only if expected sales are such as to give the values of $I_e(= S_e)$.

Solow–Swan

There were two principal early reactions to Harrod's instability problem and the non-equality of g_w and g_n. The best known is, first, the neo-classical model of economic growth associated with Robert Solow (1956) and Trevor Swan (1956)[15] – two eminent Keynesian economists, it should be noted. They asked the following questions: suppose an

---

[15] John Pitchford, who was at the seminar which led Swan to develop his 1956 article, has edited and published a larger and more wide-ranging paper by Swan (2002) out of which the published article came (see Pitchford 2002). The previously unpublished paper is remarkable for its insights and prescience and reveals, yet again, what a superb mind Swan had.

all-wise, Keynesian-inspired, government were to keep the economy at full employment in all short periods. Would then the operation of neo-classical forces, Marshall's 'dynamical principle of 'Substitution' . . . seen ever at work' (Marshall 1890; 1962, xv), responding to appropriate signals through the price mechanism, lead to a change in q so as to give it a value that makes $g_w = g_n$? As is well known, at least in a simple one-commodity model, the price mechanism does the trick by so changing the relative prices of the services of labour and capital as to lead busi-nesspeople, faced with different techniques of production, to choose the value of q that, given the value of s, brings about the desired equality. Solow argued that Harrod's assumption of a constant value of q was too strong, too *ad hoc* and likely to be the cause of the instability result, that a capitalist economy is immensely unstable, either pushing upwards to an inflationary Heaven or downwards to a deflationary Hell. This is not really fair to Harrod, for he was considering a point in time so that q could be momentarily both a constant *and* the outcome of sensible economic choice in a given situation.

We now examine Swan's way, his version of the issues involved, for I have always thought, even after discounting for Australian nationalism, that Swan's diagram (see figure 7.5) brings out the processes involved in a wonderfully clear manner, even better than Solow's diagrams which now adorn most textbooks.[16] There is a well-known tale of the mathem-atician who burst into tears at the sight of the binomial theorem 'because it is so beautiful'. I have had occasion to remark that economists at least get a lump in their throats at the sight of the Cobb–Douglas production function because it has such beautiful properties: the expo-nents of K and L measure the respective shares of wages and profits in national income; the marginal products of K and L measure, respect-ively, the return to capital and the wage rate; the marginal products themselves relate in a very simple way – proportionally, where the factors of proportionality have clear economic meaning – to their respective average products. Moreover, in growth theory the Cobb–Douglas func-tion allows simple measures of the contributions to growth in output per head of the respective growth in capital and labour. Swan's algebra and diagrams neatly exploit these properties (and more) in order to illuminate the processes being analysed – and, in particular, to show why competitive markets give out stabilising signals which guide g_w towards equality with g_n by affecting the choice of technique (as reflected in capital–output ratios).

---

[16] Generations of Australians have been brought up on this and other famous Swan diagrams, invaluable pedagogic tools for teachers and taught alike.

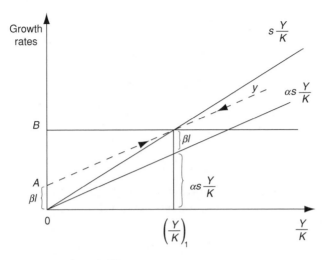

Figure 7.5. Swan's Way.

Swan wrote his economy-wide aggregate production function as:

$$Y = K^\alpha L^\beta$$

where Y = output, K = capital and L = labour. Swan avoided the problems associated with the measurement (if not the meaning) of capital by adopting a one, all-purpose commodity model, akin to corn as seed corn, corn as output. (Swan in the appendix to the article explicitly dodged capital measurement problems by using the analogy of Meccano sets.) The Cobb–Douglas production function exhibits constant returns to scale, so that $\alpha + \beta = 1$ and $\beta = 1 - \alpha$. If we also assume that perfect competition reigns in all markets, we know that r (the return to capital) equals the marginal product of capital and w (the real wage) equals the marginal product of labour. Moreover, with Cobb–Douglas:

$$\frac{\delta Y}{\delta K} = \alpha K^{\alpha-1} L$$

But

$$\frac{Y}{K} = K^{\alpha-1} L^{1-\alpha}$$

So

$$\frac{\delta Y}{\delta K} = \alpha \frac{Y}{K} (= r)$$

and the share of profits in national income is

$$\frac{rK}{Y} = \frac{\alpha \frac{Y}{K} K}{Y} = \alpha$$

Similarly, it may be shown that:

$$w = \beta \frac{Y}{L} = (1 - \alpha) \frac{Y}{L}$$

and the wage share

$$\beta = (1 - \alpha)$$

We obtain the relative contributions of the growth of capital and labour to the growth of output by logarithmic differentiation of the production function:

$$\frac{1}{Y} \cdot \frac{\delta Y}{\delta t} = \alpha \frac{1}{K} \frac{\delta K}{\delta t} + \beta \frac{1}{L} \frac{\delta L}{\delta t}$$

or

$$y = \alpha \frac{I}{K} + \beta l = \alpha \frac{sY}{K} + \beta l$$

where y is the rate of growth of output, $\frac{sY}{K}$ the rate of growth of capital and l the rate of growth of labour.

Now consider Swan's diagram (see figure 7.5). On the vertical axis we measure *rates* of growth, on the horizontal axis the output–capital ratio, $\frac{Y}{K}$. $s\frac{Y}{K}$ is the growth line of capital, showing what value of the rate of growth of capital will be obtained for any given values of Y, K and s. The resulting contribution to the growth of output is given by $\alpha s \frac{Y}{K}$. Note, too, that $\alpha s \frac{Y}{K}$ tells us (indirectly) what the value of r is at any rate of growth and value of K/Y. Now put in the exogenously given rate of growth of labour (no Malthus here), $0B$ (see the horizontal line starting from B on the vertical axis). We add the (constant) contribution to the growth of output of the growth of labour (βl) to the contribution line of the growth of capital to give the rate of growth of output associated with each value of $\frac{Y}{K}$ (see line y).

Then, because $\alpha + \beta = 1$, when labour and capital grow at the same rate, so too does output, so that all three lines intersect at the value of $\frac{Y}{K}$ marked on the diagram, $\left(\frac{Y}{K}\right)_1$. To the left of the intersection output grows faster than capital (and slower than labour), to the right the ordering of rates of growth is reversed. Because Swan (and Solow) assume the substitution possibilities between capital and labour given by the production function, these relative growth rates imply changes in relative factor prices such that through cost-minimising, profit-maximising choices of technique, the values of the capital–labour and capital–output ratios 'change' in such ways as always to lead the economy towards the intersection point of the three lines where we have steady equal rates of growth of output, capital and labour – the neoclassical steady state. For example, suppose $\frac{Y}{K}$ were momentarily above $\left(\frac{Y}{K}\right)_1$. Then, capital would be growing faster than output (and labour slower). The output–capital ratio would be falling (and $\frac{Y}{L}$ rising). These moves in turn imply that r is tending to fall and w to rise, inducing the choice of a more capital- and less labour-intensive technique–i.e. a lower $\frac{Y}{K}$. Similarly, it may be shown that the appropriate relative price signals would be given to the left of the intersection point, leading to the choice of higher $\frac{Y}{K}$s.

Note that

$$\frac{sY}{K}\left(=\frac{s}{q}\right)$$

is Harrod's g_w and that l is his g_n (we abstract from the impact of technical progress). The gs are, of course, equal at the intersection point, and anywhere away from it the price signals are such as to change g_w so as to drive its value towards that of g_n. This is the neoclassical, Solow/Swan solution to one of Harrod's problems – the forces of substitution do the trick by changing the value of $\frac{Y}{K}$. Seemingly Harrod instability has also also been banished in the sense that the intersection point is a stable equilibrium point (in a one-, all-purpose, commodity model). So much, it seems, for Marx, Harrod and the actual behaviour of capitalism. Not that either Swan or Solow ever believed this literally for a moment. Here is Solow's take on the issue, one that has been shamefully neglected by his surrogates (and his critics) ever after:

Everything above is the neo-classical side of the coin. Most especially is it full employment economics – in the dual aspect of equilibrium condition and frictionless, competitive, causal system. All the difficulties and rigidities which go into modern Keynesian income analysis have been shunted aside. [It was not Solow's] contention that these problems don't exist, nor that they are of no significance in the long run. [Solow's] purpose was to examine . . . the tightrope view of economic growth and to see whether more flexible assumptions about production would lead to a simple model. Underemployment and excess capacity or their opposites can still be attributed to any of the old causes of deficient or excess aggregate demand, but less readily to any deviation from a narrow 'balance'. (Solow 1956, in Sen 1970, 189–90).

Kaldor, Mark 1

The second main response to Harrod's writings came from the other Cambridge, through Kaldor, Joan Robinson, Kahn, Pasinetti and Goodwin. In this section we examine Kaldor's initial response to Harrod and his problems. As we saw in chapter 2 on macroeconomic theories of distribution, in Kaldor's classic 1955–6 article, 'Alternative theories of distribution', he developed a long-period, full-employment, 'Keynesian' macroeconomic theory of distribution. By having the economy at full employment in the long term, the Keynesian saving–investment relationship, with investment leading and saving responding, came about through changes in the distribution of long-period full employment income between wages and profits, with accompanying changes in the values of the aggregate saving ratio. Kaldor supposed that the economy was induced to accumulate at a rate and as a share of income $(\bar{I}/Y_f)$ that would keep it on the natural rate of growth, g_n, where the value of g_n was exogenously given.

Then g_w, if not equal initially to g_n, would be brought to such an equality by changes in the value of S/Y_f. So Kaldor accepts a constant value of q – indeed, goes further in the article, making its value independent of economic signals through profits, putting all the emphasis on adjustment through the value of S/Y_f. Thus, as we saw, if at full employment, planned S/Y_f were to be, say, less than $\bar{I}/Y_f$, the resulting excess demand situation would tend to make prices rise faster than money-wages, redistributing income from wage-earners to profit-receivers and raising the value of g_w to equality with g_n where $S/Y_f = \bar{I}/Y_f$.

Kaldor had an especially fertile period in the 1950s and the 1960s when he developed a number of different models of growth (or, rather, different-in-detail versions of the same underlying 'vision').[17] In doing so, Kaldor moved away from concern with Harrod's models as such, by developing models in order to explain a set of 'stylised facts' which he felt characterised the development of modern capitalist economies.

By 'stylised facts' Kaldor meant broad empirical generalisations which hold, in a rough and ready way, often for long runs of historical time and require situation-specific theories and accompanying models to explain them. It was Kaldor's particular genius to discern more of these than probably any other economist of the twentieth century. Like the classical

---

[17] Indeed, Bob Solow in his (1963) Marshall Lectures on a mythical creature called 'Nicky' and another called 'Joan' pictured 'Nicky' in a Sputnik circling the earth, dropping off growth models at frequent intervals, with a new one on the way even before the preceding one had reached the earth.

political economists, Marx and also Marshall, Kaldor preferred to start from empirical generalisations about systemic behaviour and the behaviour of decision-makers and then to build on them theory and accompanying models, in order to see whether the inferences deducible from the latter matched in a general way the observations to be explained.

In the 1950s and 1960s the 'stylised facts' his models of growth were meant to explain were the observed constancies (there was some dispute as to whether the observations were in fact constants or not) in capital–output ratios, the distribution of income and rates of profits on capital. There were three broad features of his models: first, as we have seen, having the Keynesian saving–investment relationship help to explain the distribution of income instead of the level of income and employment. Secondly, having rejected the traditional (neoclassical) idea that we may distinguish movements *along* the production function from movements *of* the function itself when analysing the relationship between the growth of productivity, capital accumulation and technical progress, Kaldor put in its place a technical progress function (see, for example, Kaldor 1957). It described the relationship between proportionate rates of growth of productivity and of capital over time (in the last form he gave it in Kaldor and Mirlees 1962, the relationship was between the proportionate rate of gross investment per operative and the proportionate rate of growth of the productivity of labour operating the new machines, an idea which has much in common with Salter's analysis which we discussed above on pp. 37–42, see also Salter 1960). Thirdly, Kaldor regarded scarcity of resources rather than lack of effective demand as the principal obstacle to economic growth, so that, as we saw, full employment is the long-period equilibrium position of a growing economy, a view Kaldor clung to tenaciously for well over ten years, despite being unable to establish clinching arguments to explain why this should necessarily be so. (Modern economists now just assert that it *is* so.)

We have already examined the details of the distribution mechanism. It has to be said that in Kaldor's models of growth he extended the distributive mechanism to include the short period while still assuming full employment and ignoring the peculiar pricing behaviour that the assumption of full employment implies for different sectors of the economy in order for the mechanisms to work and planned investment each short period to become actual investment (see Harcourt 1963; 1982).

The initial form of the technical progress function was constructed as follows: Kaldor assumed that the flow of new ideas over time occurred at a steady rate but that their impact on productivity depended on the rate at which capital was accumulated. He drew the technical progress

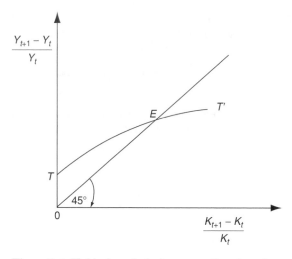

Figure 7.6. Kaldor's technical progress function, first model.

function, TT' (see figure 7.6), in which the proportionate rate of growth
of output, $(Y_{t+1} - Y_t)/Y_t$, is an increasing function of the proportionate
rate of growth of capital, $(K_{t+1} - K_t)/K_t$. Even without capital accumulation, productivity grew at the rate of $0T$. Faster rates required
accumulation. At E capital and output grew at the same proportionate
rate. Kaldor's main purpose was to show that there are forces at work
in capitalist economies which make E the position of long-period equilibrium. At E, K/Y is constant, as is I/Y; this implies in turn constant
distributive shares and a constant rate of profits on capital.

The technical progress function, which shows how output will change
if certain rates of investment are implemented, is complemented by an
investment function, itself complemented by the distributive mechanism. The investment function determines the *planned* investment of
each period, the distributive mechanism, whether it becomes *actual*
investment. Actual investment determines the position of the economy
on the technical progress function in each period. The length of the
period is such that the actual capital by the end of the period is brought
to the level of desired capital at the beginning of the period. After a
false start in his (1957) article, Kaldor specified a plausible investment
relationship which ensured the approach to E (see Kaldor 1961;
Harcourt 1963; 1982, 71–2).

The most explicit argument that Kaldor used to justify his belief that
long-period growth implied full employment involved the use of a 'representative firm' model (see Kaldor 1959a, 1961). The 'representative

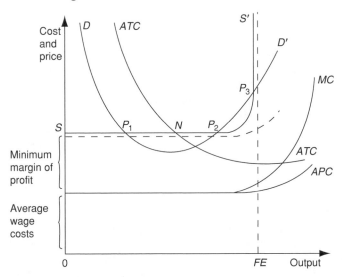

Figure 7.7. Kaldor's representative firm.

firm' behaved like a small-scale replica of the economy as a whole so that variations in its output reflected variations in aggregate output. Its supply curve consisted of average prime costs and a minimum margin of profit below which businesspeople would not go for fear of spoiling the market (see figure 7.7). Cost and price are measured on the vertical axis, output on the horizontal axis. Average prime costs are wages only, as raw material costs and intermediate goods generally net out for the economy as a whole (Kaldor assumes a closed economy). The constancy of average prime costs up to near full employment reflects his (then) view that employment rather than physical capacity was the principal constraint on output.

The corresponding demand curve, DD', is U-shaped showing, first, that the lower are prices relative to money-wages, the greater is the level of income associated with any given level of autonomous investment; secondly, that once normal profits are being received (at the point N, where the average *total* cost curve, including normal profits, cuts SS') induced investment will occur. However, there must be a shift to profits in order to bring forth the required planned saving, since in this range of output the marginal propensity to invest at any *given* distribution of income will exceed the corresponding marginal propensity to save (Kaldor 1959a, 219; 1961, 200). There are three possible equilibrium positions – namely, P_1, an underemployment one with no induced investment; P_2, an unstable one; and P_3, a full-employment one with positive induced investment. Kaldor argues that only P_3 is consistent with the observation that the national incomes of capitalist economies have, in fact, grown over time, for only at P_3 does induced investment occur and capacity grow; 'it . . . is impossible to conceive of a *moving* equilibrium of growth to be an under-employment equilibrium' (Kaldor 1959a, 220 emphasis in original).

While at first sight Kaldor's argument is attractive, it is vulnerable to criticisms that, as we noted, led him to change his mind (not necessarily because of *these* criticisms). The major criticism is the use of the 'representative firm' as a replica of the whole economy – does it represent the capital goods sector, the consumption goods sector, or a mixture? How can its output change at the same rate as national output which at best is a mixture of the outputs of the two sectors, the rates of output of which change at different rates to each other at different levels of overall activity? Moreover, if the distributive mechanism is to work in the short period, pricing behaviour must differ as between the two sectors (see Harcourt 1963; 1982) and so the pricing behaviour of the economy cannot be represented by the model.

Unless autonomous investment is unproductive, the point P_1 *can* exhibit both growth in output per head and underemployment, so that observed growth does not necessarily imply full employment. Indeed, *ceteris paribus.*, rising productivity will lower the SS' curve so that P_1 will move to the right over time, again showing that growth and under-employment equilibrium can go together. The section of the demand curve between P_1 and P_2 cannot exist because the price levels needed to establish outputs in this range are *below* the minimum supply price. P_3 could not exist either. The upward-sloping portion of DD' implies a shift to profits to allow investment to offset saving. It must therefore rise faster than the prime-cost curve APC (and SS') so that it would never cut from above.[18] So Kaldor's model shows that capitalist economies tend either towards an underemployment equilibrium or full employment with inflation. Finally, it is hard to see the logic of using the distributive mechanism which assumes full employment to ensure that the economy gets to full employment.

In the years after the late 1960s, Kaldor became more and more dissatisfied with this approach to designing models which provided long-term steady growth. He now thought that the problem of steady growth arose not from the saving–investment balance, but from the

---

[18] Eric Russell pointed this out to me.

difficulty of keeping the growth of the availability of primary products in line with the growth of the absorptive capacity of the industrial (and service) sectors of the world. He rejected both neoclassical and Keynesian growth models because they could not handle the basic complementarity of an integrated world. This required a multi-sector model to tackle the mutual independence of different sectors where the development of each depends upon, and is stimulated by, the development of others.

However, before we discuss Kaldor, Mark 2 in detail, we discuss the approaches of Joan Robinson, Goodwin and Pasinetti.

Joan Robinson (as told to Donald Harris)

Joan Robinson's and Donald Harris' writings preceded those of Marglin we discussed in chapter 6. Marglin used a very similar apparatus to discuss the concept of conflict inflation. Joan Robinson, and especially Harris, used the apparatus to indicate the sources of certain sorts of crises that were potentially possible in capitalism.[19]

Harris' neat diagram (see Harris 1975), allows us to bring in happenings in the sphere of production where the state of technology, the class war, the conditions of work and the creation of the potential surplus are intertwined; and to combine this with the Kaleckian, Keynesian, and Robinsonian construction of the 'animal spirits' function and the saving–investment relationship in the sphere of distribution and exchange. The determinants of effective demand and the distribution of income together determine whether the potential surplus will be realised or not in actual accumulation and profits and whether the conditions there are such as to create irreconcilables that lead to different forms of crisis.

Thus, on the left-hand side of figure 7.8 we have the sphere of production. At any moment of time technology and social factors between them allow a particular combination of wages and rates of profits potentially to be established. Here, we suppose the current state of the class struggle dictates a wage $w^\star$, what Marglin called the 'conventional wage'; it implies that the maximum rate of profits which may be received is $r^\star$. On the right-hand side we have the sphere of distribution and

---

[19] Their writings also bear on the methodological dispute between Joan Robinson and Kalecki, on the one hand, and Garegnani, Eatwell, Kurz and others, on the other, concerning the role of the classical Marxist concept of centres of gravitation and the use of the long-period method in economic theory (see Harcourt 1985; Kurz and Salvadori 1995 for further discussions).

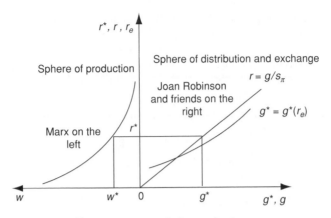

Figure 7.8. Class war, accumulation and crises.

exchange which we have already met. We show, first, in terms of rates of growth of the stock of capital goods, the rate of profits that would be established from the post-Keynesian expression $r = g/s_\pi$. We also show the accumulation or 'animal spirits' function, $g^\star = g^\star(r_e)$ – the desired rate of accumulation is a function of the expected rate of profits, for any given financial situation and state of long-term expectations. Provided the economy is within the area bounded by $g^\star$, $r^\star$ and is below $r = g/s_\pi$, no contradictions arise; but once it is outside it, a variety of crisis situations are created and changes must occur in order to resolve the contradictions which gave rise to them in the first place.

Even if the saving-investment line were to be intersected by the 'animal spirits' function at $r^\star$, $g^\star$, though the potential surplus would be realised there is no guarantee that full employment of labour would be achieved. We are only, as we saw in chapter 4 (pp. 63–5), on Joan Robinson's version of g_w, for the factors determining the rate of growth of the labour force are a largely independent set. As the economy moves on in historical time it remains to enquire whether the various relationships move and whether the actual rate of growth is such as to absorb or add to the reserve army of labour over time. If it is absorbing it, sooner or later an inflationary situation will ensue. If it is adding to it, the ensuing reaction depends very much on how a growing reserve army affects the class war in the sphere of production and the 'animal spirits' function in the sphere of distribution and exchange. The respective movements of these relationships over time are a dynamic illustration of Keynes' shifting equilibrium model. Finally, suppose that the 'animal spirits' function were to be *above* the saving–investment line. This would

imply a crisis marked by a deflationary, contractionary downward movement, and ultimately by a deep slump.[20]

Goodwin's eclecticism

I once described Richard Goodwin as a twentieth-century eclectic (see
Harcourt 1985; 1993, 105), a description intended as a great compli-
ment. For Goodwin not only had a fine analytical mind,[21] he also had a
deep knowledge of the conceptual contributions of past greats and his
contemporaries – Marx, Wicksell (his favourite economist), Marshall,
Walras, Keynes, Harrod, Leontief and Schumpeter, his two teachers at
Harvard (to whom he taught mathematics), Sraffa, Joan Robinson and
Kahn. Throughout his life he blended insights from these mentors
with original contributions of his own, taking in new developments in
both physics (which he taught at Harvard during the Second World War)
and mathematics. Because he was also an excellent abstract painter,
again with a great knowledge of past masters, with which was allied his
love of Italy, he preferred to teach using geometry, 'Marshall brought
up to date', as he described his approach in his (1970) book based on his
lectures to the second year at Cambridge.

Goodwin's principal preoccupations over many years were concerned
with the 'laws of motion of capitalism'. In the later years of his life he
and Lionello Punzo produced a grand synthesis that brought together
the two main but parallel strands of his earlier contributions – aggregate
models of cyclical growth, on the one hand, and the analysis of the
structure of production interdependence, on the other. Early signs of
his recognition of the need for such a connection was his well-known
article 'The multiplier as matrix' (Goodwin 1949; 1983), in which the
induced expenditures associated with the Kahn–Keynes–Meade multiplier operating on the multiplicand were traced through the interrelated
production patterns of the economy.

One theme that dominated Goodwin's thinking from early on, reflecting his readings of Marx and Schumpeter in particular, was his
insight that the trend and cycle were indissolubly mixed, *not* determined
by separate, independent factors. This implied that time series could
not analytically (as opposed to descriptively) be broken down, either
additively or multiplicatively, into trend components and cyclical

[20] Harris (1978) has a long chapter, 'Reproduction, accumulation and crises', discussing
all these possibilities.
[21] He is credited with at least one original discovery in mathematics (see Goodwin 1982,
186, 196).

components. (Here he was at one with the later Kalecki who, though he started by analysing a trendless cycle, eventually came to the view succinctly and accurately expressed in his last article on the subject, that the long-run trend was not an independent entity, that it was a statistical measure coming out of the happenings and interrelationships of successive short periods, see Kalecki 1971, 165.)

Already in a most lucid article in the *Yorkshire Bulletin* (Goodwin 1953; 1982), Goodwin addressed himself to the problem of trend and cycle, moving inevitably towards the concept of a growth cycle. In the (1953) article, he emphasised 'Marshall's famous principle that the short period is very much shorter [in real time] for expansions than for contractions' (Goodwin 1953; 1982, 117), as are the time periods associated with the distinction between fixed and variable costs.

Goodwin admired Harrod for combining the multiplier and the accelerator in his growth theory. To this, he added on Schumpeter's views on the role of technical progress through innovations in business cycle analysis. Goodwin thought that new ideas came forth smoothly (as did Kaldor later, in his technical progress function), but their embodiment was periodically bunched as existing capacity was used up in production and expenditures were rising in the upturn and expansion. This inevitably led to overshooting in the laying down of capacity, to a build-up of excess numbers of machines to back up new higher levels of activity, making the downturn and contraction inevitable. He was critical of Hicks' use of a rising floor and ceiling of activity associated with autonomous investment which did not affect overall productivity but did affect capacity, arguing that they were illogical – and unnecessary – in order to obtain endogenous cycles in capitalism (see Goodwin 1953; 1982, 115).

Because of his understanding of Marx, especially the roles of the reserve army of labour and of the sack as disciplinary devices on the factory floor, including restraining increases in money-wages, and of the fight over the distribution of income associated with class war, Goodwin was drawn more and more to an analysis of the symbiotic relationship between populations – 'the Volterra case of prey and predator' (Goodwin 1967; 1982, 167). In Goodwin's case the relationship was between wages and profits, workers and capitalists, bringing about cyclical developments. His masterpiece was his short contribution, 'A growth cycle', to Maurice Dobb's *Festschrift* volume (Feinstein 1967, reprinted in Goodwin 1982), in which the application of Volterra's model brought about a growth cycle – alternating periods of fast and slow, sometimes even negative growth. As Goodwin (1967; 1982, 167) wrote: 'the symbiosis of two populations – partly complementary, partly hostile – is helpful in . . . understanding . . . the dynamical contradictions of capitalism, especially when stated in a . . . Marxian form.' His essay spawned a literature that is still growing today.

Joan Robinson criticised him for 'falling' for Say's Law, just like Marx – and, as we have seen, Marglin. So Goodwin responded by integrating effective demand considerations in the analysis as part of his synthesis of aggregative models and production-interdependent ones which constitute the centrepiece of his major book with Punzo, *The Dynamics of a Capitalist Economy: A Multi-Sectoral Approach* (1987).

Pasinetti's grand synthesis[22]

Pasinetti has great clarity of mind and vision; they have allowed him to carry out a unified research programme, encompassing several strands.

His forty-and-more-year-old research programme has followed a co-herent pattern, first outlining the weaknesses of the marginalist model, and then laying step by step the foundations of the reconstruction, on mixed classical/'pure' Keynesian bases, of a 'more general theory' in order to identify, explain and analytically recompose the mechanisms and dynamics of modern economic systems. Pasinetti has used powerful tools of analysis, in particular the method of vertical integration, in order to understand a number of complicated phenomena taking place in economies – for example, the unequal distribution and pace of technical progress, non-linear variations in the composition of demand, a great variety of asymmetric behaviour and the complex role of institutions (although Pasinetti begins with a core model free of institutions). He may well be the last of the great system-builders of our trade. He is, of course, the senior living heir to the original post-Keynesian tradition.

Pasinetti's study of the 'long-term evolution of industrial economic systems' originated in 'a combination of three factors – one factual and two theoretical' (Pasinetti 1981, xi):

The factual element was provided by the extremely uneven development – from sector to sector, from region to region – of the environment in which I lived (post-war Europe) at the time I began my training in economics. The . . . theoretical factors are represented by the two types of theories – specifically the macro-dynamic models of economic growth and input–output analysis – . . . Both the macro-dynamic growth models and input–output analysis impressed me . . .; but they left me profoundly dissatisfied when I tried to use them in order

---

[22] This section draws heavily on the introduction that Mauro Baranzini and I wrote to the (1993) *Festschrift* for Luigi Pasinetti's sixtieth birthday (Baranzini and Harcourt 1993). As typical economists (vaguely right rather than precisely wrong) we started the project five years before and presented it to him three years after his actual birthday.

to understand what was going on in economic systems with a very high degree of dynamism, i.e. of technical progress. And I began to think that an attempt might be made to develop a theoretical scheme which, while retaining the analytical character of input–output analysis, could also deal with uneven increases in productivity, in the way the macro-dynamic models had begun to do, but only for the very simplified case of a one-commodity world . . . from this determination to look for new tools of analysis . . . the present work has come into being. (Pasinetti 1981, xi)

Step by step this work has become a 'theoretical essay on the dynamics of industrial systems'; its publication was delayed by two elements, which account for the long time that elapsed since it was first written as a PhD dissertation at Cambridge. The first is connected with the publication of Sraffa's *Production of Commodities by Means of Commodities* (1960), which emphasised the concept of 'circularity' in economic theory. Pasinetti's dynamic analysis had already avoided the fixity of coefficients which had forced inter-industry analysis 'into a strait-jacket'. In Pasinetti (1973) he established a link between Sraffa's analysis and worked out, without any loss of generality, all analytical inter-industry connections.

The second problem is connected with a distinctive feature of Pasinetti's approach, a 'level of investigation which is so fundamental as to be independent of the institutional set-up of society', the so-called 'natural' feature. In his well-known (1962) article 'Rate of profit and income distribution in relation to the rate of economic growth' Pasinetti, starting from Kaldor's income distribution theory, defined a 'natural' rate of profits at the macroeconomic level, determined by the natural rate of growth of the system and the propensity to save of the 'pure' capitalists' class. However, this was not satisfactory since, as Pasinetti (1981, xiii) points out, he soon realised 'that introducing behavioural (savings) relations did not fit consistently into a theoretical framework which was basically conceived independently of institutions'.

In Pasinetti (1980–1), he situated the concept of 'natural' at the industry or sector level where there logically exists a whole series of 'natural' rates of interest, at a stage which precedes the process of capital accumulation. Indeed, in a pure labour economic system characterised by structural dynamics of technology and prices there exists a rate of interest on interpersonal loans that keeps 'labour commanded' equal to 'labour embodied' through time. This natural rate of interest, obtained independently of any institutional framework, allowed the completion of Pasinetti's theoretical scheme.

Pasinetti (1981, xiii) emphasised the relevance of an institution-free scheme of inquiry: 'For the first, more fundamental, stage of analysis a complete and self-contained theoretical scheme has at least clearly emerged.' For these first important steps towards a full-scale reconstruction of political economy allow for a more comprehensive methodological approach. Alternative schemes of analysis provide a general rule (such as the equality between marginal productivities and factor payments) and successively are constrained to modify such a rule in order to take into account a number of exceptions (the presence of market imperfections, and so on). On the contrary, in the case of the 'natural' system approach the presence of a particular institutional set-up does not modify the basic framework, but simply provides additional information. And in the case of a modification of the institutional set-up the framework does not require modifications that are bound to alter its 'scope and method'.

This approach allows sharp differentiation between those economic problems that have to be solved on the ground of logic alone – for which economic theory is autonomous – and those economic issues that 'arise in connection with particular institutions, or with particular groups' or individuals' behaviour – for which economic theory is no longer autonomous and needs to be integrated with further hypotheses, which may well come from other social sciences' (Pasinetti 1981, xiii).

Pasinetti's contributions grew out of a thorough study of Ricardo and classical political economy generally. We have already used his early work on Ricardo (Pasinetti 1960), on pp. 89–94. The article itself – only the skeleton appears above – shows Pasinetti's theoretical skills and mastery of the interconnections between value, distribution and growth. The principal object of the article was to show how an analytical model could capture the ingredients of Ricardo's system and produce his results. The model contained the essence of Ricardo's theory of value – embodied labour. It highlighted Ricardo's stress on persistent and permanent or dominant factors at work in the economy which expressed themselves in the forces which determined natural prices. The short-term factors associated with supply and demand and the determination of market prices were relegated to a secondary position. This was especially so in Ricardo's theory of the natural wage and changes in population *cum* labour force, with which was associated his theory of accumulation. In Pasinetti's model, the Malthusian principle of population works instantaneously so that the wage is *always* at its natural level even though accumulation is occurring. This simplification allows, as we saw, a clear-cut picture of the accumulation process and the approach to the stationary state.

Two- and then *n*-sector versions of the model show the results of the simple model to be robust (*n*-sector models for Pasinetti are also the crux of structural dynamic analysis). Pasinetti used Ricardo's theory of value to illustrate the dichotomy in value theories, as between the two dominant traditions, which has become a feature of his own work. (He has been criticised for this, see Bliss 1986.) Many modern economists find it impossible to accept that there *is* a distinction between the notion of price as an 'objective' index of reproducibility in the classical tradition and as a 'subjective' index of scarcity in the neoclassical tradition; and that this implies a difference between the surplus that is relevant for distribution and consumption theory, on the one hand, and for production theory, on the other. The factors which determine growth which Pasinetti through Ricardo captures create a process which makes more sense of the world than that which emerges from the Fisherian model. As we noted above, in the former it is decision-making by the entrepreneurial class which explicitly drives the system along (landlords played a more dominant role then than now, of course). Certainly this seems to capture more of what the world is like than the notion that all activities and institutions in capitalism exist only as the agents who serve the purposes of utility-maximizing consumers trying to allocate their consumption in an optimal manner over their life-cycles.

Pasinetti's most widely known contribution is in the field of income distribution, profit determination and growth theory. I do not go here into details of the development and extensions of his and Kaldor's models (for an account of the theory itself, and some early reactions, see Harcourt 1972, 45; for later developments, see Baranzini 1991).

In his seminal paper 'Rate of profit and income distribution in relation to the rate of economic growth' (Pasinetti 1962), starting as a critique of Kaldor's growth model where there exist two different saving rates, one for workers and one for capitalists, Pasinetti showed that the equilibrium rate of profits is totally independent of the saving behaviour of the working class; it is determined only by the saving rate of the pure capitalists (s_c) and by the rate of growth of the system (n). (The solution $P/K=n/s_c$ is known as Pasinetti's Theorem or the New Cambridge Equation.)

In summing up, it should be stressed that, over a span of more than four decades, the Kaldor–Pasinetti post-Keynesian model has been developed and refined in order to include a number of issues associated with the distribution of income and wealth and with the determination of the rate of profits in a steady-state growth model. The historical, demographic and institutional aspects of these models have come under close scrutiny and a number of relevant questions seem to have received adequate answers.

The core of Pasinetti's contributions on structural dynamics and vertical integration was stressed by him as early as 1961 in his PhD dissertation (which was partly published in 1965 and finally completed in 1981). He studied the conditions under which an economic system may reach and maintain full employment and full capacity utilization over the long period when it is subject to the main pressures leading to structural change – i.e. technical progress, non-uniform productivity increases and changes in the consumption structure (or consumers' preferences) according to Engel's law. His approach left aside the analytical tools of marginalist economics, tackled technical change by giving up the input–output scheme and focusing instead on the 'vertically integrated sectors' approach. (On this point, see Baranzini and Scazzieri 1990.) This allowed Pasinetti to bring into the modern literature the truth contained in the classical theory of value, to devise a tool with which to handle technical progress in a complex model, and to provide a bridge between a 'world' of production of commodities by means of commodities and the characteristics of the Keynesian system with its flows of final expenditure, production and incomes.

Pasinetti started from Sraffa's ingenious device of a subsystem whereby the total direct and indirect labour content of a particular commodity in a given production and technical situation may be obtained immediately. Suppose that we consider an economic system of circulating commodities, each one of which is produced in a single commodity industry – i.e. the model underlying much of classical political economy. In the actual economic system we suppose there to be produced, over a given production period, a gross product of such size and composition as to provide a net product. With this particular level of production will be associated a total amount of labour units, distributed in a technically determined way between each industry as its direct labour content. We wish to find, though, the direct and indirect labour content of each particular commodity in the net product. Therefore, we notionally construct a system in which the net product contains one (or more) units of the commodity that we are interested in *but no other*. The total amount of labour associated with the subsystem is the direct and indirect labour content of the commodity that constitutes its net product.

Pasinetti demonstrates that we may see also the capital requirements in terms of a unit of (vertically integrated) productive capacity of each unit of final good. In this way, we come to rearrange our way of looking at the production process so as to form a series of 'notional' vertically integrated activities, one for each commodity. We have also 'redistributed' the total labour force employed in the economy into its vertically integrated components, as obtained from the subsystem corresponding to each commodity in the original net product. The same process also may be repeated, as many times as we like, for the 'composite commodity' of each subsystem. Pasinetti exploits this approach and variations on it in order to discuss the implications of the theoretical concept of vertical integration for value, distribution, capital accumulation and growth theory.

In particular Pasinetti (1986b, 11–14) shows that the concept of vertical integration results in a vertically integrated sector which may be represented by one physical unit of its final good, one physical unit of vertically integrated productive capacity for the final good, and one physical quantity of labour for the final good. Put this way, the components of the sector have the property (which a subsystem has not) of being unaffected by technical progress.[23] This thus makes possible 'an economic analysis that may encompass, at the same time, the circular process of production and the evolution of the economic system through time' (Pasinetti 1986, 14). It has the added advantage, Pasinetti argues, of linking onto Keynesian analysis, if we reclassify the final goods within that framework in terms of those associated with the Sraffian production interdependent model.

The use of vertically integrated sectors permitted Pasinetti to overlook the network of inter-industry transactions which may obscure the picture when we use the input–output approach. Additionally, it provided a logical framework in which both technological and demand conditions may be integrated in order to give a comprehensive interpretation of the dynamics of the 'wealth of a nation' concerning both its absolute level and possible changes in its composition. Finally, it is an analytical device that permits us to focus on the 'natural' properties of the economic system, leaving aside institutional mechanisms such as the tendency towards the equalization of the rate of profits in a competitive market economy.

Indeed, by starting from the analytical scheme described above, Pasinetti next put forward a 'pure' labour theory of value and distribution, around which his more recent work has centred. Pasinetti (1986, 1988) first introduced a set of 'newly defined subsystems', much more comprehensive than those considered in Pasinetti (1973) and (1981, chapter 7) since 'they include not only the labour and the means of

---

[23] Sraffa (1960) seemed to have shown with the concepts of the Standard commodity and the Standard system that Ricardo's search for an invariable standard of value, invariable to *both* 'changes' in distributive shares and to changes in levels and composition of output and methods of production over time, was a search for a will-o'-the wisp. Pasinetti now seems to have shown that this is not necessarily so.

production for the reproduction of each subsystem, but also the labour and the means of production necessary to its *expansion* at its particular rate of growth' (Pasinetti 1988, 126–7).

By additionally assuming that (a) the rate of growth of these 'newly defined subsystems' may be different (due to a different rate of growth of technical progress and changes in the level and/or composition of demand), (b) there will be a particular natural rate of profits for each hyper subsystem (where a natural rate of profits is defined as a rate of profits which is equal to the rate of growth of demand for the corresponding consumption good) and (c) defining by $\mathbf{1}^{(i)}$ the vector of the vertically hyper-integrated labour coefficient for commodity i, Pasinetti (1988, 129) obtained the specific set of natural prices $\mathbf{p}^{(i)} = \mathbf{1}^{(i)} \cdot w$, where w is the wage rate. This result is a complete generalization of the pure labour theory of value; each physical quantity of any consumption good is shown to be unambiguously related to a physical quantity of labour. '[T]he two [i.e. physical quantities of consumption and of labour] have, between them, a physically self-replacing, and expanding, circular process' (Pasinetti 1988, 130). Consequently the whole set of natural prices of the means of production appear as performing in each hyper-subsystem 'a sort of ancillary role with respect to the corresponding price of the consumption good. Formal symmetry has been re-established perfectly between all aspects concerning physical quantities and all aspects concerning prices'. Pasinetti's analysis reveals a strong intellectual sympathy with Adam Smith; first for the representation of the productive system as a set of vertically integrated sectors, and then for the associated concept (common to both) that labour may be considered as the ultimate source of wealth. Pasinetti is working on a further generalization of the above model which, besides introducing a fully fledged model of capital accumulation on the lines of his (1988) *Cambridge Journal of Economics* article, should also show how the analysis may be taken beyond the natural system to include relations referring to the institutional framework of the various economic systems and their relations with each other.

Linked with this issue in (Pasinetti 1980–1), in which he shows that at a stage which precedes the introduction of capital accumulation and thus the emergence of any rate of profits, the theoretical scheme of a pure dynamic labour economy (see p. 128) contains already a comprehensive theory of the rate of interest and hence a theory of income distribution which is not yet linked with the existence of profits. Pasinetti considers a simple economic system in which all goods are produced by labour alone (a pure labour economy) and proves that the theoretical scheme of such a simple economic system contains ('as had been known since Adam Smith') a pure labour theory of value. Such a simple theoretical model, by avoiding the complications relating to capital accumulation and hence the emergence of any rate of profits, logically contains both a 'pure theory of the rate of interest' and a 'pure labour theory of the distribution of income'. Pasinetti points out that these theories 'necessarily follow from exactly the same postulate as that on which Adam Smith's pure labour theory of value is founded: namely, from the postulate that "labour commanded" be equal to "labour embodied"' (Pasinetti 1980–1, 181). In a pure labour economic system characterised by structural dynamics of technology and of prices, there exists a rate of interest on interpersonal loans – i.e. a rate of interest equal to the growth rate of the wage rate, which Pasinetti calls the 'natural' rate of interest – that keeps 'labour commanded' equal to 'labour embodied' through time. Hence there exists a level of interest on interpersonal loans (i.e. a 'natural' interest) which 'if paid annually by debtors to creditors, keeps income flowing to each single individual, through time as well as at any given point of time, in proportion to labour contributed to the production process' (Pasinetti 1980–1, 181).

Finally, it may be noted that in *Structural Economic Dynamics: A Theory of the Economic Consequences of Human Learning* (Pasinetti 1993), he offers a theoretical investigation of the development through time, as a consequence of human learning, of a 'pure labour economy' – that is to say, an economy in which production activity is carried out by labour alone, 'labour unassisted by any intermediate commodity'. The theory is simple; yet its aim is to catch a number of basic features of industrialised societies. Economists have known for a long time of two basic phenomena at the root of the long-term movements of our industrial societies: *capital accumulation* and *technical progress*. But, according to Pasinetti, the privileged position has always been given to capital accumulation. Pasinetti's volume (1993) reverses this approach, and technical progress is assigned the central role. Within a multi-sector framework he first describes (against a background of 'natural relations') the structural dynamics of prices, of production and of employment (implied by differentiated rates of productivity growth and of expansion of demand); he then discusses a whole series of problems that arise at the institutional level. 'Individuals' and social learning, know-how and diffusion of information emerge as the fundamental factors accounting for the features and fates of industrial societies – the source of their troubles, and the source of their wealth. The pure labour theory of value allows Pasinetti to shift the theory of long-term economic development from a traditional framework based on capital accumulation to new foundations based on learning, technical progress and diffusion of knowledge.

So Pasinetti, as with Kaldor, is the source, rarely acknowledged, of the conceptual basis of neoclassical endogenous growth theory that has been developing over the past twenty years and more (and which was behind Ed Balls' advice, early on, to Gordon Brown).

We now reassess the significance of Pasinetti's research programme. We may talk of 'new foundations' of economic analysis. Pasinetti has provided a new theoretical framework capable of synthesizing the works of Smith, Ricardo, Marx, Keynes, Sraffa and Kaldor, by appropriately modifying parts of their foundations and completing still other parts so as to arrive at a whole, coherent framework. The scheme itself is, however, so enormous that it is unrealistic to expect it to be completed by Pasinetti himself.

It has been often pointed out that Pasinetti has, among other original contributions, successfully achieved the difficult task of providing a bridge between two different levels of analysis, sharing the same scope but not the method – i.e. that of Keynes and Kaldor on the one side and of Sraffa on the other; the former was characterised by a mainly macro-economic scheme built in order to explain the working of actual economies and also founded on simple, though revolutionary, foundations. The latter was based instead on an extremely refined system of inter-industry relations, not so much directly concerned with the most pressing problems of the modern economic systems but more with the construction of a lucid and self-contained model within which the oldest questions of our subject may find answers.

The tentative bringing together of the two complementary schemes may, among other things, be connected with the following basic features of Pasinetti's theory:

(1) The use of vertically integrated sectors permits us to focus on the input requirements for producing any given vector of final commodities. Additionally it shows there is no need for Keynesian analysis to be carried out exclusively in macroeconomic terms; the vertically integrated approach, besides the consideration of different socio-economic classes of savers, provides a first step towards the construction of the micro-foundations of the model, where the dynamics may be much more easily described and understood. The full disaggregation of the post-Keynesian model will require necessary additional information and assumptions about consumers' allocation of income between consumption, saving and inter-generational

bequest, consumers' choice of goods and producers' choice of techniques. (On this point, see Pasinetti 1962, 268–9).[24]

(2) The theory of economic dynamics outlined by Pasinetti permits the analysis of how an economic system may maintain full employment and full capacity utilization through time and in the presence of uneven technical progress, growing population and changes in consumption patterns, according to Engel's Law. Short-run difficulties – unemployment, spare productive capacity and the rapid rise or fall of particular industries – have hence to be considered as necessary conditions for long-run growth in which there is a continuous modification of the productive structure. Concernings the linkage between growth and the system of prices (i.e. distribution), Pasinetti (1965, 692–3) maintains that:

> In the theoretical scheme I am proposing (a theoretical scheme for the long period), relative prices are determined by technology. Demand (i.e. consumers' preferences) then determine the relative quantities to be produced. Prices, therefore, emerge as a sort of indexes of *relative efforts* that society is obliged to put into each single unit of the various commodities.[25]
>
> (emphasis in original)

Hence the relationship between the uneven dynamics of technology on the one hand, and the non-linear evolution of consumers' preferences on the other, becomes crucial. From this comes the difficulty of maintaining over time a productive structure compatible with the structure of demand, which helps to explain both short-run problems, such as the alternation of booms and recessions, and the fact that an industrial economy must follow a long-run development path along which structural change is necessary.

(3) The focus on the natural properties of an economic system allows the analysis to reach beyond certain institutional mechanisms such as the tendency towards the equalization of the rate of profits. As Pasinetti has repeatedly pointed out, the introduction of the concept of vertically integrated sectors implies a radical change in the meaning of the rate of profits with respect to a standard multi-sector model. As Scazzieri (1983, 87) has pointed out, the interpretation of the overall historical dynamics of an economic system leaves

---

[24] The similarity to Goodwin's contributions is obvious, and indeed it was Goodwin who initially set Pasinetti off on this trail.

[25] This is quite different from what happens in the 'pure' marginalist scheme with scarce goods, where endowments are accepted as given by nature and prices emerge as sorts of indexes of scarcity with respect to consumers' preferences.

space for a full-scale analysis of those patterns of expansion that are to be expected as a result of the interaction between the fundamental factors of change (common to all industrial systems) and the special behavioural principles characteristic of each particular institutional and technological set-up. The role of the 'natural rate of profits' had been stressed by Pasinetti (1962), when he closed his essay on income distribution and profit determination by saying that:

> In a full employment economic system in which all net revenues that accrue to the organizers of the process of production are saved, there exists one particular rate of profit[s], which we may indeed call the *natural rate of profit[s]* – since it turns out to be equal to the rate of growth – which . . . if it is applied both in the process of pricing and in the payment of interest on loans, causes the system, *whatever the individual decisions to save may be*, to produce a total amount of [saving] which is exactly equal to the amount of investment needed to cope with technical progress and population growth.   (emphases in original)

In Harrod's terms, the conditions for g_w to equal g_n.

Pasinetti's contribution remains fundamentally (and 'passionately') 'at the roots' of post-Keynesian economics, or rather at the roots of the work Keynes started with his 'revolutionary' approach to economic thinking:

> Post-Keynesian economics starts when the 'revolutionary' change – i.e. the switch from the old to new foundations – has already taken place. And post-Keynesianism inherits all the problems that a revolutionary change implies. Provided that Keynes had perceived 'very clearly that the centre of the new foundations were those of an advanced *monetary theory of production*' post-Keynesians were faced with two distinctive tasks:
> Firstly, there was the task of putting together a coherent 'production model', that the earlier literature had proposed but rather sketchily singled out. This was the task of so to speak completing the foundations. Secondly, there was the task of 'shifting', on to a new basis, what may be called a 'superstructure' of arguments that had been constructed during years of solid work, but had been laid on what now appeared shaky, weak and deficient foundations. In so doing, it could not be immediately clear which elements of the 'superstructure' also had to go and which elements could be kept, and made use of.
>
> (Pasinetti 1990, 7)

According to Pasinetti, the contribution of Sraffa was concerned with the first task and that of Kaldor mainly, though not exclusively, with the second, while Kahn, Joan Robinson and Goodwin were concerned with both. To the latter list we add Luigi Pasinetti himself.

Kaldor, Mark 2

In the section on Kaldor, Mark 1 (pp. 114–19), we noted that Kaldor had changed his mind on the sources of growth and on the difficulties of attaining and sustaining steady growth, rejecting both the 'early' neo-classical and his own post-Keynesian approaches. He now argued for an approach that would tackle the mutual interdependence of different sectors where the development of each depends on, and is stimulated, by the development of the others.

In his last book (Kaldor 1996),[26] Kaldor used a simple two-sector model of agriculture and industry in order to bring 'to light aspects of the economic problems that tend to be neglected both in micro- and macro-economics' (Kaldor 1996, 41). There is dual interdependence between the sectors, each being a market for the other's product and a supplier of the means necessary for the other's production. The industrial sector needs material inputs as its means of production and wage goods – 'food' – for its employees; the primary sector depends on the industrial sector for capital goods. Technical progress is 'land-saving' in agriculture. There is assumed to be a stream of innovations, the adoption of which requires additional investment for their realisation. The agricultural sector produces 'corn', and industry, 'steel' (capital goods). Kaldor abstracts from the production of consumption goods in the industrial sector and from investment goods such as irrigation or larger herds in agriculture. He assumes a community with surplus labour, most of which is attached to agriculture, so that industry may hire workers in unlimited numbers at a wage in 'corn' sufficiently above real earnings in agriculture to induce whatever migration is needed.

While both sectors accumulate capital by saving part of current income, there is an important difference: in agriculture, saving requires a decision to refrain from consuming part of 'corn' output. The 'corn' so released is sold on the market in exchange for the capital goods which the introduction of new accumulation requires. Its rate of accumulation is therefore determined by the amount of corn so saved and the rate of exchange – terms of trade – between corn and steel. In industry, investment comes first, it creates the profits from which saving then comes (a third commodity, money, has yet to be introduced). Steel producers accumulate capital by retaining a proportion of their current output in order to expand their own capacity and sell the remainder on the market.

---

[26] But he had developed these ideas long before, see the relevant articles in part IV of Targetti and Thirlwall (1989).

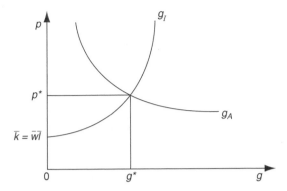

Figure 7.9. Kaldor's two-sector complementary model.

Their costs consist of the payment of wages (fixed in corn) so that the total amount of corn sold by agriculture determines total employment. If steel output per worker is given, the total output of steel is given irrespective of the price of steel. Its minimum price is wl, where w is the wage in terms of corn and l is the labour requirement per unit of steel, below which no steel is produced. At prices above wl we have a relationship between the degree to which price exceeds costs and the proportion of steel reinvested, with the resulting profits being just sufficient to provide the saving to match the investment undertaken. (There are similarities here with the writings on the determination of the size of the mark-up in chapter 3.)

Kaldor developed a neat diagram (1996, 44) in which the price of steel in terms of corn (p) is on the vertical axis and the associated rate of growth of each sector (g) is on the horizontal axis (figure 7.9). The cheaper the agricultural sector can obtain steel, the faster it can grow for a *given* saving ratio, but because of diminishing returns the g_A curve will shift inwards unless this is offset by 'land-saving' innovations which *ceteris paribus* shift it out. The g_I curve slopes upwards, because the cheaper is corn, the more labour for making steel can the sector buy and the more of its own output it can invest, and so the faster it can grow.

The price is written as $p = wl(1 + \pi)$, where π is the mark-up. (The g_I curve shifts when either the real wage or labour productivity, $1/l$, changes.) At the point $p^\star$, $g^\star$, where the two curves intersect, we have rates of growth in both sectors and terms of trade between sectors which allow the supply and demand of agricultural and industrial goods to balance.

In telling the stability stories – convergence on the intersection of the two curves – Kaldor emphasises that the steel producers are quantity-adjusters, acting so as to bring the growth in capacity in their sector in line with sales, whereas competition between agricultural producers tends to bring the price of corn in terms of steel to a point where the growth rates are equal–and, more fundamentally, demand and supply match.

An important feature of the model is its dependence on the persistence of 'land-saving' innovations which in the model keeps the system growing at a constant rate as long as growth is not hampered by scarcity of labour in the world as a whole. Kaldor says that we are nowhere near such a problem, that unemployment is a growing problem even though, he argues, the rate of growth of world population had passed its peak (when he wrote in the mid-1980s).

Kaldor then uses his model to illustrate the effects of 'labour-saving' innovations in steel (associated with Verdoorn's Law and the induced rise in the rate of growth of productivity in the economy as it grows) and to consider the destabilising effects of the inherent instability of both curves due to, for example, weather, a non-steady rate of technical innovations in both sectors and the different pricing behaviour as between the sectors.

Suppose we bring in money so that corn is sold for money which *can* be used to buy steel. We consider the effect of a new super crop which shifts the g_A curve to the right by a 'large' amount. We suppose that the price of corn also falls by a 'large' amount because the market-making middlemen are unwilling to increase their commitments until the price falls to abnormally 'low' levels. Steel producers find their sales restricted by 'effective demand' and emerging surplus capacity unleashes a downward spiral which is both contractionary – investment plans are revised downwards – and deflationary.

If both corn and steel had had the *same* regime for marketing, this 'absurd' result would not have occurred, because the price of one commodity could not have fallen so much as to reduce the producers' purchasing power over the other. The remedy is to reduce the large fluctuations in the prices of primary products by the use of buffer stock schemes, *not* to go back to market-determined prices for manufactures (as the modern world increasingly seems to have done, and to have been told by economists to do). Buffer stock schemes actually do what the market-making merchants are supposed to do. Kaldor points out that the great slump of 1929–32 had many of the features of his examples and concludes that: 'in a well-functioning world economy it is the availabilities of primary products which should set the limit to industrialisation – the expansion possibilities of which are limitless, or rather are only limited by demand – and not the other way round' (1996, 54).

Kaldor discerned in the 1970s another set of causes of deep troubles which he discussed in the context of the spatial aspects of the economic problem. He regarded primary products as land-based commodities which are geographically spread while industrial activities are concentrated in urban areas, so that exchange between primary products and manufactures is also an exchange between the products of town and country. Industrial producers devote only a part, if any, of their activities to their own consumption. The greater part is obtained by exchange. Agricultural producers could produce *only* for their own consumption while industrial producers can operate *only* in a social setting with activities dependent on demand from others through the market, their success or failure depending on the strength of this demand.

We then come to typical Kaldorian generalisation and insight: that the world may be divided into relatively rich and relatively poor areas and that this is a matter of relatively recent occurrence, reflecting persistent differences in rates of growth over the past two–three centuries. The basic cause is neither differences in resource endowment nor a reward for virtuous thrifty behaviour (as opposed to spendthrift expenditure); rather, it results from the process of industrialisation and its 'fall-out' in terms of political and educational institutions. Industrial activities are not self-sustaining but depend upon demand for goods coming from outside the industrial sector, the ultimate causal factor which accounts for all other activities. It involves a sort of multiplier process. Industrial activities are concentrated in urban areas because of the growth of marketing activities and the social economies gained by division and subdivision of the making of articles into a number of separate operations. Kaldor also mentions the advantage of having highly specialised workers in close proximity to one another together with small and specialised firms. He cites the Italian industrial districts and Marshall's analysis of a similar phenomenon, engulfing the static and dynamic economies of large-scale production *and* the economies of large production.

The existence of increasing returns makes a large difference to the way markets develop and competition operates – the remarkable thing, says Kaldor, is only why its consequences are so largely ignored. Businesspeople, unlike our trade, would never ignore the existence of diminishing costs. With increasing returns a rising market share means success but a falling one, failure. In a growing market, a business can never stand still – indeed, it must grow if it is to survive (1996, 64). Kaldor comments that only Marx fully recognised this in the nineteenth century – in neoclassical theory each firm has an optimum size so that the number of firms has to increase when the industry grows. (Marshall tried to have it both ways with the analogy of trees in a forest and the concept of the representative firm; Pigou undermined him by turning the latter into the equilibrium firm.) So we move on to success meaning more success, failure meaning more failure – Gunnar Myrdal's 'principle of circular and cumulative causation' (1996, 64), the hallmark of Kaldor's later work.

Having earlier shown the very special circumstances in which free trade benefits all, Kaldor now argues that free trade in the field of manufacturing goods allied with the process of cumulative causation begets a process of polarisation which inhibits growth of such activities in some areas while concentrating them in others. In a nutshell, this is what happened during the industrial and transport revolutions of the nineteenth century. Kaldor reviewed the history of UK manufactures and their export and the role of tariffs when other countries industrialised. The successful ones were discriminating in their use of tariffs, as were Japan and then the newly industralised countries (NICs) in the post-war period. The Latin American countries made indiscriminate use of tariffs and the resulting costs of their products in terms of primary products made them too expensive to enter world markets successfully.

Thus Kaldor is led to the key role of export-led growth in successful development and to the ultimate constraint imposed by the value of the import income elasticity of demand. He used Harrod's foreign trade multiplier analysis of (1933), three years *before The General Theory*, which was brought to fruition in the post-war period in the work of John McCombie and Tony Thirlwall (1994). The balance of payments is seen as the effective constraint on growth, the rate of which will be higher the greater is the export income elasticity and the lower is its import counterpart, reflecting differences in non-price competitiveness.

Kaldor recognises that price elasticities are important for trade in traditional goods such as textiles and shoes where the newly developed countries may copy the latest technical advances in other countries and have huge advantages because of the lower price of labour services. Kaldor quotes with approval Hufbauer's classification of 'low wage' trade and 'technological lead' trade (1996, 69). But, in the large picture, it is income – quantities – not prices which are the basic clue to the nature of growth processes and the success or otherwise of development.

Endogenous growth theory[27]

In Ricardo's theory of distribution and growth, in the absence of periodic technical advances, accumulation and growth come to an end because diminishing returns to the application of additional doses of labour-and-capital to the fixed amount of land imply the disappearance of both the incentive (profits) and the ability to accumulate. In the Solow–Swan model, in the absence of technical progress, growth reaches a steady state equal to the exogenously given rate of growth of the labour force, essentially because of diminishing returns to capital so that as the capital–labour and capital–output ratios rise, the rate of profits would fall and output per person will (eventually) cease to rise.

Both Solow and Swan recognised that technical progress would enable growth in output per head for ever, but that increases in the saving ratio could never (eventually) achieve this.[28] The transition from an economy with one value of the saving ratio to another with a higher value, however, would be characterised by rising output per head even in the absence of technical progress.

Solow (1957) developed an ingenious method for estimating the respective contributions of (exogenous) technical progress – exogenous in the sense that it affected all capital goods alike whether new or old – and rising capital–labour and capital–output ratios – deepening – to observed rises in productivity (see Harcourt 1972, 47–51 for Solow's algebra and diagrams). He also developed vintage models that allowed technical progress to be embodied through the accumulation process itself. As is well known, a huge literature is based on these two developments. Together all these developments were subsumed under the rubric of 'old' (modern) growth theory. As we have seen, Kaldor followed a different tack back to classical political economy and emphasising the complementarity of demands and supplies and the role of increasing returns. Many of Kaldor's and the classicals' insights have been subsumed in 'new' or endogenous growth theory which took off in the 1980s, following the two seminal papers of Romer (1986) and Lucas (1988), placed in a neoclassical setting. The latter requirement reflects

---

[27] In writing this section I have drawn heavily on Charles Jones's 'answers-to-a-teacher's-prayer' volume (Jones 1998), and the illuminating writings and insights of Heinz Kurz and Neri Salvadori (see, for example, Kurz and Salvadori 2003, Salvadori 2003). The object is to relate in outline the new developments to what has gone before, not to exposit them as such.

[28] Tom Russell (personal communication, May 2005) tells me that with CES production functions, the elasiticities of substitution of capital for labour of which are greater than unity, growth *can* go on for ever. Perhaps this is why Solow has not been that keen on endogenous growth theory.

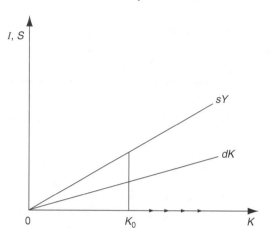

Figure 7.10. Growth for ever: 1.

the hegemony of the mainstream, including especially the aftermath of Lucas' (and others') work on rational expectations and the new classical macroeconomics, in which explicit microeconomic foundations involving optimising behaviour became essential for respectability. Any other procedures were contemptuously dismissed as *ad hoc*.

As we noted above, the 'old' neoclassical models imply that *levels* may be changed by policy or private sector changes but not ultimately *rates* of growth. By contrast, the 'new' growth theories argue that *permanent* changes are possible.[29] The simplest case builds on the Solow–Swan model and is known in the literature as the '*AK*' model.

We write $Y = AK$ which implies that $\alpha = 1$ and A is some positive constant. We ignore population growth and write accumulation (where S is I) as $\dot{K} = sY - dK$ (see figure 7.10).

In figure 7.10, gross investment (sY) exceeds depreciation (equals replacement) (dK). Growth in this model *never* stops because there are no diminishing returns to capital as in the Solow–Swan model, because α is no longer less than unity. Rather, there are constant returns to the accumulation of capital – its marginal (and average) product is equal to A.

The capital accumulation function is:

$$\frac{\dot{K}}{K} = s\frac{Y}{K} - d$$

---

[29] But see n. 28, p. 139 above.

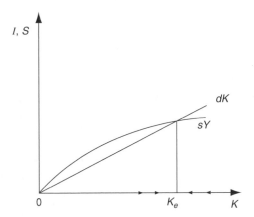

Figure 7.11. The steady state in Solow's model.

But

$$\frac{Y}{K} = MP_K = A$$

So

$$\frac{\dot{K}}{K} = sA - d$$

In the steady state,

$$g_y = \frac{\dot{Y}}{Y} = sA - d$$

That is to say, the rate of growth is a simple increasing function of the rate of accumulation, s – which is also true of Harrod's model in the sense that g_w is also greater, the greater is the value of s.[30]

In Solow's model (see figure 7.11), we have an equilibrium value of K_e where the economy has reached the steady state – the transition has come to an end. In the AK model this *never* happens and so we need neither technical progress nor population growth to get endogenous growth.

---

[30] It should be noted that the AK model was already to be found in the modern literature – it is also in Ricardo! – in Kenneth Arrow's classic paper, 'The economic implications of learning by doing' (Arrow 1962). It was rejected by him as being too special a case, as Solow in his Arrow Lectures (Solow 1997a), pointed out, so unrobust as to be a curiosum only. Indeed, Solow's arguments for so dismissing it are akin to those he directed at Harrod's apparently constant capital–output ratio.

Lucas (1988) exploits these results in order to show that the more education the labour force has, the higher will be its growth of output per person. He shows that a policy that leads to a permanent increase in the time individuals spend obtaining skills generates a permanent increase in the growth of output per worker. Those writers who are more sympathetic to the approach of Solow and Swan – for example, Jones – are sceptical of the inference that growth rates (as opposed to levels) can differ *permanently* as a result of government and private educational and research and development (R & D) policies. Nevertheless, they accept that economic growth is the endogenous outcome of an economy in which profit-seeking individuals who are allowed to receive rents – monopoly profits – search for newer and better ideas. *In this sense*, the process of growth is *endogenous*, but it is also an insight which comes from Marx and, especially, Schumpeter. Hence an important part of the 'new' growth theories consists of putting Schumpeter's ideas into 'new' growth models (see, especially, Aghion and Howitt 1998).

Barro and Sala-i-Martin (1998) also argue that the key property of endogenous growth models is the absence of diminishing returns to capital – i.e., the absence of any falling long-term tendency of the rate of profits, seen as measured by the marginal product of capital.

As we saw above, in Ricardo's writings it is the rate of accumulation that is endogenously determined; the demand for labour is governed by the pace at which capital accumulates, while the long-term supply of labour is regulated by the Malthusian population mechanism. The only limit to growth comes from the presence and role of non-accumulable factors of production – natural resources, especially land. This contrasts with the Solow–Swan model, where labour is the non-accumulable factor – its rate of growth is exogenous – and, as we have seen, the rate of profits falls as capital grows relative to labour. In the steady state the rate of profits and the wage rate are determined endogenously as they are the prices which are consistent with the steady-state capital–labour ratio.

In the 'new' growth theory it is the steady-state rate of profits which is *exogenous* and the steady-state rate of growth which is *endogenous*. So we need arguments that guarantee that the rate of profits is either constant; or falls, but is bounded from below so that it never reaches the level where accumulation ceases; or it actually rises. We illustrate this with *AK* models.

If labour were either not 'needed' in production or were a free good, the marginal product of capital would not fall as capital accumulates (relative to labour). So one class of these models assumes that all inputs are 'capital' of some sort. The most elementary version assumes, as we have seen, a linear relationship between gross output (Y) and a single factor capital (K), both of the same commodity,

$$Y = AK\frac{1}{A}\left(=\frac{K}{Y}\right)$$

is the amount of the commodity required to produce itself. Surplus product is

$$Y - dKso = \frac{Y}{K} - d = A - d$$

If s is given, we get $g = s(A - d) = sr$ (saving *is* investment), which as $r = \frac{g}{s}$ looks remarkably like the Cambridge equation! r is given by technology (just as in Ricardo's corn model) and the saving–investment relationship determines the rate of growth.[31]

So the difference from Ricardo's corn model is that, first, the input of 'corn' is treated as a durable capital good and, secondly, land is a free good. So, if $r > r_{min}$ the system grows forever (see figure 7.12). (Ricardo recognised that, if there were no limit to the supply of the best land and so no extensive margin to constrain production, the same result would be obtained.)

Ricardo once imagined a world in which machine power displaced labour power. There would be no demand for labour and no one who was not a capitalist who could hire or buy machines would be able to consume. (Marx's variant was a world of robots.) In some 'new' growth models all people are capitalists of some sort so the economy is analysed by a 'representative agent'. But as there are different kinds of agents – there are even people – workers are subsumed under capitalists by conceiving of the capacity to work as a *special* kind of capital, 'human capital'. When we have machine capital and human capital as the only inputs, there are no non-accumulable factors (such as simple labour and land). Instead, there is a choice of technique problem – the rate of profits is the outcome of technology and profit-maximizing behaviour and the saving–investment relationship then determines the rate of growth of the system as ever. Common or unskilled labour is thus treated as a free good.

In neoclassical economics, this means that the wage rate equals zero; in classical economics, there was at least a *positive* minimum wage, for

---

[31] Sometimes s is the outcome of an intertemporal maximisation assumption which complicates the algebra (and satisfies the Lucas approach) but does not change the conceptual story.

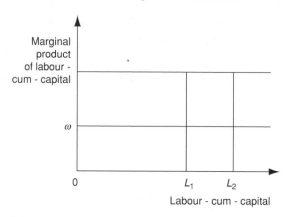

Figure 7.12. Growth for ever: 2.

then it was explicitly recognised that labour provides labour services and must be kept alive.[32]

Finally, by using the concept of externalities which impinge on the economy as a whole but are not taken into account in individual decision-making, the 'new' growth theorists are able to include the optimising behaviour of decision-makers of steady-state models with constant returns. The combination of these two factors lies at the source of the 'market failures' identified in modern theory and the case for designing policies and creating institutions with which to tackle their effects. As Kurz (forthcoming, 7) notes, 'While capital accumulation is still at the centre of the analysis these wider issues which figured prominently in the classical authors have been brought back into the picture': whether in the most illuminating setting and with the most appropriate tools of analysis is still an ongoing debate.

---

[32] Sraffa (1960) recognised this by distinguishing between this element and the share of wages above this in the distribution of the surplus. '[B]esides the ever-present element of subsistence, [wages] may include a share of the surplus product' (1960, 19). Only the latter may vary.

8   Applications to policy

The vital link between 'vision' and policy

It is probably fair to say that Keynes never completely threw off the vision of the working of economies in terms of an equilibrium framework. He did, of course, argue that government intervention was needed to help attain a satisfactory full employment equilibrium (internal balance) in each economy – left alone, less satisfactory equilibria or rest states would emerge. This was an essential step towards equilibrium associated with external balance in the international system and the possibility then to take advantage of the classical principles of free trade on which he had been brought up. (Skidelsky 1992, xv called him 'the last of the great English liberals.') The proposals Keynes put forward at Bretton Woods were designed to provide the institutions and the orders of magnitude of, for example, the provision of liquidity that would make all this possible. That the Americans, principally through Harry Dexter White, won out on both the institutions and the orders of magnitude adopted for the post-war period was a tragedy; for this ensured that the Bretton Woods system contained within it the seeds of its own eventual destruction from its very inception.

One of the major changes in vision since Keynes' death about how markets, economies and even whole systems work, associated with Keynes' followers, especially Kaldor and Joan Robinson, is, as we have seen, the concept of cumulative causation. The concept has its origins in Adam Smith (what has not?) and was brought into prominence in the modern era by Allyn Young, Kaldor's teacher at the London School of Economics (LSE), and subsequently championed by Kaldor and independently by Gunnar Myrdal, especially in their post-war writings. We may illustrate the essential idea of the concept by the analogy of a wolf pack (as I am not a zoologist, this may be completely wrong about how wolves behave; but as I am an economist, let us assume I am right). There are two major views on the workings of markets and economies– that is to say, whole systems. The dominant one is that akin to a wolf pack running along. If one or more wolves get ahead or fall behind, powerful forces come into play which return them to the pack. (The parallels with the existence of an equilibrium that is unique and stable, and that the forces responsible for existence are independent of those responsible for stability are, I hope, obvious.) The other view has it that the forces acting on the wolves who get ahead or fall behind make them get further and further ahead or fall further and further behind, at least for long periods of time. This view captures the notion of virtuous or vile processes of cumulative causation. (It also corresponds with Goodwin's and Kalecki's approach that the trend and cycle are indissolubly mixed, not separable concepts determined by independent factors.) My contention is that, according to which view is 'correct', makes a drastic difference to our understanding of the world, and how specific policies may be perceived, recommended and evaluated.

We illustrate this with an example, the case for freely floating exchange rates. A classic paper arguing for such rates is by Milton Friedman (1953). Underlying his argument is the first wolf pack analogy, that in a competitive setting there exists a set of long-period stable equilibrium exchange rates that quickly would be found and then kept by a free float. Moreover, in this setting the systemic effects of speculation would be beneficial, for speculators with their superior knowledge, intelligence and information would help the system to reach the equilibrium pattern more quickly than in their absence, and then sustain it there.

But suppose that the second wolf pack analogy is the correct – or, at least, the more correct description – of how foreign exchange markets work. Then there is no set of stable equilibrium exchange rates 'out there' waiting to be found and now a float combined with speculative activity will be systemically harmful, accelerating the movements away in both directions of exchange rates from one another and also of systems, at least for long periods of time. I submit that the second scenario is more akin to what has happened over much of recent decades, and provides a rationale for various schemes suggested to curb the action of speculators. (My own suggestions may be found in Harcourt 1994; 1995a; 2001b. In effect, I generalised the Tobin tax proposal without, I must confess, being aware of its existence at the time!)

It is not only in markets characterised by cumulative causation processes that speculation may be systemically harmful. Any market in which stocks dominate flows and expectations about the behaviour of other participants in the market dominate the more usual economic factors – preferences, costs of production – in the setting of prices may experience periods when speculation is harmful. (The seminal and classic paper on this is Kaldor 1939.) An obvious example is the stock exchange. On this, we may recall Keynes' famous description in chapter 12 of *The General Theory* of what may happen when 'enterprise becomes a bubble on a whirlpool of speculation' (Keynes 1936; *CW*, vol. VII, 1973, 159).

Keynes' solution was to suggest tax incentives that would induce people to hold bonds and equities for long periods of time and so look to the longer-term prospects of the firms, the profitability of whose real assets the values of these financial assets ideally ought to reflect. I extended his argument to the property market by proposing tax incentives and disincentives to purchasers, sellers and real estate agents that would induce them to look at the provision of housing services rather than to speculative prospects in their transactions (see Harcourt 2001b, 259–60).

Package deals: a solution to the Kaleckian dilemma?

We close with another example of how Keynes and Keynesian/Kaleckian/ Marxian – i.e. post-Keynesian – ideas are still relevant for both our understanding and policy-making. The ideas are based on Kalecki's famous 1943 paper, 'Political aspects of full employment' and the writings of my two greatest Australian mentors, Eric Russell and Wilfred Salter, both devoted Keynesians (see Harcourt 1997a; 2001b for the arguments and references).

Kalecki set out graphically the vital difference between the political economy of getting to full employment after a deep slump, when all classes are in favour of this – wage-earners in order to get jobs, businesspeople in order to receive higher profits, the government in order to reduce the risk of serious social unrest – on the one hand, and the political economy of sustaining full employment, on the other:

The assumption that a Government will maintain full employment in a capitalist economy if only it knows how to do it is fallacious. (Kalecki 1943; 1971, 138)

In the second situation, economic, social and political power shifts cumulatively from capital to labour. The capitalist class – indeed, conservative elements generally – get more and more uneasy about the emerging situation.

As Kalecki wrote:

the *maintenance* of full employment would cause social and political changes which would give a new impetus to the opposition of the business leaders. Indeed, under a regime of permanent full employment, 'the sack' would cease to flag its role as a disciplinary measure. The social position of the boss would be undermined and the self assurance and class consciousness of the working class would grow. Strikes for wage increases and improvements in conditions of work would create political tension . . . true . . . profits would be higher under a regime of full employment than they are on average under *laisser-faire*; and even the rise in wage rates resulting from the stronger bargaining power of the workers is less likely to reduce profits than to increase prices, and thus affect adversely only . . . rentier interests. But 'discipline in the factories' and 'political stability' are more appreciated by the business leaders than profits. Their class instinct tells them that lasting full employment is unsound from their point of view and that unemployment is an integral part of the normal capitalist system.

(Kalecki 1943; 1971, 140–1, emphasis in original)

An environment is created in which, for example, Monetarist ideas will be well received, and more than one economist will be prepared to be a hired prize fighter in support of them as government (and central bank) actions. As Kalecki put it, 'big business and *rentier* interests . . . would probably find more than one economist to declare that the situation was manifestly unsound' (Kalecki 1943; 1971, 144, emphasis in original)

The approach we set out in earlier chapters culminating in the linkages between the happenings in the sphere of production, on the one hand, and those in the sphere of distribution and exchange, on the other – for example, Harris' exposition of key Marxian and Robinsonian ideas – help to explain one of the paradoxes of recent decades. As we saw, Monetarism has rightly been called by Thomas Balogh (1982) 'the incomes policy of Karl Marx'. Ostensibly, the theory was meant to justify policies designed to rid the system of inflationary tendencies. In fact, it was associated with the attempt to swing the balance of economic, social and political power back from labour to capital. (The reverse swing had occurred cumulatively in many advanced capitalist economies during the years of the long boom or 'Golden Age' of capitalism, see chapter 6.) The means to this end was the recreation of the reserve army of labour, so making the sack an effective weapon again and creating cowed and quiescent workforces and greater potential surpluses for national and, increasingly, international capital accumulation.

What was not realised was that the emergence of heavy and sustained unemployment, initially ostensibly to push short-run rates of unemployment above so-called 'natural' rates and then let them converge on natural rates where inflation could be sustained at steady rates and accelerating rates of inflation would be things of the past, would simultaneously have such an adverse effect on the Keynesian 'animal spirits' of businesspeople, the ultimate determinants of rates of accumulation. Hence we have had decades in many economies in which inflation has been drastically reduced yet accumulation has been sluggish, certainly well below the levels needed to offset full employment saving and the levels achieved during the years of the long boom itself. In those countries where this had *not* occurred, despised Keynesian policies continued to be used, sometimes unintelligent ones such as those implemented, for example, during the last six years of Ronald Reagan's Presidency in the USA and now by President Bush the Second.

Since attaining full employment by the use of fiscal policies was no longer on the agenda in the former countries and monetary policies were mainly directed at general price levels and exchange rates, contractionary forces were widely prevalent in these countries, as the politicians and their advisors waited (or said they waited) in vain while the impersonal forces of competitive markets allied with Monetarist rules allowed the economies to seek and find their natural rates.

Is there a possible answer to this, on the face of it, inescapable dilemma in our sorts of economies? Keynes and his followers recognised that attaining and then maintaining full employment would carry with it cumulatively rising risks of inflationary pressures associated with rising money-wage demands. It is no accident that Joan Robinson always said that from 1936 on, 'Incomes Policy' was her middle name. Kahn gave lectures on incomes policies for many years in the post-war period. Russell and Salter recognised the dilemma and argued in Australia for a full employment policy that included an incomes policy implemented through the centralised wage-fixing body (then the Australian Arbitration Commission). In broad outline, as a starting point, money incomes were to be adjusted periodically for changes in prices and in *overall* productivity. Not only is this adjustment equitable, it is also efficient. Basically, the aim was to provide a package deal of policies which allowed sustained full employment with agreeable rates of inflation and more satisfactory rates of growth of gross domestic product (GDP) and productivity. A necessary corollary of achieving these is to raise the overall level of accumulation.

We move now to the more detailed analysis.[1] We start by reminding ourselves of Salter's analysis (see Salter 1960; 1965). The problem Salter set himself to explain was why, in situations in which technical progress is steadily occurring, old machines of an inferior vintage are to be found operating alongside new best-practice techniques in most industries, a problem which was never clearly stated nor satisfactorily solved either in classical analysis (including Marx) or by neoclassical

[1] I draw heavily on Harcourt (1997a, 2001b) in what follows.

analysis, and especially not by Marshall. In fact we may read into both sources that in the final long-period position,[2] if it were ever reached, we would only find operating machines incorporating current best-practice techniques. The capital–labour and capital–output ratios associated with these machines would have been determined by the expected movements in long-period prices and wages at the beginning of the analysis (and period). As we saw in chapter 3 (p. 39), the state of knowledge – the capital–labour and capital–output ratios of the array of best-practice techniques – is summed up conveniently in terms of either a family of isoquants or, if there are constant returns to scale, a unique isoquant of various associations of inputs per unit of output.

Salter's crucial contribution was to show that if we suppose that technical progress in each industry is steady but discrete (and if, for the moment, we abstract from cyclical effects), investment in the current best-practice techniques chosen in the existing situation will, in competitive conditions, be pushed to the point where the prices established for the output which these machines and the accumulated vintages from past bursts of accumulation help to produce only allow the normal rate of profit to be received on the best-practice techniques. That is to say, *total* long-period costs including normal profits are just covered by the prices set and sales receipts received. The sales receipts associated with the outputs of previous vintages which are still operating and contributing to the current supply have to cover only their existing *variable* costs in order to remain operating – 'Bygones are bygones'. Of course, all but the marginal vintages will do better than this. Machines are retired and, sometimes, scrapped *only* when their quasi-rents are less than zero. In this way the benefits of technical progress are embodied in the stocks of capital goods and passed on to consumers in lower prices, yet some older vintages are able to exist side by side with the new improved ones.

Both at the level of each industry and, even more, at the level of the economy as a whole, the levels and rates of increase of wages are crucial to the process. (Wage movements may legitimately be regarded as exogenous at the level of the firm or even of the industry in many cases, but are obviously endogenously determined at the level of the economy as a whole.) They are among the principal determinants of variable costs, both directly and indirectly, and therefore of which machines remain in operation and of how far investment in new machines may go before

---

[2] It is an equilibrium of long-period supply and demand in the neoclassical case. The discussion in the text is only part of a series of papers on policy in which modern regimes of floating exchange rates and increasingly free movements of capital internationally are explicitly taken into account (see Harcourt 2001b, Part V).

prices reach levels where only normal profits are received so that accumulation comes temporarily to a halt: temporarily, because technical progress is a continuing process so that new sets of best-practice techniques become available over time and the accumulation and retiring/scrapping processes start up anew.[3]

The analysis is essentially Marshallian in spirit but overcomes the vagueness and misleading inferences of Marshall's own long-period analysis.[4] Moreover, Salter (1960, 90–3) shows that if we have imperfectly competitive or even oligopolistic market structures, much the same processes tend to occur though the forces driving decision-makers to install and retire may be neither as strong nor as persistent as in the competitive situation. This view was first set out by Marx, though not as explicitly or as convincingly. Salter considers either profit-maximisation or strategic behaviour in the non-perfectly competitive situations. We consider later the implications of some of the mark-up theories which link the profit margin and price-setting to investment requirements.[5]

For our present purposes, it is the systemic implications of these industry processes which are relevant.[6] From what we have argued so far, if we are interested in overall growth of output as a whole and of output per head,[7] the most favourable conditions for achieving high rates of growth in both is that declining industries and expanding

---

[3] Of course, this is an artificial way of putting it – first, because individual industries are not synchronised by time and period so that, *overall*, accumulation and embodiment are continuous; and, secondly, because we have made the simplifying assumption that technical advances occur at discrete intervals in order to make the analysis of output, accumulation and price-setting tractable. We have also concentrated on the volume of accumulation determined by wage movements, keeping at the back of our heads the effect of relative prices on the choice of the best-practice techniques.

[4] But see Dennis Robertson's defence of the master (1956), that there were two concepts of the long period in Marshall, one abstract, theoretical, the other more attuned to real life. John Nevile has also proved that it is, as ever, 'all in Marshall', by referring me to n. 1, p. 352, of the 8th edn. (Papermac) of the *Principles*.

[5] Brian Reddaway pointed out to me that both Salter and I are 'assuming away' a host of problems which spring from the presence of imperfect competition, especially the implications of non-homogeneous commodities. I do rather feebly try to tackle this later in the chapter. He added that 'uncertainty is largely responsible for non-investment and retention of old models'. I can only respond by saying that if the analysis of this chapter is correct, and if the package deal of policies proposed were to be implemented, the environment so created might well reduce the effects of uncertainty and allow higher rates of accumulation to occur.

[6] Salter extended his analysis to the system as a whole in (1965).

[7] Not only are they desirable in themselves, they are also the necessary prerequisite for obtaining and sustaining full employment and for having some chance of implementing an incomes policy which is consistent with an overall rate of inflation that maintains the competitiveness of the economies concerned.

industries do so quickly. For this to occur, the last thing we want is a flexible labour market for its proponents tell us that the money-wages of labour should reflect the respective levels and rates of change of productivity in their particular industries (or even firms, as stressed by the proponents of enterprise bargaining on all sides of the political fence in Australia). But this means that money-wages *for the same sorts of labour* will be low and the rates of increase low in the declining industries, so that they linger on, their existing vintages still profitable to keep operating, *ceteris paribus*. By contrast, the industries that should be expanding rapidly have the required accumulation process held back by high money-wages based on the capacity to pay! The outcome is certainly a lower level of productivity in the economy overall and probably a lower rate of increase of productivity overall, than would be the situation if the levels and advances of money-wages were to follow the more efficient and equitable course for which we argue below.[8]

In brief, the guiding principle should be that money-wages are adjusted for changes in the cost-of-living and effective productivity – the overall change in productivity adjusted for any permanent change in the terms of trade. Thus Salter drew these basic policy conclusions from his analysis (see Salter 1960, 153–4) which may be summarised as follows:

(a) Government economic policy should be directed towards creating a flexible economy which enables an easy transference of resources from declining, high-cost and price industries to expanding, low-cost and price ones.

(b) Wages policy should be national in scope rather than related to the circumstances of particular industries. Relating earnings to the 'capacity to pay' of particular industries tends to bolster declining industries and hamper expanding, progressive ones. It delays the introduction of new techniques and has a harmful effect on overall economic growth.

(c) A high rate of gross investment is necessary to allow the structure of production to change quickly and, given the structure of demand, increase the output and productivity of those industries where technical advances are most rapid.

---

[8] Bryan Hopkin has pointed out a potential *non sequitur* here: it is low-productivity industries which should go, high-productivity ones which should grow and they are not necessarily synonymous with declining and expanding industries, respectively. Salter obliquely covers himself on this point (see Salter 1960, 153).

In Salter's 1960 book the level and rate of growth of aggregate demand were external to each industry. But when discussing pay policy and full employment, this cannot remain so. It is here that Kalecki's distinction becomes vitally relevant. While businesspeople are happy (or at least, used to be!) for some government activity to be taken to lift an economy out of a deep slump that has reduced their profits and dimmed their 'animal spirits', they are not at all happy with the social and political conditions which emerge when full employment is reached and then sustained, despite the obvious advantage which high demand brings them. Yet if 'animal spirits' are to be revived and maintained, the maintenance of something akin to sustained full employment is necessary – witness, for example, the experience of the 'Golden Age' of capitalism. But unless continual and persistent action is taken about pay policy, the situation will be increasingly threatened by cumulative inflationary pressures associated especially with the setting of money-wages. For though real wages are an ultimate determinant of the standard of living and increases in it, in a monetary production economy – that is to say, our world as we know it – the wage bargain may be made only in monetary terms, as Keynes taught us long ago.

So we must be able to implement an incomes policy, despite the fact that each employer would like to be free of the inconvenience which the policy brings. The policy must include as one of its features increases which are consistent with the control of inflationary pressures, as determined by our international situation, yet which also allow the great potential benefits of the Salter processes to be realised in the growth of productivity associated with operating at full-employment output levels. Such a position will, of course, be favourable for the support of the 'animal spirits' necessary to allow the accumulation processes identified by Salter to be implemented. All this coming together will reward the economic communities for agreeing to money-income restraints, so allowing everyone to share fairly and fully in the rising prosperity – a virtuous, cumulative, reinforcing process will have been created.

An obvious implication of Salter's analysis is that the guiding principle of wage–setting – indeed, money-incomes-setting in general – should be that, *ceteris paribus*, money-wages change by amounts dictated by changes in the cost-of-living and effective productivity. This guiding principle *is* just, as well as efficient. At the level of the economy as a whole, capital and labour are complements and so jointly contribute to the rise in overall productivity. It is just, therefore, that all citizens should share in the benefits that flow from this. Including the change in the cost-of-living insures people who are unable to protect themselves against a decline in their real incomes from sustained inflation, thus removing a major cause of anxiety and insecurity and, incidentally, making it easier for people generally to agree to money-incomes restraint in an overall package policy deal.[9] This deal nevertheless will not be easy to secure because it has to pay some heed to past ruptures of established relativities, the need to match job opportunities with some (limited) financial incentives and the need to have a floor to the level of money-wages (and other incomes) in a minimum wage, for reasons which are related to the efficiency-wage hypothesis.[10]

As to the main guide line, while it may be *relatively* easy to get agreement on what constitutes the cost-of-living index and its increases – certainly that is something which trade union, employer and government representatives could profitably get together on – a real problem of principle may arise in the measurement of effective productivity changes in a world dominated by floating exchange rates. Why? Because with floating exchange rates and deregulated financial markets, we have, as we have seen, a classic case of markets where stocks dominate flows and speculative influences dominate real economic factors in the setting of both day-to-day market prices and the average of prices over the medium-to-longer term. This state of affairs is compounded when we take into consideration that in a dynamic world economy in which the Salter processes are of very unequal strength as between different countries and regions, the notion that there exists an underlying set of stable long-period equilibrium exchange rates, only awaiting to be found by market forces, is, to say the least, problematic.

It follows that the idea of effective productivity – domestic productivity adjusted for changes in the terms of trade – is an elusive concept in theory and certainly in practice as far as agreed-upon estimation is concerned. Yet some rough agreement, some compromise, would need to be found between interested groups. No doubt the institutions set up to tackle the problem of ruptured relativities could also be expected to make reviews and periodic adjustments for the effects of revisions of estimates of effective productivity as well. Clearly this requires people

---

[9] The confident tone of this argument probably reflects Australian experience where we have had many periods in which cost-of-living adjustments have been an integral part of national wage cases and/or automatic. Bryan Hopkin is deeply sceptical, calling the proposals the 'principle of hope over experience' in the light of UK experiments in the post-war period; but he does favour an incomes policy in principle.

[10] Willy Brown has pointed out that there are serious social problems for some regions as well, in that even if there were to be full employment, children may have to move from regions dominated by declining industries in which their parents were initially employed. This could be offset, to some extent anyway, by encouraging investment in new industries to go to the regions containing these communities.

of good will – are there any left? – but all consensus and sensible and, ultimately, efficient policy-making requires this anyway.[11]

We mentioned earlier that Salter processes are at their most effective when competitive market structures, or something akin to them, may be assumed to be present. But much effort has been devoted in post-Keynesian circles (and others, of course) to describing non-competitive (or imperfectly competitive) market structures and their implications for pricing and the investment decision. Much of this work is micro-economic in character and the systemic effects have at best only been sketched. Nevertheless, there are some disquieting aspects that need to be thought about.[12] Before doing so, let me conjecture that with the increase in international competitiveness of the past three decades, in both goods and services, especially financial services, the world econ-omy *may* be closer to the competitive model, albeit a ruthless jungle red in tooth and claw, than it was when the writings referred to above were first developed. If so, our minds may be put more at ease on that score.

The most disquieting microeconomic result is an implication of the work which I did with Peter Kenyon. There, as we saw, it is argued that prices in oligopolistic industries characterised by large price-leaders are set by profit margins designed to raise the internal funds needed to finance investment, and that there was a process of mutual determin-ation involved. It follows that margins would be greater, the greater was the investment that was planned, *ceteris paribus*. But investment would be less, the higher were the margins and therefore the prices set, because this would allow older vintages to remain in operation that much longer, thereby reducing the shortfall in expected output which new investment would be needed to cater for. In microeconomic terms at least, this is a limitation on accumulation, productivity growth and attaining and sustaining full employment. Moreover, the higher price levels, *ceteris paribus*, may make the control of inflation more difficult. I am not sure that these arguments go through at the level of the system as a whole but, at the very least, they need to be explored.

---

[11] John Wells kindly pointed out to me that *Economic Trends* carries estimates of the terms of trade by quarters from 1970 on and drew my attention to an annual series of UK GDP *per capita* in real terms adjusted for the terms of trade from 1950 on. Bryan Hopkin reckons that I have over emphasised the difficulties (this reflects the fierce debates on this issue in Australia in the 1960s) and that some rough approximation could well be agreed to.

[12] At this point Reddaway made a typically down-to-earth comment: 'The fact that commodities are not homogeneous and have varying amounts of services attached to them is particularly awkward for the would-be producers of elegant analysis.'

There may also be another source of inflationary bias involved in non-competitive situations. Firms with below-average increases in productivity will have rising costs which may be passed on in prices in order to avoid bankruptcy. Those with above-average increases may nevertheless not allow the consequent lower-than-average rise in costs to be fully reflected in prices because they wish to retain profits for extra investment. Overall, therefore, the price level will tend to rise – or, at least, be higher than it would otherwise have been. How important this tendency is depends on how fast demand for particular commodities is growing, and on the feedback effects of this on systemic behaviour.[13] Another limitation is that, because services have risen in importance, we need, but do not yet have, a comprehensive analysis of Salter processes in service industries.

To conclude: by relating the nature of Salter processes to their policy implications for incomes policy we have identified inter-relationships which promise a virtuous, cumulative performance of higher growth and higher employment, a performance which has some possibility of being sustained, if reasonable skill is shown over macroeconomic policies (notably demand management). For the policy measures promise to create an environment where 'animal spirits' may be more consistently robust, even dynamic, and the resulting potential rise in the standard of living rewards the community for acquiescing in a policy of money-incomes' restraint. I do not wish to overstress the cosy side of the story. There are deep-seated structural problems present in many advanced industrialised countries, not least the UK and Australia, so that bottlenecks and balance of payment constraints are only too real, and often bite. Moreover, while it may be possible to create favourable climates for businesspeople, there is no guarantee that they will necessarily do their thing or do it properly – this was certainly the experience of Australia during many years of the Accords when the level and composition of investment were far from what was needed. It may be that governments can give some general pointers by the use of broadly based investment-incentive schemes (see Harcourt 1995a, 38, n. 3). But whatever misgivings we may have,[14] what is proposed is surely more efficient and more just than the present hotchpotch of non-policy and one-sided

---

[13] I am indebted to Peter Kriesler for this argument.

[14] Andrew Glyn has drawn my attention to Rudolf Meidner's (1993) paper on 'Why did the Swedish model fail?' The economic analysis is similar to that of this chapter and some salutary lessons from history are documented; but see Rowthorn (1992) and Stegman (1987), the conclusions of which made me more optimistic about the possible success of the policies proposed.

attacks on the standard of living and employment opportunities of wage-earners.[15]

In any event, I hope that this sketch of a package deal of policies, underlying which are the approaches analysed in the preceding chapters, illustrates that the post-Keynesian way does provide a relevant framework for thinking about both the light-bearing and the fruit-bearing aspects of what Keynes once called 'our miserable subject'. He immediately and always belied such a description with his own cheerful, optimistic and imaginative approach to the puzzles and issues that perpetually face us, its practitioners.

---

[15] John King (personal communication, 27 March 1997) feels there is 'a significant flaw in the argument: the pressures for increasing wage inequality are so powerful that even centralised wage determination . . . proved unable to overcome them [so that my] argument is stronger as a statement of principle than as a practical proposal'. Still, you have to try.

Appendix I: Biographical sketches of the pioneers: Keynes, Kalecki, Sraffa, Joan Robinson, Kahn, Kaldor

John Maynard Keynes, 1883–1946[1]

John Maynard Keynes, the eldest child of John Neville and Florence Ada Keynes, was born into a professional middle-class English household in Cambridge on 5 June 1883. There were three children, all gifted and destined to make their own mark, but Maynard Keynes excelled. He was his parents' favourite and modern students of sibling rivalry no doubt could have a field day analysing the consequent impact on his brother, Geoffrey and sister, Margaret. John Neville Keynes was a university lecturer in the Moral Science Tripos when Keynes was born (in the year that Karl Marx died). He was to be the author of two 'minor classics', *Studies and Exercises in Formal Logic* (1884) and *The Scope and Method of Political Economy* (1891). He was also a colleague of Alfred Marshall, whose pupil Maynard Keynes became. He subsequently became the Registrary of the University in 1910. Florence Ada Keynes was a remarkable person and citizen of Cambridge – 'the busiest woman in Cambridge' (Skidelsky 1983, 425). Among many other activities she was Mayor of Cambridge in 1932–3. Both Keynes' parents outlived him, his father dying in 1949 and his mother in 1958.

Maynard Keynes went to Eton, where he excelled intellectually and socially, and then to King's, Cambridge to read mathematics. He seems to have spent as much time on philosophy as on mathematics and he continued his hectic social and intellectual life. He was elected to the Apostles, spoke at the Union and made lifelong friends in King's and Trinity. His tripos result – 12th Wrangler – was respectable but disappointing for such a gifted person and for his father. Keynes himself aimed to get exactly this result, the first of the instances he had used rational expectations. (Another instance was in his theory of investment, see chapter 4, p. 60.) He stayed on in Cambridge to read for the civil service examinations in 1906, so having his first contact with economics. He was supervised by Marshall, who quickly realised that he had a genius on his hands. Characteristically, in effect, Marshall said, 'We old men must kill ourselves' – the usual mixture of grudging admiration and envy which characterised this great economist and awful person. Nevertheless, Keynes's lowest mark in the civil service examinations was in economics (presumably, he said, because the examiners knew less about the subject than he did) and, as he came second in

---

[1] I have drawn heavily on my entry in Cate (1997) (see Harcourt 1997).

the examinations as a whole, he had to settle for the India Office rather than his first love, the Treasury. While in the civil service, Keynes started work on a fellowship dissertation for King's (it became *A Treatise on Probability* in 1921). He was elected in 1909, at his second attempt. He had already returned to Cambridge in 1908 to become a lecturer in economics, paid for by Marshall out of his own pocket (here he *was* generous), and then by Pigou who had succeeded Marshall when Keynes took up the post. Keynes was primarily interested in monetary theory and policy, though he lectured on a wide range of topics.

His social life continued apace, as he was a core member of the Bloomsbury Group and a friend of many of the up-and-coming artists, theatre people and, subsequently, psychoanalysts – Keynes was vitally interested in the cultural and intellectual developments of his time, especially, of course, the philosophical developments associated with G. E. Moore, Bertrand Russell, Frank Ramsey and Ludwig Wittgenstein.

During the First World War, Keynes worked in the Treasury (to the disgust of many of his friends who were pacifists and conscientious objectors). Keynes thought the war was an unspeakable crime but that, if the UK had to be in it, the war effort should be guided by rational and humane principles provided by intelligent and educated people who accepted the 'old presuppositions of Harvey Rd' (Keynes' birthplace) as Harrod (1951, 183) put it. Keynes was one of Lloyd George's advisors at Versailles; he was so appalled by the vindictive and destructive provisions of the Treaty that in the end he resigned and wrote *The Economic Consequences of the Peace* (1919), which made him world famous. In doing so he changed from being just an extraordinarily clever but often superficially flip and cynical young man into a serious maturity which can only be described as admirable. His beautifully written polemic is still worth reading for its passionate anger, power and application of theory in its best sense to explanation and policy.

Keynes returned to Cambridge in the 1920s, resigning his lectureship but maintaining his fellowship in King's (of which he was now senior bursar) and the editorship of the *Economic Journal* (to which he was first appointed in 1911). He performed an enormous number of roles – speculation, journalism, director of an insurance company, bibliophile, patron of the arts, theatre and ballet (in 1925, he was to marry Lydia Lopokova, the Russian ballerina, a mutually supportive partnership based on love and laughter) – all while he 'settled down' in order to write the three books which were to make him an immortal: *A Tract on Monetary Reform* (1923), *A Treatise on Money* (1930) and *The General Theory of Employment, Interest and Money* (1936). (We should also mention *Essays in Persuasion*, 1931 and *Essays in Biography*, 1933.)

Initially Keynes worked on monetary matters within the Marshallian paradigm as he saw it, yet reacting to his teacher by concentrating more and more on happenings in the short run for policy recommendations. His most famous line – '*In the long run* we are all dead' – is to be found in a passage where he exhorts economists to live in and work and advise on the here and now. But he put the general price level at the centre of what was to be influenced by monetary policy and had not yet arrived at a coherent theory of an integrated monetary production economy where both the general price level and activity were entwined – *that* was to come with the writing of *The General Theory*.

Keynes' marriage in 1925 marked a major sea change in his personal life. Prior to this Keynes had been actively gay, as Skidelsky tells us in graphic detail in his Volume One (1983), repairing the deliberate omission of this aspect of Keynes' life by Roy Harrod in the first 'official' biography in 1951. The happiness associated with his marriage had, it may be conjectured, a crucial impact on his creativity and understanding, so that his *magnum opus* was both a true work of genius and the work of a contented man, who was therefore all the more passionately angry about a system which brought mass unemployment and poverty to others. Keynes was also supremely confident that he could teach us why these evils happened and what we could – and should – do about them.

In 1937, he had the first of several severe heart attacks and the next two years or so were wiped out – relatively; that is to say, he only did what normally clever people would have done. In particular, though he replied to those he considered the most important of his critics in some important articles, including a summary restatement of his theory in the *Quarterly Journal of Economics* (1937), he never did write those 'footnotes' to *The General Theory* which he told Ralph Hawtrey in August 1936 he was intending to do (see *CW*, XIV, 1973, 47). Then came the Second World War in which (reluctantly at first, because of his health) Keynes became more and more involved. Not only did he 'generalize' *The General Theory* to tackle the inflationary problems of wartime scarcities but he also took a larger and larger role in the actual running of the wartime economy and in the design of institutions to make the post-war world better and more just – Bretton Woods and all that.

Keynes literally killed himself for his country and the world by his efforts. His last major task was to get the British government and people to accept the harsh conditions of the American loan: his speech to the House of Lords on this issue was crucially important for the acceptance of the conditions. He then went to the inaugural meetings of the IMF and World Bank, the Savannah Conference, 'the most exhausting conference that he had attended' (Austin Robinson 1947, 65). Exhausted, he returned to his country home, Tilton, in Sussex (in 1942, he had become Baron Keynes of Tilton) and on Easter Monday 1946 he had his last and this time fatal heart attack, dying far too young, at 62. Yet, as Austin Robinson (1947, 66) told us, those 'whom the gods love should die young' – 'a great economist and a very great Englishman', as the *Times* obituarist put it, a man whose life and works provide a resounding 'yes' to the Moorean puzzle with which Keynes and his contemporaries grappled: is it possible both to *be* good and to *do* good?

Michal Kalecki, 1899–1970[2]

Michal Kalecki was born in 1899; he was the son of a small textile manufacturer. Two major happenings in his youth shaped his personality and influenced his attitudes: the separation of his parents (he then lived with his father) and the

---

[2] I have drawn heavily on the late Josef Steindl's illuminating and affectionate essay (Steindl 1981) on his sometime colleague at Oxford, mentor and friend.

collapse of his father's business in 1923. This meant that Kalecki could not finish his course on civil engineering at, first, the Warsaw Polytechnic and then, after serving as a conscript in the Polish army, the Polytechnic School in Danzig. Steindl writes that these misfortunes 'became sources of strength', that 'the deep distrust of life they created [spawned his] life-long scepticism and relentless questioning' (Steindl 1981, 590).

Kalecki had to support himself by working for a company that sold information to creditors – Kalecki enquired about the solvency of relatively small businesses – and writing newspaper articles on practical economic problems and for a socialist journal. Steindl sees 'his socialist conviction – his innate revulsion at the iniquities and the brutalities of the existing capitalist society and his wish for a better system – [as] the basic inspiration of Kalecki's [life] work' (Steindl 1981, 595). In the later 1920s Kalecki moved to Warsaw. He married Ada Sternfeld, his inseparable and devoted companion who was to prove a 'counterweight to so many adverse circumstances'. In 1929 he was appointed to the Institute for Business Cycle and Price Research, of which Edward Lipinski was Director and 'who instinctively saw the merits of Kalecki's candidacy' (1981, 595).

As a student Kalecki read Tugan-Baranowski; this led him to Marx and especially to his departmental schemas. Steindl thinks that Kalecki knew little of other economic doctrines at this time but he was already publishing in what we would now regard as Brownie-point journals – *Econometrica* and *Revue d'Economie Politique* in 1935. He received a Rockefeller grant that took him to Sweden in 1936. Then, on learning of the sacking of two of his friends at the Warsaw Institute for political reasons, he resigned 'in a show of solidarity' (1981, 591), the first of three times in his lifetime that he resigned from posts on principle.

The publication of *The General Theory* in 1936 caused him disappointment, understandably, as he had independently discovered the main propositions of Keynes' book. But as he quickly pointed out, it was the propositions that mattered and Keynes, a well-placed insider, was in a much better position, politically *and* socially, to get them known, to propagate their essential message.

He came to the UK in 1936, first to the LSE, where he met George Shackle, who much admired him. Kalecki had asked the research students at the LSE whether there was someone who could help him brush up the written English of his papers, written and to come. Shackle went to Kalecki's rooms to do so, receiving, he said, a superb education in economics as Kalecki paced about the room arguing out loud points of theory with himself. Shackle's own superb command of English which no doubt imprinted itself on Kalecki was an appropriate *quid pro quo*.

Kalecki then went to Cambridge where his long and deep friendship with Joan Robinson began. She was amazed as this outsider who understood the new theory as well as if not better than the Cambridge insiders and who even came up with some of their in-jokes – Kalecki was one of the greatest crackers of jokes and writer of witty remarks – with a point – of our trade.[3]

---

[3] My favourite is that after Kalecki heard a lecture by an Indian economist that did *not* impress him, he said: 'I have no racial prejudice, I think I can say that this man is an ass.'

In 1940 he went to the Oxford Institute of Statistics, then a haven for economists from continental Europe (Steindl was one). Kalecki was the 'guiding spirit'. They worked on economic problems of the war and post-war period from a left-wing (Labour Party) perspective, knowing 'what [they] wanted and how it should be done' (1981, 591). They developed reformist policies that read, even more so today, as enlightened, humane and common sense. In the 1977 issue of the *Bulletin* of the Institute in honour of Kalecki some of his former colleagues pay tribute to his integrity, inspiration and contributions.

After the war there was something of a purge of the asylum seekers as the Institute (nothing new under the sun?) and Kalecki, sensing that there was neither recognition nor a future for him in Oxford, went to the ILO in Canada. In 1946 he became Deputy Director of a section of its Economics Department, responsible for its *World Economic Reports*. In 1950 he was working as an official at the UN in New York. Steindl tells us that this was the 'tensest period of the cold war' and that 'Kalecki found the atmosphere of McCarthyism repugnant' (1981, 592). Rather than submit to political pressures on him and the work of the institutions, he resigned in 1955 and returned to Poland, to Warsaw.

His FBI files[4] show that he was likely to be a victim not only of McCarthyism but also of anti-semitism. Thus, he is summed up as follows:

Name:	Michal Kalecki
Alias:	Michal Kalecki
Age:	40–50 years
Nationality:	Polish
Height:	5'4"
Weight:	150 pounds
Hair:	Dark
Complexion:	Swarthy
Build:	Medium
Eyes:	Small, dark, intense, solemn
Features:	Prominent nose
Mannerisms:	Not sociable, speaks very loudly.

Kalecki is said, 'according to a confidential informant of the New York office, [to have] the general reputation in the United Nations of being a communist'. The same informant doubted that he 'would return to Poland [but] would prefer to live in the United States . . . because although KALECKI is a Marxist he is also a theorist, and [would] not 'buckle down' to communist theories in all instances'–!!

In Poland his task as economic advisor to the chairman of the Planning Commission was to work out a long-term plan for the years 1960–80. He wanted consumption goods production and employment in that sector to be such that real wages could rise modestly but steadily and investment expenditure to take up the rest of the labour force to ensure full employment. He devised rational

---

[4] I am indebted to Jan Toporowski for giving me a copy of the files. They are dated July 13, 1951 and name Kalecki as Assistant Director of the Division of Economic Stability in the Department of Economic Affairs, Division of Economic Stability, United Nations, Lake Success, New York.

investment-decision mechanisms for managers in both sectors. Kalecki's plans ran into the 'Stalinist heavy industry ambitions of Gomulka and his political minions, whose preference for ambitious investment projects could not be reconciled with Kalecki's figures' (1981, 592). He lost this 'unequal political battle', and resigned in 1961 to become a professor at the School of Planning and Statistics. He had a serious heart attack soon after his sixty-fifth birthday and 'was never the same vigorous and dynamic man again'. One last noble act lit up the unhappy years of the end of his life. In 1968 there was a purge of Jewish intellectuals from their jobs; they were chosen as scapegoats for 'the reformist opposition of intellectuals and students' to the government's plans. Kalecki was too eminent to be directly affected but he retired early in protest. 'He saw his world crumbling. The brilliant man who had keenly analyzed . . . the history of his time now felt that the world his mind had nourished had collapsed . . . His despair and [subsequent] retreat . . . measure . . . the depth of disillusionment and disorientation of our time' (1981, 592).

Kalecki died in 1970. Six months later, Gomulka was forced from office by street demonstrations by workers against insufficient real wages and widespread scarcity of consumer goods. 'Kalecki's logic had come back with a vengeance' (1981, 593).

In my view, Kalecki has a strong claim to be regarded as the greatest all-round economist of the twentieth century. Not only is there his independent discovery of the principal propositions of *The General Theory*, there are also his outstanding contributions to planning democratic socialist societies and his many contributions to the solutions of the problems of developing countries, both as a direct advisor and as a theorist of the political economy of development. Jerzy Osiatynski has edited in seven volumes the *Collected Works of Michal Kalecki* (1990–7). Always a 'horses for courses' person, whenever he was asked on arrival in a country to which he had been invited as an advisor, what he intended to recommend, he would say, in effect, 'How can I answer that now? Come back in six months and ask me again after I have had a chance to absorb the characteristics of your history, politics and sociology and make myself familiar with your institutions and the orders of magnitude of the key components of your national output and industries.' This contrasts starkly with those who, as Eric Russell used to say, give advice as they step off the plane because they have model, will travel.

Steindl (1981, 595–6) described him as 'a very powerful personality concealed behind an unpretentious and unassuming appearance . . . a very kind and sympathetic man [who nevertheless] could be . . . uncompromising when his convictions were involved'. He could be 'most sociable . . . [was] interested in people . . . The results of his astounding political analyses came across through his powerful voice like the clatter of a machine gun . . . His . . . predictions . . . invariably turned out to be true. . . . His anecdotes and stories . . . always [fitted] the situation exactly'.

Steindl contrasted these traits with the succinctness and clarity of his writings, so that Kalecki has never inspired a literature about what he *really* meant because he was so crystal clear. Yet his contributions and Kalecki himself remain 'relatively obscure', first, because of his social position, especially in England in the 1930s – 'a Jew, [an] "outcast" from the east in an era seething with Hitlerian hates' and, secondly, because he 'was too blunt in his reformist socialist zeal' for our conservative and conformist trade. Nevertheless Steindl thought, and I agree (otherwise I would not have written this volume), that 'his work . . . will influence thought for years to come' (1981, 596).[5]

Piero Sraffa, 1898–1983[6]

Piero Sraffa was born in Turin on 5 August 1898, the only child of Angelo Sraffa, from Pisa, a professor of commercial law at several Italian universities, and his wife, Irma Tivoli, from Piedmont. Both parents came from well-known Jewish families. He was educated in Parma, Milan and Turin, and at the University of Turin, where he graduated as doctor of law in 1920. He became associate professor of political economy at the University of Perugia in 1924 and then professor at the University of Cagliari (Sardinia) in 1926. After offending Mussolini (see below) he migrated to England in 1927 and, through the initiative of Keynes, was appointed to a university lectureship in the Cambridge faculty of economics and politics. In 1930 he resigned his lectureship (he was agonisingly shy about lecturing) and was appointed Marshall Librarian and, soon after, assistant director of research to act as mentor to research students. In 1939 he was elected to a fellowship at Trinity College, Cambridge. He was made FBA in 1954 and a reader in economics at Cambridge in 1963. In 1961 he was awarded the prize of the Stockholm Academy of Science, which was equivalent to receiving the Nobel prize.

Sraffa had a major influence on the intellectual developments of the twentieth century. He was an intimate friend of Antonio Gramsci, Keynes and Ludwig Wittgenstein, and indeed played an important part in persuading

---

[5] Should it be thought that only the FBI files were 'beyond the pale' in their evaluation of Kalecki, we quote here, again through kind permission of Jan Toporowski, a British Ambassador's evaluation in 1959 in 'Notes on leading Personalities' which are in Kalecki's papers:

A Vice-Chairman of the Economic Council. Member of the Planning Commission.

Born 1899 in Lodz. Perhaps Poland's only world-class economist. Created a sensation as a post-graduate student at the London School of Economics just before the war with his passionate and bigoted advocacy of his own ideas. Led a statistical research group at Oxford during the war, and enjoyed the highest reputation among British economists. Worked after the war in the United Nations and the ILO [International Labour Organization] before returning to Poland in 1955. A member of the group of Polish planners who visited the United Kingdom as guests of Her Majesty's Government in February 1958.

Professor Kalecki is now in charge of the Polish Fifteen-Year Plan, 1960–75. He is a firm believer in a planned economy, and is not hampered by Marxist beliefs. Is not a member of the Communist Party, and will not hesitate to advocate what he believes to be economically right whatever its political implications. His importance in Poland is likely to increase.

A small bird-like Jew, with a harsh personality and no social graces. He is prejudiced against the United States and what he believes to be the British moneyed classes, but is impressed by postwar British development. Now more mellow than in his youth. His Jewish wife is pleasant. Speaks excellent English.

[6] This essay is based on my entry on Sraffa in the *Oxford Dictionary of National Biography* (Harcourt 2004a).

Wittgenstein to change his philosophical views as between the *Tractatus logico-philosophicus* (1922) and the *Philosophical Investigations* (1953). Sraffa was the most important critic of the orthodox theory of value and distribution in the twentieth century. Yet, though he was to make outstanding contributions to pure theory, about the rigour and coherence of which he had well-defined ideas, the object of his theorizing always had a political and social aspect to it.

From his schooldays he had taken a keen interest in political issues and early on became a socialist. He fought in the Italian army during the First World War and, as a result of his experiences, became a pacifist. He opposed Mussolini's Fascist regime; his friendship with Gramsci came about because of this. In even his earliest economic work – his dissertation 'L'inflazione monetaria in Italia durante e dopo la guerra' (1920) – important political, institutional, and sociological ingredients were already present. And though the analytical structure was the then dominant form of the quantity theory of money, Sraffa's own particular contribution was to integrate the sociological and institutional determinants of wages and employment into this framework. He incurred the wrath of Mussolini by exposing the corrupt practices of the pre-Fascist and Fascist state with regard to the private banking system in his 1922 *Economic Journal* and *Manchester Guardian* articles on the bank crisis in Italy. It was his interest in monetary matters that first attracted Keynes' attention and while they were later to follow different lines of research in economics, their friendship remained as close as ever, not least because they were both passionate bibliophiles. Sraffa translated Keynes' *A Tract on Monetary Reform* (1923) into Italian in 1925.

In the mid-1920s Sraffa commenced his critique of the orthodox theory of value and distribution. First, he attacked the partial equilibrium analysis of Alfred Marshall and then the general equilibrium framework, all different examples of the dominant supply and demand theories. As a challenge to these theories, Sraffa spawned the imperfect competition revolution which others developed, in a manner probably not to his liking. Then, changing tack, Sraffa developed a coherent account of the surplus approach of the classical political economists – the contention that the surplus of commodities is the core concept of economic theory around which theories of value, distribution, production, employment and growth may, and should, be set. In Sraffa's view, this approach reached its highest form in Marx's work, only to be superseded in mainstream economics by the rise to dominance of the supply and demand theories. By stressing the production interdependencies of the economy as a whole (commodities produced by means of commodities) Sraffa set out a system which gave precise coherence to the surplus concept, allowed the analysis of the effect of different values of a distributive variable on prices to be examined and, at the same time, provided a critique of the marginal theories in so far as they were directed to answering classical questions about the origin and size of the rate of profits. The development of these ideas occupied many years. They were published as *Production of Commodities by Means of Commodities* (Sraffa 1960).

From 1930 Sraffa also worked on his magnificent eleven-volume edition (1951–73) of the works and correspondence of David Ricardo, in later years collaborating with Maurice Dobb, who did not share Sraffa's extreme inhibitions against writing for publication. It is one of the finest examples of sustained and meticulous scholarship in the discipline. The arguments of the introduction to vol. I, published in 1951, are important complements to those of the 1960 book. In attempting this sustained research programme of both criticism and revival Sraffa may have had in mind Gramsci's injunction to attack at its logical core the very best expression of a rival philosophical system.

Sraffa was a remarkable personality. He had the capacity to evoke great affection and to inspire people to perform at their full potential. He had a subtle original wit and he made wholly unexpected responses to points raised in discussion. He was fluent in four languages. Though he lived in England from 1927 on, he always regarded himself as Italian, reading the Italian papers daily and never changing his nationality (indeed, he was interned on the Isle of Man in 1940, until Keynes succeeded in having him returned to Cambridge). Sraffa died in Cambridge on 3 September 1983. He was unmarried.

Joan Robinson, 1903–1983

Joan Robinson was born on 31 October 1903 into an upper-middle-class family with a tradition of dissent. She herself was the rebel with a cause *par excellence*. As Joan Maurice, she read history at St Paul's Girls' School and came up to Girton College, Cambridge in 1922 to read economics because she wanted to know why unemployment and poverty abounded. She did not think the economics or the economists of that time provided satisfactory answers. She graduated in 1925, married Austin Robinson, one of her teachers, in 1926 and they went to India for two years. This started her life-long love affair with the subcontinent and her interest in the problems of developing countries. Though Cambridge was always to be her base, her love of travelling meant she visited China several times in the post-war years and in her later years she spent part of each year in Kerala State in India. Her first visit to the USA is still remembered with awe and, sometimes, affection. Joan Robinson became a university assistant lecturer at Cambridge in 1934, a university lecturer in 1937, a reader in 1949 and a professor in 1965. She 'retired' in 1971, remaining active into the last years of her life, despite poor health in her last few years. She died in August 1983.

Joan Robinson said of Alfred Marshall, 'The more I learn about economics the more I admire Marshall's intellect and the less I like his character' (Joan Robinson 1953; *CEP*, IV, 1973, 259). Marshall had a profound influence on the development of her thought through his *Principles* and the teaching and writings of A. C. Pigou, Maynard Keynes, Gerald Shove, Dennis Robertson and Austin Robinson. Even as an undergraduate she showed she understood him only too well, see her delightful 'spoof', 'Beauty and the Beast' (Joan Robinson, *CEP*, vol. I, 1951).

In her first major publication, *Economics is a Serious Subject* (1932), Pigou's tool-making imagery is dominant. She is wary of applying theory directly to explanation and policy, discerning a conflict between reality and tractability and warning that there must be a trade-off between them.

Yet it was a real problem that led her to develop what became *The Economics of Imperfect Competition* (Robinson 1933a) – why had not more firms closed down in the depressed conditions of the 1920s and 1930s in the United Kingdom, an inescapable inference of Marshallian–Pigovian theory? Piero Sraffa's 'pregnant suggestion' in 1926 that demand rather than rising marginal costs determined levels of production of firms provided the springboard for her analysis of mini-monopolies operating in competitive environments. The core tool of her book was the marginal revenue curve, and the most important influence on her as she wrote it was Richard Kahn. That the unfit were not necessarily eliminated by the slump was a damning indictment of the workings of competitive capitalism, second in importance only to the Keynes–Kalecki theory of effective demand, especially of its unsatisfactory level, in such economies. Joan Robinson subsequently repudiated *The Economics of Imperfect Competition*, especially the 'shameless fudge' (Joan Robinson had something of a 'who's for hockey' vocabulary) whereby demand curves stayed still while businesspeople groped for equilibrium prices by trial and error. In later years this critique, as we saw, was summed up as 'History versus equilibrium' (Joan Robinson, 1974; *CEP*, vol. V, 1979b, 48–58).

Keynes' *A Treatise on Money* was published in 1930. Joan Robinson saw Keynes as trying, guiltily, to break out of the Marshallian dichotomy between the real and the money in order to analyse the causes and cures of prolonged unemployment as well as deflation and inflation of the general price level. The discussion of *A Treatise on Money* by the 'Circus' in the early 1930s and Keynes' lectures as the embryonic *General Theory* emerged were an obvious outlet for Joan Robinson's passionate search for truth. She wrote two perceptive interim reports in the early 1930s, (Robinson 1933b, 1933c), arguing that Keynes was trying to make a theory of output and employment but that, still under Marshall's influence, it was a long-period theory. By the time *The General Theory* was published in 1936 it had become short-period analysis in its own right with Joan Robinson providing in *Essays in the Theory of Employment* (1937) a long-period exercise to try to show that the new, short-period, results held in principle in the long period, too. The same volume of essays contained a discussion of disguised unemployment (it brought together understanding from her time in India and the new theory) and an exposition of what is now known in the literature as the Harris–Todaro model of migration (1970) (see Tahir 1999).

As we have already noted, Joan Robinson first met Michal Kalecki in 1936 and the beginning of their long, close intellectual friendship and vigorous debates was probably the single most important stimulus for the sea change in her views that started about then. (She was the greatest champion of the clear-cut case that Kalecki had independently discovered the principal propositions of *The General Theory*.)

Joan Robinson came to feel that the Marxian framework through which Kalecki solved the realisation problem was more appropriate than Keynes' Marshallian-based approach for an understanding of the capitalist process. The mastery of this former approach and framework is exemplified in her superb account of Kalecki on capitalism (Robinson 1977a; *CEP*, vol. V, 1979b, 184–96) (see chapter 2, pp. 11–15). Joan Robinson shows how the price policies of firms, the different saving behaviour of wage-earners and profit-receivers and the dominant importance of profit-making and accumulation may be combined in a short-period model of employment and the distribution of income to illustrate the possibility of an underemployment rest state. The same structure underlies the analysis of her *magnum opus*, *The Accumulation of Capital* (1956), and its sequel of 1962, *Essays in the Theory of Economic Growth* (1962a). Moreover, as we have seen (see chapter 4, pp. 60–5), Kalecki's critique (1936, 1990–7; Targetti and Kinda-Hass, 1982) of the structure of Keynes' theory of investment is mirrored in her own, that it is an unholy mass of *ex ante* and *ex post* factors which need to be separated by taking into account the two-sided relationship between profitability and accumulation. On the one hand, actual accumulation creates actual profitability; on the other, expected profitability creates planned accumulation, the ingredients of her famous banana diagram (see Joan Robinson 1962a, 48, and chapter 4, p. 64). All this had been preceded by her 1942 *An Essay on Marxian Economics* (1942), criticised by Shove (1944) for its lack of understanding of Marshall rather than Marx and praised by Keynes (in a letter to Mrs Austin [*sic*], Robinson of 20 August 1942) for how well written it was 'despite [how] . . . boring [is] an attempt to make sense of what is in fact not sense'.

Keynes' ideas were developed by Joan Robinson in at least two directions in the post-war years. First, she had a deep understanding of money and its roles in economic systems. Her main concern was with the determination of the rate of interest (Robinson 1952). She responded to Keynes' injunction to be on guard against the fallacy of composition and explained how the equilibrium rate of interest was to bring about an uneasy truce between bullishness and bearishness in financial markets at each point in time.

The other development, as we have seen, was 'generalising *The General Theory* to the long period', the distinctively Cambridge, England, contributions by Kahn, Kaldor, Joan Robinson, Sraffa, Goodwin and, later, Luigi Pasinetti to post-war theories of growth. Real post-war problems and Harrod's theoretical contributions (1939, 1948) were the stimuli. As we argued in the text, all of these issues and analyses of them constituted a return to classical and Marxian preoccupations renewed in the light of the Keynes–Kalecki revolution.

Parallel with these developments were the fights over the theory of distribution and the meaning of capital (side-tracked into questions of measurement) in the neoclassical supply and demand approach as compared to the Marxian–Kaleckian–Keynesian view of the world, see Appendix 2. The Wicksellian analysis in Joan Robinson's article on 'The production function and the theory of capital' (1953–4), and in *The Accumulation of Capital* (1956) concerned the choice of techniques aspect of her theory of growth, the most difficult but not the most essential part of her analysis. But the Cambridge controversies in the theory of capital which her writings and the publication of Sraffa's *Production of Commodities by means of commodities* (1960) threw up overshadowed her positive contributions, especially when the controversies 'hotted up' in the mid-1960s with the 1966 *Quarterly Journal of Economics* symposium on capital-reversal and reswitching. Though she contributed both early and late to the debates, she increasingly came to feel that they were all beside the point, see her 'The unimportance of reswitching', (Robinson 1975). She pursued relentlessly her methodological critique, the illegitimacy of using comparisons (differences) to analyse processes (changes), the need to be clear about the limitations and applicability of models set in logical time *vis-à-vis* those set in historical time. The former are concerned with what would be different if . . . ?; the latter, with what would follow if . . . ? (This naturally leads to consideration of path-dependence, though neither Kaldor 1934a nor Joan Robinson received credit for their early awareness of this when path-dependence became all the rage in the 1980s and 1990s.)

There was, however, a practical aspect to her work on the choice of techniques, as well. In the 1950s, on a visit to China, she gave three lectures, the second of which was devoted to this question (see Tahir, Harcourt and Kerr 2002). It was set within the context of the analysis associated with Dobb (1954), Galenson and Leibenstein (1955) and Sen (1960) of the appropriate techniques to embody in accumulation in developing economies. Joan Robinson argued for a middle way, giving weight to employment as well as to increasing the annual surplus to be reinvested. The first lecture was concerned with the nature of interdepartmental flows which planners need to have at the back of their heads – and the forefront of their minds. The third lecture was in outline her difficult but profound essay, 'The philosophy of prices' (Robinson, *CEP*, vol. II, 1960, 27–48), in which she discusses the role of the price mechanism in development, especially its role in the creation of incomes and expenditures. In outline and content, the lectures, together with her views on population control, are close to the pragmatic, gradualist, trial-and-error use of the market, openness and central control that now characterises the Chinese economy.

In 1979 she published *Aspects of Development and Underdevelopment* (1979a), in which she spelled out in detail the approach she had taken in the 1950s lectures in China and later. The pages are filled with a mixture of acute analysis, usually well-chosen empirical examples, and a feel for what ought to be done, coupled often with realistic analysis combined with *Realpolitik* but also influenced by her growing pessimism about what was likely to happen.

Joan Robinson was ill for much of the last decade of her life and deeply distressed about the arms race (see Robinson 1981). She became more and more pessimistic, even nihilistic concerning economic theory. Two late papers (Bhaduri and Robinson 1980; Robinson 1980; 1985) reflect this mood. The first is the more optimistic; it contains her final assessment of where the writings of possibly her greatest influence and certainly her most feared critic, Piero Sraffa, might be combined with those of Marx and Kalecki to form a schema through which to understand the laws of motion of capitalism. The latter article was much more radical. Initially titled 'Spring cleaning', it is a plea to clear out the whole house, not just the attic, and start again.

Joan Robinson taught us always to look at the conceptual basis of our theories. The latter should start from actual situations, actual societies with explicit 'rules of the game', institutions, past histories and defined sociological characteristics. When analysing these societies, we should ask what levels of abstraction are appropriate to the questions we are trying to answer. We should aim to construct theories that contain the essential elements of reality, expressed in a sufficiently simple form to allow us to see clearly the relationships at work, and how they intertwine. Most of all, perhaps, we should remember her injunction that: 'The purpose of studying economics is not to acquire a set of ready-made answers to economic questions, but to learn how to avoid being deceived by economists' Robinson 1955; *CEP*, vol. II, 1960, 17). I hope these injunctions have been reflected in the chapters of this volume.

Richard Kahn, 1905–1989[7]

Richard Ferdinand Kahn was born in London on 10 August 1905, the second child and only son of four surviving children (two younger sons died) of Augustus Kahn, inspector of schools, and his wife, Regina Rosa Schoyer, of Germany. His father was an extremely orthodox Jew, an adherent to a form of Judaism that 'combined strict observance of the laws of the Torah with an openness to secular learning' so that Kahn 'was brought up in a household which had a commitment to communal service and combined punctilious and decorous orthodoxy with a thirst for education and culture' (from the Address by Professor David Tabor at Richard's funeral). Kahn was educated at St Paul's School, London and at King's College, Cambridge. He read mathematics for one year, obtaining a First in part one in 1925, physics for two years, obtaining a Second in part two of the natural sciences tripos in 1927 and economics, obtaining a First in part two in 1928, a remarkable performance after only one year. Keynes and Gerald Shove, his King's supervisors, and Piero Sraffa encouraged Kahn to write a fellowship dissertation for King's, of which he became a fellow in 1930.

In only a year and a half, Kahn produced 'The economics of the short period' (1929), a remarkable contribution to the then emerging theory of imperfect competition. It was associated with the beginning of Kahn's close intellectual friendship with Joan Robinson. Kahn's dissertation contained many of the results in her *The Economics of Imperfect Competition* (1933a) and the subsequent literature spawned by it and Edward Chamberlin's *The Theory of Monopolistic Competition* (1933): the use of a reverse L-shaped cost curve, the kinked demand curve and the procedure of explaining empirical observations in terms of businesspeople's perception of their situations rather than starting from a simple axiom. Showing that the unfit were not purged in a slump was the most grievous blow dealt to *laissez-faire* until Keynes and Kalecki established the possibility of underemployment equilibrium in 1936. Kahn's dissertation was not published in English until shortly after his death in 1989. (An Italian translation was published in 1983.) In retrospect, Kahn regretted that he had not published it at the time. In his introduction to the 1989 book he described it as an impressive performance for its time and (economic) age of its author.

Kahn became a university lecturer in the faculty of economics and politics in 1933, second bursar to Keynes in 1935, and a teaching fellow at King's in 1936. He was the key figure in the famous 'Circus' which 'argued out' the propositions of *A Treatise on Money* (1930) and discussed and criticised Keynes' drafts as Keynes moved from *A Treatise on Money* to *The General Theory of Employment, Interest and Money* (1936). Kahn also went regularly with Keynes to Tilton (the Sussex home of Keynes and Lydia Lopokova) to give him 'stiff supervisions' on the emerging drafts.

Cambridge was the scene for two theoretical revolutions in economic theory in the 1920s and 1930s. Kahn played crucial roles in both. His lifelong

---

[7] I have drawn on my entry on Kahn in the *Oxford Dictionary of National Biography* (Harcourt 2004b).

scepticism about the quantity theory of money as a causal explanation of the general price level increasingly sapped Keynes' acceptance of it (and Say's Law) from his teacher Alfred Marshall. In a famous article on the multiplier, 'The relation of home investment to unemployment' (1931), Kahn used the apparatus of Keynes' *Treatise on Money* to put a precise order of magnitude on the total increase in employment that would ultimately occur if a primary increase was created by public works. He showed, under carefully specified conditions, that the investment expenditure itself would create a matching volume of new saving. This concept allowed Keynes to create a key innovation, the propensity-to-consume schedule, which became an integral part of the theory of employment as a whole in *The General Theory*.

During the 1930s Kahn wrote a number of seminal papers on imperfect competition, welfare economics, and international trade. The Second World War saw Kahn, on Keynes' recommendation, in Whitehall. He started as a temporary principal in the Board of Trade. Oliver Lyttelton liked his work and had Kahn seconded to him in a number of different sections: the Middle East supply centre (as economic adviser, 1941–3), then the Ministry of Production, the Ministry of Supply, and finally the Board of Trade again in 1945. Kahn ended the war with the administrative grade of principal assistant secretary. He took to Whitehall like a duck to water, drafting memos, scheming to get his views through, while still having enough time and energy for the minutiae of administration. This intense interest in detail and a reluctance to delegate stayed with Kahn for the rest of his life. He had excellent ideas, was an acute and incisive critic, but was often difficult to work with, especially when his notorious anger was aroused.

After the war Kahn returned to Cambridge for the rest of his life (there were extended periods away working for the United Nations in the 1950s and 1960s). He became first bursar of King's in 1946 when Keynes died, a position which he held until he was elected to a chair in 1951. (He retired from this post in 1972.) He was created a life peer in 1965, sitting on the cross-benches as an independent. He remained, as he himself wished to be known, a disciple of Keynes, devoting himself, particularly through his selfless input into the work of others, to extending Keynes' ideas into the theory of the long period – especially with Joan Robinson and also with Kaldor, Sraffa and Pasinetti – and to extending and defending Keynes' ideas on money and the stock market generally. Kahn had a substantial impact on the views of the committee of inquiry into the monetary and credit system (1957–9), chaired by Sir Cyril Radcliffe. He also discussed the need for an incomes policy as he spelled out the implications for inflationary pressures and the balance of payments of successfully sustaining full employment, as opposed to reaching it (for obvious reasons, Keynes' main objective in the 1930s). In the 1970s and 1980s Kahn turned increasingly to the history of theory, providing authoritative evaluations of Keynes' achievements for the British Academy (1978), in the *Journal of Economic Literature* (1978) and in his Raffaele Mattioli Foundation Lectures in Italy, *The Making of Keynes' General Theory* (1984).

Kahn lived in a splendid set of rooms in Webb's Court at King's until his final illness. To those who did not know him well, he seemed an intensely private person. Deafness and ill health in his last years made him a rather solitary public figure. In reality, he was kind, generous and hospitable, a meticulously considerate host and, in his younger days, a vigorous walker and rock climber. He never lost his interest in what was happening in King's and the faculty, or ceased to disapprove if things did not turn out as he would have wished.

As we noted above, Kahn came from a deeply religious Jewish family who were devoted to education. Up until the Second World War Kahn's orthodoxy was a byword among Jewish students and others. After the war his strict observance fell away. In his last years, though, he returned to his earlier faith and asked that he be buried in the Jewish section of the Cambridge cemetery. Kahn never married but he never lacked agreeable female company either. He died in Cambridge, on 6 June 1989, and was buried in accordance with his wishes.

Nicholas Kaldor, 1908–1986[8]

Nicholas Kaldor was born in Budapest on 12 May 1908, the son of Dr Julius Kaldor, a lawyer, and Mrs Joan Kaldor. He attended the famous 'Model Gymnasium' as a boy, studied economics in Berlin in 1925–6 and then moved to London, to the LSE, in 1927. He graduated with a First in 1930, and was appointed as an Assistant in economics in 1932. This later became an assistant lectureship, and he was made a lecturer in economics in 1938. During the Second World War the LSE was evacuated to Cambridge and Kaldor taught there until near the end of the war when he served as chief of the economic planning staff of the US Strategic Bombing Survey. After two years in Geneva from 1947 to 1949 as Director of Research at the Economic Commission for Europe (ECE) under Myrdal, Kaldor was elected to a Fellowship at King's College, Cambridge, and became a university lecturer in economics and politics in 1949, reader in 1952, and was awarded a personal chair in 1966. Kaldor was elected a Fellow of the British Academy in 1963 and he was President of the Royal Economic Society from 1974 to 1976. He had two important spells in government as Special Adviser to the Chancellor of the Exchequer (1964–8 and 1974–6). He was also an adviser to many overseas governments. He was made a Life Peer (Baron Kaldor of Newnham in the City of Cambridge) in 1974. Kaldor retired in 1975. In 1934 Nicholas Kaldor married Clarissa Goldschmidt; they had four daughters and eleven grandchildren.

Kaldor resembled Keynes more than any other twentieth-century economist because of the breadth of his interests, his wide-ranging contributions to theory, his insistence that theory must serve policy (his best-known book is *An Expendure Tax* 1955), his periods as an adviser to governments, his fellowship at King's and, of course, his membership of the House of Lords. Kaldor was a highly original theorist, full of ideas of his own and making important modifications to and criticisms of the theories of others; he was also fortunate in his mentors, as he generously acknowledged.

Among them were Allyn Young, his teacher at the LSE; John Hicks (as an undergraduate at the LSE, Kaldor came to know John Hicks. They became

---

[8] I have drawn heavily on the obituary article of Kaldor I wrote for *Economica* (Harcourt 1988).

inseparable companions until Hicks went to Cambridge in the mid-1930s, meeting most days and discussing economic theory, often at excellent Italian restaurants near where they lived); John von Neumann; and, when he came to Cambridge, Joan Robinson, Richard Kahn and, most especially, Piero Sraffa. Robbins and Hayek were also important influences early on in his career and through whom (as well as through Hicks) he became familiar with the writings of Walras, Wicksell and Pareto, the British classical economists, Marx, and von Mises and the Austrians generally. He parted company with Robbins and Hayek ideologically and theoretically in the mid-to late-1930s, mainly because of his absorption of the method and message of *The General Theory* (but also because he had come to know the work of Myrdal and the Swedish monetary theorists through Hicks and Brinley Thomas).

There were three stages of Kaldor's career. First, there was the young orthodox theorist at the LSE who made seminal contributions to the theory of the firm, the emerging theory of imperfect competition, welfare economics and capital theory. Second, there was the enthusiastic Keynesian (after a slow start) who absorbed Keynes' message and added significantly to the corpus of Keynesian thought: his model of the trade cycle, Kaldor (1940) and, what is probably his greatest theoretical article (he certainly thought so and so do his most discerning admirers), 'Speculation and economic stability' (1939b), and its sequel on 'Keynes' theory of the own-rates of interest' ((1960b, 59–74)). Third, there was Kaldor of the post-war period (about whom I have written in this volume), who painted on increasingly larger canvasses, absorbed with the theory of distribution and accumulation, first for capitalist economies, then for developing ones, and finally for the world as a whole. It was principally during this period that he became increasingly critical of the 'vision' and the methods of mainstream economic theory.

Observers of the Kaldor phenomenon part company at this point. First, there are those who regret his transformation into the Kaldor of the third stage. They feel that he lost his grip on modern developments and so his influence, as a theorist, on the post-war generation. But there are those who would put his early Keynesian articles near the pinnacle of his achievements, but who think that the mature Kaldor, who strayed explicitly from the orthodox fold (and explained cogently why), was the greatest of them all. They admire the maturity of his vision and the extraordinary fertility and ingenuity of his mind, and his 'feel' for economic issues, processes and their outcomes and/or solutions, often set out in conclusions that, as with Keynes, ran ahead of his arguments.

One of Kaldor's earliest papers (1934a, on the determinateness of equilibrium) has a very modern ring to it. It concerned existence and stability and dealt principally with the question of whether the ultimate equilibrium in a market (or an economic system) is or is not independent of the path that is taken to it. This eventually was to become in Kaldor's view a conviction that equilibrium itself did not exist (one of his last books was entitled *Economics without Equilibrium*, Kaldor1985), and that to pose economic questions in the usual way of whether there is an equilibrium (or several) and, if so, whether it is (they are) stable was to place our thinking in a straitjacket. Ultimately, Kaldor was to proceed from empirical regularities – his famous 'stylised facts' – to explanations that themselves should be the most reasonable ways capable 'of accounting for the facts independently of whether they fit into the general framework of received theory or not' (1985, 8).

In the 1930s, Kaldor also wrote several fine critical articles on the theory of the firm (1934b), and on imperfect competition (1934c, 1935), in which he emerged as a sympathetic critic of both Joan Robinson and Chamberlin. His survey of capital theory (1937) is noteworthy. First, there was the anticipation of the post-war criticism from Cambridge of the lack of coherence of the notion of a quantity of 'capital' and its marginal product. Secondly, at the end of the article he independently discovered von Neumann's result (von Neumann, 1945–6) that $r = g$, where $r =$ rate of profits and $g =$ rate of growth – in Kaldor's case in a slave society, though the intuition of both authors was the same.

Kaldor's contributions to Keynesian economics fall into two distinct periods. First, there is the enthusiastic convert who significantly extended (e.g. in his article on the trade cycle, 1940) and modified the basic structure of *The General Theory* (e.g. in his 1939 article on speculation and stability, 1939) and who contributed the important empirical appendix C to Beveridge's *Full Employment in a Free Society* (1943). Kaldor was one of the earliest to explore stock and flow relationships and their effects on the desired rate of accumulation, with increases in expected profits and output encouraging accumulation while increasing stocks as a result of past accumulation discouraging it, so that for each short period the position of the relationship between I and Y was affected by the stock of capital goods. In the shape of the corresponding dynamic saving–income relationship there was a hint of the role that the distribution of income was later to play in his work. What was missing was a systematic role for monetary factors, a limitation that was later to be remedied by Hugh Hudson (1957), the editor of the first two volumes of Kaldor's papers (Kaldor 1960a, 1960b).

Kaldor was attracted to the work of Keynes not only because of his appreciation of its insights but also as a reaction to his increasing dissatisfaction with the parallel work of Hayek.

An emphasis that was to run through Kaldor's work for the rest of his life made an early appearance in his paper on speculation and stability (1939) – namely, the importance of the existence of established 'norms' for the attainment of stability in economic systems. There, it was applied to Keynesian concerns, especially the theory of interest rates; in the post-war period, it was to be applied to the prices of primary commodities and to the foreign exchanges. Kaldor attributed the great increase in the volatility of fluctuations of these prices in this period, and especially since the 1970s, to the lack of 'norms'. Without them, speculation leads to enhanced rather than to dampened fluctuations.

The second stage of Kaldor's contributions to Keynesian economics concerns Kaldor as the scourge of Friedman's Monetarism and Mrs Thatcher's policies. Balogh and, later, Kaldor were prominent among the few economists who were prepared to see Monetarism for what it is – as we have seen, Balogh called it 'the incomes policy of Karl Marx' – rather than pussyfoot around at a purely technical level as most of the economics establishment did. In these debates, Kaldor explored what he considered to be the theoretical and tactical weaknesses of *The General Theory* from the point of view of allowing the Monetarist attack successfully to occur on both the theoretical and the applied policy fronts.

Especially important here are Kaldor's views on the endogeneity of the money supply in a credit economy; the inappropriateness of Keynes' assumption of free competition and the consequent neglect of the role of increasing returns, a neglect that would not have occurred had the microeconomic foundations been imperfectly competitive from the beginning; and the limitations of using a closed economy model so that the sources of both employment and growth contributed by exports were neglected. Kaldor incorporated ideas that stemmed from Allyn Young (on dynamic increasing returns, whereby demand interaction between markets led to accumulation which incorporated technical advances) and Myrdal on cumulative causation, from Harrod's foreign trade multiplier and later from Verdoorn. (The last formed the basis of his Inaugural Lecture at Cambridge in the 1960s (1966b) as well as being the theoretical rationale for the introduction of the selective employment tax (SET) by the Wilson Labour government in the 1960s.)

Coinciding with Kaldor's interest in developing Keynesian theory and policy were his post-war contributions to the theory of distribution and growth, for which he is probably best known and which are discussed in chapters 2 and 7 of this volume. Certainly his *Review of Economic Studies* paper, 'Alternative theories of distribution' (1955–6), must be his most referred to (and criticised) paper.

Eventually, though, as we saw above (see chapter 7), Kaldor moved away from the unnecessarily restrictive constraint of requiring full employment. Instead, he emphasised the notion of cumulative causation. He became more and more dissatisfied with equilibrium economics, the notion of balance of forces, the strong tendency of economies to return to former resting places following shocks, or to seek out new ones following changes in underlying conditions. In its place he put the notion that, once economies get a run on (or off), they keep it up rather than return to the pack. His 'fairly drastic' changes in theoretical ideas formed for many years the basis of lectures to undergraduates at Cambridge, although he himself was 'not . . . able to present the results in the comprehensive form of a model' (1960a, xxv).

Kaldor's best friend at Cambridge was Piero Sraffa, and Kaldor's understanding of Ricardo's contributions owes much to him. Kaldor's attitude to *Production of Commodities by Means of Commodities* (Sraffa 1960), changed over the years. Given Kaldor's own interest in capital theory, his knowledge of von Neumann's views and 1945–6 article and his independent discovery of the result $r = g$, he was inclined to interpret Sraffa's basic model as a von Neumann model caught in suspended animation. Because he was also concerned with distribution and accumulation, he welcomed Sraffa's 'more comprehensive model' in which variations in the division of the product are considered, and especially Sraffa's final move, whereby the rate of profits is made exogenous to the sphere of production, following the initial moves of, first, no explicit subsistence wage, and then a wage that is in principle split into two parts – the ever-present element of subsistence, and a variable share of the surplus with profits. Kaldor was also to make accumulation and profits have first claim on the use of the national product, with the wage-earners receiving the residual – exactly the opposite of the procedure in the Physiocratic, Classical and Marxian systems. Finally, Kaldor was to see in Sraffa's writings a rigorous statement of part of his own critique of orthodox theory, and of his reasons for breaking with it.

Kaldor was progressive and humane. He hated stupidity, muddle and injustice. He was immensely clever and confident, an extraordinarily tough arguer, saying exactly what he thought. He was sometimes an intellectual bully, yet generous when he was persuaded that he was wrong and never reluctant to jettison his own intellectual capital. He had an infectious sense of humour. Indeed, he was much loved by those who knew him best – and was sometimes viewed as an ogre by those who did not, and whose policies and vested interests he opposed.

Appendix 2: The conceptual core of the post-Keynesian discontent with orthodox theories of value, distribution and growth

The discontent surfaced most notably in the so-called 'Cambridge controversies' in the theory of capital, the debates between the two Cambridges (England and MA) which occurred principally between the 1950s and the 1970s. They started with Joan Robinson's article 'The production function and the theory of capital (1953–4)'; they really 'hotted up' with the publication of Piero Sraffa's classic, *Production of Commodities by Means of Commodities* (1960). They 'ended' with the publication of Christopher Bliss' volume, *Capital Theory and the Distribution of Income* (1975), as a result of which Avinash Dixit (1977) pronounced the quasi-rents of previous writings on the issues to be either zero or, in the case of the Cambridge, England, protagonists, negative. That the 'end' may have been prematurely dated is argued by Harcourt (1995a) and Cohen and Harcourt (2003) and is, I hope, borne witness to as well in the present volume.

With hindsight, we may say that the issues related not so much to the *measurement* of capital as to its *meaning*. This carried with it further questions about how the accumulation process in capitalist society may best be envisaged, and so modelled. There are, as we have seen, two principal competitors: On the one hand, Marx–Keynes–Kalecki–Schumpeterian ruthless swash-buckling entrepreneurs and capitalists, for whom profit-making and accumulation are ends in themselves, who call the tune to which all other classes in society must dance. On the other hand, the consumption and saving behaviour of lifetime utility-maximising agents dominates, and all other actors and institutions in the economy–firms, the stock exchange, for example – are but the agents through which they achieve their ends. To both views must be coupled the question: what is the appropriate method with which to analyse the processes of accumulation, distribution and growth?

The first question posed historically was: can we find a technical unit in which to measure capital which is independent of distribution and prices? For, if we are to use a demand and supply approach to explain the origins and the sizes of the distributive variables – the rate of profits (r), the wage rate (w) – and also the distributive shares; if we are to make explicit the intuition of the supply and demand approach that price is an index of scarcity; and if we accept that in a competitive situation there is a tendency to equality of rates of profit in all activities so that we have to explain the origin and size of the overall, economy-wide r; *then* we need to know *before the analysis starts* what we mean by a 'quantity of capital', in order that it may be a determinant of r (an exogenous, given variable), and one of the reasons why r may be high or low relative to w is that we have a 'little' or a 'lot' of capital. If it is not possible to find such a unit (the debates showed that outside one-commodity models it is not), it is not possible to say that r takes the value it does partly because we have so much 'capital' and because 'its' marginal product has a particular value.

This aspect of the debate was related to the methodological critique associated with the distinction between differences and changes. The results of the debate were mostly drawn from comparisons of long-period positions which reflect differences in initial conditions. It is argued that they can tell us nothing about processes – changes – in particular, the processes of accumulation. As we saw, Joan Robinson (1974) was to characterise this critique as 'History versus equilibrium'. Its implications are reflected in the econometric practice of collapsing the short period and the long period into one. Then, for certain forms of the aggregate production function, exactly the same values of key parameters (and therefore variables) are involved, whether we are considering greater or lesser utilisation of a given stock of capital goods in the short run – i.e. movements up or down what Joan Robinson called the utilisation function – or changing capital–labour and capital–output ratios as the result of differential rates of growth of accumulation and the labour force over time. In the second process there may not only be more capital per head and per unit of output but also better capital per head and per unit of output. Such a specification, allied with the assumptions of competitive market structures in the economy concerned and static expectations about the future courses of the prices of products and of the factors of production, so that the simple marginal productivity implications of cost-minimising and profit-maximising may go through, allow the use of actual 'real world' statistics on wages, profits, capital and so on when fitting the specified model. This in turn allows the estimation of key parameters– e.g. the exponents of the variables of the function; the elasticity of substitution of capital for labour; and so on.

The reaction to the criticism of the aggregate production function and the meaning of 'capital' in its construction was to try to avoid the use of 'capital' and 'its' marginal product and make the social rate of return – Irving Fisher's central concept – a key concept. It provides on the productivity side of the story what the rate of time preference does on the psychological side (see Solow's de Vries Lectures, Solow 1963). Joan Robinson (1964) criticised Solow's procedures, arguing that, for much of the book of the lectures, he used what she called a 'butter model' in the theoretical sections and in the specifications of his empirical work. (The main objective of Solow's de Vries lectures was to develop theoretical measures of the Fisherian social rate of return on investment in a number of different scenarios. He treated it as a technocratic measure – the potential return to a bit more saving–investment at full employment. He estimated its values in what was then West Germany, and in the USA. As the resulting values were considerably greater than those of near-riskless returns on certain financial assets, empirical proxies for the orders of magnitude of the rate of time preference, the inference was that more investment should be encouraged in both countries.)

In the model, butter was both input (B) and output (B') and the parameters of the model were usually functions of key *ratios* only, $B'/_L$ and $B/_L$, where L was the potential workforce. Ignoring technical progress for the moment, it did not matter whether the thought experiment was concerned with running up and

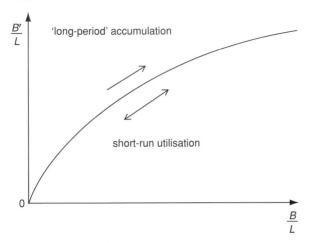

Figure A2.1. Short-period utilisation possibilities doubling up for long-period accumulation possibilities.

down the short-period utilisation function with varying values of B'/L and B/L or whether the changes in the values of B'/L and B/L were due to accumulation over 'time' so that B'/L was taken to be increasing as deepening occurred ('moving down the production function' as Joan Robinson, 1959; *CEP*, vol. II, 1, 1960 once put it).

The 'real world' observations are, by definition, observed points on the existing utilisation functions of each instant of time since, though in the long run we are all dead, the living are always to be found in the short run. Nevertheless, they were meant to serve as well as observations of long-period values taken from, in effect, the same production function (see figure A2.1).

We do not have to go into the intricacies of the capital-reversal and reswitching debates and results (see, for example, Harcourt 1972, 1995a; Cohen and Harcourt 2003) in order to criticise the conceptual basis of this standard procedure. I reviewed for the *Economic Journal* (Harcourt 1964, Bagicha Minhas' book, *An International Comparison of Factor Costs and Factor Use* (1963), in which he exploited the properties of the famous CES production function, which came from an article he wrote jointly with Arrow, Chenery and Solow (1961) (hereafter, ACMS). (I don't suppose many PhD students have such illustrious research students these days.) In 1962 (Harcourt 1962; 1982), I had published a review article of Salter's classic, *Productivity and Technical Change* (1960). Salter's book (which grew out of his early 1950s Cambridge PhD dissertation, supervised by Brian Reddaway) was a pioneering account of vintage (putty-clay) models and their application at firm and industry levels. As a result of what I learned from Salter then, I argued in the review of Minhas (Harcourt 1964), that though the data used in Minhas' study came, of necessity, from existing short-run utilisation functions incorporating stocks of existing capital goods of different vintages associated with past accumulation, it was being used to estimate the values of the characteristics of what Salter called the iso-quants of the latest 'best-practice' techniques. These were, of course, the most up-to-date ways known in various industries of producing different levels of output, or output per unit of input if we assume that the *ex ante* production function – Salter's iso-quant – exhibits constant returns to scale. As a result of the choice of technique in each short run, the additions through accumulation at the margins of the stock of existing capital goods reflect the then 'optimum' point on the iso-quant.

Minhas (and his co-authors) were interested in a number of theoretical and empirical possibilities. Paul Samuelson (1948) had shown for the case of two countries which produce the same two commodities, use the same factors of production and have the same production functions in each industry, but different factor endowments, that free trade will equalise their absolute and relative factor prices. He assumed constant returns to scale and that, at any given ratio of factor prices, the chosen ratio in one industry is always greater or less than the corresponding ratio in the other. Minhas *et al.* showed that if the two commodities are produced with two CES production functions which have different elasticities of substitution of capital for labour, there will always be a critical ratio of factor prices at which their factor intensities are equal, and above (or below) are reversed, requiring, for this case, modifications of Samuelson's factor-price equalisation theorem. Minhas was concerned in his book to fit relationships derived from the CES production function to observed data which came from the same industries in different countries. He wanted to estimate the values of the elasticities and to see whether factor reversals occurred within the observed range of factor prices. He purported to show that the CES production functions fitted the data well (if it is assumed that the efficiency of factors used between countries differed neutrally); that the elasticities were usually significantly less than unity (bye bye, Cobb–Douglas); and that the critical price ratio was within the observed range of factor prices. For our present purposes we note that the 'real world' data were interpreted as points around the 'best-practice' iso-quant in each industry in different countries. The short period and the long period have been collapsed into one another, where by 'long period' I mean the choices available at any moment of time for investment in 'best-practice' techniques – i.e. the choice is made in the short period but long-period factors are its dominant determinants.

I followed the review with an article (Harcourt 1966), in which I said in effect: let us grant neoclassical economists every assumption they make in these investigations (I had ACMS and Minhas especially in mind), except that we allow for different vintages of 'best-practice' techniques to have been embodied by past bursts of accumulation into the total stocks of capital goods of the utilisation functions which directly or indirectly had thrown up the data used by ACMS, and Minhas, in their estimates of the values of the elasticities of substitution. Will the equations they fitted to such data be 'good' fits – i.e. provide unbiased estimators of the elasticities of substitution of the 'best-practice' iso-quants, which is their claim? ACMS found a close association between the logarithms of labour productivity (value added per unit of labour used) and money-wage rates in the *same* industries in *different* countries, which was confirmed by the appropriate regressions. If the values added and labour inputs used in their analysis are assumed to be observations from CES production functions, the regression coefficients, say b, in equations of the form:

$$\log.q = \log.A + b\log.w + \varepsilon$$

where q = value added per unit of labour, w = money-wage rate and ε = error term, can be shown to be estimates of the elasticity of substitution of capital for labour (see ACMS 1961, 228–9; Minhas 1963; Harcourt 1972, 51–4). But do the estimates of b provide what is claimed for them? The answer is 'no', as I believe I established in the article and which I think Solow (1997b), in so far as I understand him, accepts. Having argued that all we ever have in the data they used are totals and averages, whereas we are really interested in relationships between marginal quantities, I made up a number of plausible (I hope) stories – Solow has his doubts – and examined how close, qualitatively, the estimates of b would be approached by the use of ACMS' procedures. I then put quantitative orders of magnitude on the biases by using Minhas' data and assuming that some of my stories had generated the data. I found biases both upwards and downwards, of considerable size, relative to what was known to be their 'true' values.

Solow has always been most candid about his procedures – for example, he wrote of his procedures in his (1957) paper: 'It merely shows how one goes about interpreting time series if one starts by assuming that they were generated from a production function and that the competitive marginal product relations apply' (Solow 1974, 121). So he is not arguing that the world is Cobb–Douglas or CES or . . . , only that if we view our observations *as if* they were observations thrown up by Cobb–Douglas *et al.*, these are the orders of magnitude of the parameters which our econometric procedures allow us to estimate. Solow does add that if the findings implied that the share of wages was 25 per cent and of profits 75 per cent, he would be less willing to trust his findings.[1]

Parallel with these developments was Samuelson's attempt (1962) to rationalise Solow's use of J. B. Clark–Frank Ramsey–J. R. Hicks' models in growth theory and econometric work (see Solow 1956, 1957). Samuelson attempted to show that the rigorously derived results of the simple model were robust, that they illuminated the behaviour of more complex heterogeneous capital models. Lying behind all this was the conceptual understanding that 'capital' and r are related in such a way that the demand curve for 'capital' is well-behaved (i.e. downward-sloping). This result as well as other neoclassical

---

[1] Nevertheless, as Thomas Michl (2002, 53, personal communication, 29 May 2002) reminded me (in this case, a euphemism for bringing it to my attention for the first time): 'Empirical research guided by the neoclassical growth model has consistently found that the apparent elasticity of output with respect to capital exceeds its predicted value, typically taken to be the share of profit in national income.'

parables derived from the simple model – the negative associations between r and the capital–output ratio and sustainable levels of consumption per head – together with the marginal productivity theory of distribution itself, were refuted by the capital-reversing and reswitching results, as Samuelson (1966) handsomely acknowledged. Capital-reversal (the Ruth Cohen *curiosum*) is that a *less* productive, *less* capital-intensive technique may be associated with a *lower* value of r. The reswitching result is that the same technique, having been the most profitable one for a particular range of values of r and w, could also be most profitable at another range of values of r and w, even though other techniques were profitable at values in between. Both refute the agreeable (neoclassical) intuition of the results of the simple models and, Pasinetti (1969, 1970) argued, of Solow's Fisherian approach as well. (Solow 1970 did not agree, see Cohen and Harcourt 2003 for later developments and the reasons why Solow still does not agree.)

Why do reswitching and capital-reversal occur? The problems arise when we consider more general models with heterogenous capital goods. Heterogeneous capital goods cannot be measured and aggregated in physical units; instead, capital valuation must be used, as Wicksell (1911) [1934], vol. I, 149) told us long ago. Their value can be measured either as the cost of production, which takes time, or the present value of the future output stream they produce. In either case, since the measure involves time, it presumes a rate of interest – which, in the simple model, is determined in a one-way manner by the quantity of capital. This additional circularity, or interdependence, causes Wicksell effects. Wicksell effects involve changes in the value of the capital stock associated with different interest rates, arising from either inventory revaluations of the same physical stock due to new capital goods prices (price Wicksell effects) or differences in the physical stock of goods (real Wicksell effects). In the Cambridge controversies, the problems created for the neoclassical parables by Wicksell effects, as we have seen, were termed 'reswitching' and 'capital-reversing'. With reswitching the same physical technique is associated with two different interest rates, violating parables 1 and 2. Capital-reversing implies that the demand curve for capital is *not* always downward sloping, violating parables 2 and 3.

Samuelson (1966) provides the intuition for why reswitching and capital-reversing occur, using the Austrian conception of *capital as time*, so that the productivity of capital is the productivity of time itself. Figure A2.2 illustrates two techniques for making champagne using only labour and time (and free grapes). In technique a, 7 units of labour make 1 unit of brandy in one period, which ferments into 1 unit of champagne in another period. In technique b, 2 units of labour make 1 unit of grape juice in one period, which ripens into wine in another period. Then 6 units of labour shaking the wine produce 1 unit of champagne in a third period.

The cost-minimising technique depends on relative factor prices. At high interest rates ($r > 100$ per cent), compounded interest on the 2 units of labour invested for three periods makes b more expensive, so a is chosen. At zero interest, only labour costs count, so a is also cheaper. But at interest rates between 50 per cent and 100 per cent, b is cheaper. The corresponding demand for capital curve would look like figure A2.3. First, notice that at different values of r along any discrete downward-sloping segment, the value of the 'capital' is

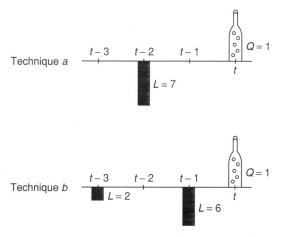

Figure A2.2. Samuelson's (1966) example of Wicksell effects in the simple Austrian model.

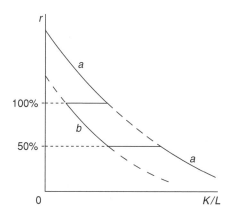

Figure A2.3. Demand for capital (per unit of labour) in Samuelson's (1966) model.

different for a physically unchanging technique, due to price Wicksell effects. Notice also that at lower values of r, the technique switches from a to b and then reswitches back to a, due to real Wicksell effects. And at a value of r just below 100 per cent, capital-reversing occurs as a lower r is associated with a lower capital–labour ratio.

Because of Wicksell effects, in models with heterogeneous capital goods (or heterogeneous output), the rate of interest depends not only on exogenous technical properties of capital, but also on endogenously determined prices such as the interest rate. The endogeneity of prices allows multiple equilibria, which complicates the one-way parable explanations of income distribution. Differences in quantities no longer yield unambiguously signed price effects. The power and simplicity of one-commodity models emanates from eliminating these endogenous price effects and measurement problems (Cohen 1989).

As early as 1936, Sraffa wrote a letter to Joan Robinson explaining the essence of this complication for neoclassical capital theory. Reswitching and capital-reversing were noted in the 1950s by Champernowne (1953–4) and Joan Robinson, but their full significance was realised only with Sraffa's (1960) book. Sraffa (1962, 479) posed the key question regarding the meaning and measurement of capital: 'What is the good of a quantity of capital . . . which, since it depends on the rate of interest, cannot be used for its traditional purpose . . . to determine the rate of interest[?]'.[2]

---

[2] Do similar valuation problems arise for heterogeneous labour? The crucial difference with capital is that there is no theoretical presumption that competition will equalise wages across different types of labour, in the way that rates of return will equalise (adjusted for risk) across investments in different capital goods/industries. To the extent that heterogeneous labour reflects differences in human capital, the valuation problems for the neoclassical parables due to interest rate changes are only exacerbated.

Bibliography

Aghion, P. and P. Howitt (1998), *Endogenous Growth Theory*, Cambridge, MA and London: MIT Press

Araujo, J. T. (1999), 'The Cambridge theory of distribution in the short period: an open economy approach', in Sardoni and Kreisler (eds.) (1999), 337–55

Arestis, P., G. Palma and M. Sawyer (eds.) (1997a), *Capital Controversy, Post-Keynesian Economics and the History of Economic Theory: Essays in honour of Geoff Harcourt, Volume One*, London and New York: Routledge

(1997b), *Markets, Unemployment and Economic Policy: Essays in honour of Geoff Harcourt, Volume Two*, London and New York: Routledge

Arestis, P. and M. Sawyer (eds.) (1992), *A Biographical Dictionary of Dissenting Economists*, Aldershot: Edward Elgar, 2nd edn. 2000

Arestis, P. and T. Skouras (eds.) (1985), *Post Keynesian Economic Theory: A Challenge to Neo-Classical Economics*, Brighton: Wheatsheaf Books

Arrow, K. J. (1962), 'The economic implications of learning by doing', *Review of Economic Studies*, 29, 155–73

Arrow, K. J., H. B. Chenery, B. S. Minhas and R. M. Solow (ACMS) (1961), 'Capital–labor substitution and economic efficiency', *Review of Economics and Statistics*, 43, 225–50

Asimakopulos, A. (1983), 'Kalecki and Keynes on finance, investment and saving', *Cambridge Journal of Economics*, 7, 221–3

Ball, R. J. (1964), *Inflation and the Theory of Money*, London: Allen & Unwin

Baloagh, T. (1982), *The Irrelevance of Conventional Economics*, London: Weidenfeld & Nicolson

Barro, Robert J. and X. Sala-i-Martin (1998), *Economic Growth*, Cambridge, MA: MIT Press

Baranzini, M. (1991), *A Theory of Wealth Distribution and Accumulation*, Oxford: Oxford University Press

Baranzini, M. and G. C. Harcourt (eds.) (1993), *The Dynamics of the Wealth of Nations: Growth, Distribution and Structural Change. Essays in Honour of Luigi Pasinetti*, Basingstoke: Macmillan

Baranzini, M. and R. Scazzieri (eds.) (1986), *Foundations of Economics*, Oxford: Blackwell

(1990), 'Economic structure: analytical perspectives', in Baranzini and Scazzieri (eds.) (1990), 227–33

(eds.) (1990), *The Economic Theory of Structure and Change*, Cambridge: Cambridge University Press

Baumol, W. J. (1951), *Economic Dynamics: An Introduction*, London: Macmillan, 2nd edn. 1959, 3rd edn. (with a contribution by Ralph Turvey) 1970

Bhaduri, Amit and J. Robinson (1980), 'Accumulation and exploitation: an analysis in the tradition of Marx, Sraffa and Kalecki', *Cambridge Journal of Economics*, 4, 103–15

Bharadwaj, K. (1978), *Classical Political Economy and Rise to Dominance of Supply and Demand Theories*, New Delhi: Longman Orient

Bliss, C. J. (1975), *Capital Theory and the Distribution of Income*, Amsterdam: North-Holland and New York: Elsevier

(1986), 'Progress and anti-progress in economic science', in Baranzini and Scazzieri (eds.) (1986), 363–76

Böhm-Bawerk, E. von (1889), *Zum Abschluss des Marxschen Systems*, transl. Paul Sweezy (ed.), *Karl Marx and the Close of his System*, New York: Augustus M. Kelly 1949

Bortis, H. (1997), *Institutions, Behaviour and Economic Theory: A Contribution to Classical–Keynesian Political Economy*, Cambridge: Cambridge University Press

Cate, T. (ed.) (1997), *An Encyclopedia of Keynesian Economics*, Cheltenham and Brookfield, MA: Edward Elgar

Chamberlin, E. H. (1933), *The Theory of Monopolistic Competition*, Cambridge, MA: Harvard University Press

Champernowne, D. G. (1936), 'Unemployment, basic and monetary: the classical analysis and the Keynesian', *Review of Economic Studies*, 3, 201–16

(1953–4), 'The production function and the theory of capital: a comment', *Review of Economic Studies*, 21, 112–35

Clark, D. A. (ed.) (forthcoming), *The Elgar Companion to Development Studies*, Cheltenham: Edward Elgar

Cohen, A. J. (1989), 'Prices, capital and the one-commodity model in neoclassical and classical theories', *History of Political Economy*, 21, 231–51

Cohen, A. J. and G. C. Harcourt (2003), 'Whatever happened to the Cambridge capital theory controversies?', *Journal of Economic Perspectives*, 17, 199–214

Cottrell, A. (1994), 'Post-Keynesian monetary economics', *Cambridge Journal of Economics*, 18, 587–605

Crotty, James R. (1980), 'Post-Keynesian theory: an overview and evaluation', *American Economic Review*, 70, 20–5

Dalziel, P. C. and G. C. Harcourt (1997), 'A note on "Mr Meade's Relation" and international capital movements', *Cambridge Journal of Economics*, 21, 621–31, reprinted in Harcourt (2001a), 72–87

Davidson, P. (1972), *Money and the Real World*, London: Macmillan, 2nd edn. 1978

(1995), 'The Asimakopulos view of Keynes's *General Theory*', in Harcourt, Roncaglia and Rowley (eds.) (1995), 40–66

(2003–4), 'Setting the record straight on *A History of Post Keynesian Economics*', *Journal of Post Keynesian Economics*, 26, 245–72

Dixit, A. (1977), 'The accumulation of capital theory', *Oxford Economic Papers*, 29, 1–29

Dobb, M. H. (1954), *On Economic Theory and Socialism, Collected Papers*, London: Routledge & Kegan Paul

Dow, S. C. 'Endogenous money', in Harcourt and Riach (eds.) (1997), vol. 2, 61–78

Eichner, A. S. (1973), 'A theory of the determination of the mark-up under oligopoly', *Economic Journal*, 83, 1184–1200

(1976), *The Megacorp and Oligopoly*, Cambridge: Cambridge University Press

Feinstein, C. H. (ed.) (1967), *Socialism, Capitalism and Economic Growth: Essays presented to Maurice Dobb*, Cambridge: Cambridge University Press

Feiwel, G. R. (ed.) (1985), *Issues in Contemporary Macroeconomics and Distribution*, London: Macmillan

Feldstein, M. and C. Horioka (1980), 'Domestic saving and international capital flows', *Economic Journal*, 90, 314–29

Fontana, G. (2003), 'Post Keynesian approaches to endogenous money: a time framework explanation', *Review of Political Economy*, 15, 291–314

(2004a), 'Hicks on monetary theory and history: money as endogenous money', *Cambridge Journal of Economics*, 28, 73–88

(2004b), 'Rethinking endogenous money: a constructive interpretation of the debate between accommodationists and structuralists', *Metroeconomica*, 55, 367–85

Friedman, M. (1953), 'The case for flexible exchange rates', in M. Friedman, *Essays in Positive Economics*, Chicago: Chicago University Press, 157–203

Galenson, W. and H. Leibenstein (1955), 'Investment criteria, productivity and economic development', *Quarterly Journal of Economics*, 69, 353–70

Goodwin, R. M. (1949), 'The multiplier as matrix', *Economic Journal*, 59, 537–55, reprinted in Goodwin (1983), 1–21

(1953), 'The problem of trend and cycle', *Yorkshire Bulletin of Economic and Social Research*, 5, 89–97, reprinted in Goodwin (1982), 112–21

(1967), 'A growth cycle', in Feinstein (ed.) (1967), 54–8, reprinted in Goodwin (1982), 165–70

(1970), *Elementary Economics from the Higher Standpoint*, Cambridge: Cambridge University Press

(1982), *Essays in Economic Dynamics*, London: Macmillan

(1983), *Essays in Linear Economic Structures*, London: Macmillan

Goodwin, R. M. and L. F. Punzo (1987), *The Dynamics of a Capitalist Economy: A Multi-Sectoral Approach*, Cambridge: Polity Press

Granger, C. W. J. (1993), 'What are we learning about the long-run?', *Economic Journal*, 103, 307–17

Hahn, F. H. (1972), *The Share of Wages in the National Income: An Enquiry into the Theory of Distribution*, London: Weidenfeld & Nicolson

Harcourt, G. C. (1962), 'Review article of W. E. G. Salter, *Productivity and Technical Change*', *Economic Record*, 38, 388–94, reprinted in Harcourt (1982), 129–37

(1963), 'A critique of Mr. Kaldor's model of income distribution and economic growth', *Australian Economic Papers*, 2, 20–36, reprinted in Sardoni (ed.) (1992), 67–82

(1964), 'Review of Minhas (1963)', *Economic Journal*, 74, 443–5

(1966), 'Biases in empirical estimates of the elasticities of substitution of C. E. S. production functions', *Review of Economic Studies*, 33, 227–33, reprinted in Harcourt (1982), 138–45

(1972), *Some Cambridge Controversies in the Theory of Capital*, Cambridge: Cambridge University Press

(1982), *The Social Science Imperialists: Selected Essays*, ed. by Prue Kerr, London: Routledge & Kegan Paul

(1985), 'Post Keynesianism: quite wrong and/or nothing new?', in Arestis and Skouras (eds.) (1985), 125–45

(1988), 'Nicholas Kaldor, 12 May 1908–30 September 1986', *Economica*, 55, 159–70, reprinted in Harcourt (1993), 35–50

(1993), *Post-Keynesian Essays in Biography: Portraits of Twentieth Century Political Economists*, Basingstoke: Macmillan

(1994), 'Taming speculators and putting the world on course to prosperity: a modest proposal', *Economic and Political Weekly*, 29, 2490–92, reprinted in Harcourt (1995a), 32–8

(1995a), *Capitalism, Socialism and Post-Keynesianism: Selected Essays of G. C. Harcourt*, Cheltenham: Edward Elgar

(1995b), 'The structure of Tom Asimakopulos's later writings', in Harcourt, Roncaglia and Rowley (eds.) (1995), 1–16

(1997a), 'Pay policy, accumulation and productivity', *Economic and Labour Relations Review*, 8, 78–89, reprinted in Harcourt (2001b), 263–75

(1997b), 'Keynes, John Maynard', in Cate (ed.) (1997), 278–81

(2000), 'Asimakopulos, Athanasios (Tom) (1930–1990),' in Arestis and Sawyer (eds.) (2000), 7–17

(2001a), *50 Years a Keynesian and Other Essays*, London: Palgrave

(2001b), *Selected Essays on Economic Policy*, London: Palgrave

(2002), 'Keith Frearson on Roy Harrod as told to Geoff Harcourt', *History of Economics Review*, Summer, 76–84

(2004a), 'Sraffa, Piero (1898–1983)', *Oxford Dictionary of National Biography*, vol. 52, Oxford: Oxford University Press, 22–4

(2004b), 'Kahn, Richard [Ferdinand], Baron Kahn of Hampstead (1905–1989)', *Oxford Dictionary of National Biography*, vol. 30, Oxford: Oxford University Press, 861–4

(forthcoming), 'The Harrod model of growth and some early reactions to it', in Clark (ed.) (forthcoming)

Harcourt, G. C., P. H. Karmel and R. H. Wallace (1967), *Economic Activity*, Cambridge: Cambridge University Press

Harcourt, G. C. and P. Kenyon (1976), 'Pricing and the investment decision', *Kyklos*, 29, 449–77, reprinted in Sardoni (ed.) (1992), 48–66

Harcourt, G. C. and P. Kerr (1996), 'Marx, Karl Heinrich (1818–83)', in Warner (ed.) (1996), 3388–45, reprinted in Harcourt (2001a), 157–68

Harcourt, G. C. and V. G. Massaro (1964), 'A note on Mr. Sraffa's subsystems', *Economic Journal*, 74, 715–22, reprinted in Harcourt (1982), 171–9

Harcourt, G. C. and P. A. Riach (eds.) (1997), *A 'Second Edition' of The General Theory*, 2 vols., London: Routledge

Harcourt, G. C., A. Roncaglia and R. Rowley (eds.) (1995), *Income and Employment in Theory and Practice: Essays in Memory of Athanasios Asimakopulos*, Basingstoke: Macmillan

Harris, D. J. (1975), 'The theory of economic growth: a critique and reformu-
    lation', *American Economic Review, Papers and Proceedings*, 65, 329–37
    (1978), *Capital Accumulation and Income Distribution*, Stanford, CA: Stanford
    University Press
Harris, J. R. and Todaro, M. P. (1970), 'Migration, unemployment and devel-
    opment: a two-sector model', *American Economic Review*, 60, 126–42
Harrod, R. F. (1933), *International Economics*, Cambridge: Cambridge Univer-
    sity Press
    (1936), *The Trade Cycle: An Essay*, Oxford: Clarendon Press
    (1939), 'An essay in dynamic theory', *Economic Journal*, 49, 14–33
    (1948), *Towards a Dynamic Economics: Some Recent Developments of Economic
    Theory and their Application to Policy*, London: Macmillan
    (1951), *The Life of John Maynard Keynes*, London: Macmillan and New York:
    St Martin's Press
Henderson, R. F. (1951), *The New Issue Market and the Finance of Industry*,
    Cambridge: Bowes & Bowes and Cambridge, MA: Harvard University
    Press
Hennings, K. (1985), 'The exchange paradigm and the theory of production and
    distribution' in Baranzini and Scazzieri (eds.) (1986), 221–43
Hilferding, R. (1910), *Das Finanz Capital*, transl. T. Bottomore (1981), *Finance
    Capital*, London: Routledge & Kegan Paul
Hudson, H. R. (1957), 'A model of the trade cycle', *Economic Record*, 33, 378–89
Johnson, H. G. (1962), 'A simple Joan Robinson model of accumulation with
    one technique', *Osaka Economic Papers*, 10, 28–33
Jones, C. I. (1998), *Introduction to Economic Growth*, New York: W. W. Norton,
    2nd edn. 2002
Kahn, R. F. (1929), '*The economics of the short period*', Fellowship Dissertation for
    King's College, Cambridge; published, London: Macmillan, 1989
    (1931), 'The relation of home investment to unemployment', *Economic Jour-
    nal*, 41, 173–98
    (1959), 'Exercise in the analysis of growth', *Oxford Economic Papers*, 11, 143–56
    (1975), *On Re-Reading Keynes, Fourth Keynes Lecture in Economics*, 6 Novem-
    ber 1975, Oxford University Press for the British Academy
    (1978), 'Some aspects of the development of Keynes' thought', *Journal of
    Economic Literature*, 16, 544–59
    (1984), *The Making of Keynes' General Theory*, Cambridge: Cambridge Uni-
    versity Press
Kaldor, N. (1934a) 'A classificatory note on the determinateness of equilibrium',
    Review of Economic Studies, 1, 122–36, reprinted in Kaldor (1960a), 13–33
    (1934b) 'The equilibrium of the firm', *Economic Journal*, 44, 60–76, reprinted
    in Kaldor (1960a), 34–50
    (1934c), 'Mrs Robinson's "Economics of Imperfect Competition"', *Econom-
    ica*, 1, 355–41, reprinted in Kaldor (1960a), 53–61
    (1935) 'Market imperfection and excess capacity', *Economica*, 2, 23–50, re-
    printed in Kaldor (1960a), 62–95
    (1937) 'Annual survey of economic theory: the recent controversy on the theory
    of capital', *Econometrica*, 5, 201–33, reprinted in Kaldor (1960a), 153–205

(1939) 'Speculation and economic stability', *Review of Economic Studies*, 7, 1–27, reprinted in Kaldor (1960b), 17–58

(1940) 'A model of the trade cycle', *Economic Journal*, 50, 78–92, reprinted in Kaldor (1960b), 177–92

(1943) 'The quantitative aspects of the full employment problem in Britain', appendix C to *Full Employment in a Free Society* by Sir William Beveridge, London: George Allen & Unwin, reprinted in Kaldor (1964), 23–82

(1955) *An Expenditure Tax*, London: George Allen & Unwin

(1955–6) 'Alternative theories of distribution', *Review of Economic Studies*, 23, 83–100, reprinted in Kaldor (1960a), 209–36

(1957) 'A model of economic growth', *Economic Journal*, 67, 591–624, reprinted in Kaldor (1960b), 259–300

(1959a) 'Economic growth and the problem of inflation: Part I', *Economica*, 26, 212–26

(1959b) 'Economic growth and the problem of inflation: Part II', *Economica*, 26, 287–98

(1960a), *Essays on Value and Distribution*, London: Duckworth

(1960b), *Essays on Economic Stability and Growth*, London: Duckworth

(1961) 'Capital accumulation and economic growth', in F. A. Lutz and D. C. Hague (eds.) (1961), 177–222, reprinted in Kaldor (1978), 1–53

(1964), *Essays on Economic Policy (I)*, London: Duckworth

(1966a), 'Marginal productivity and macro-economic theories of distribution', *Review of Economic Studies*, 33, 309–19

(1966b) 'Causes of the slow rate of economic growth in the United Kingdom' Inaugural Lecture at the University of Cambridge, reprinted in Kaldor (1978), 100–38

(1978), *Further Essays on Economic Theory*, London: Duckworth

(1983), 'Keynesian economics after fifty years', in Worswick and Trevithick (eds.) (1983), 1–28

(1985) *Economics without Equilibrium: The Okun Memorial Lectures at Yale University*, Cardiff: University College Cardiff Press

(1996) *Causes of Growth and Stagnation in the World Economy*, Cambridge: Cambridge University Press

Kaldor, N. and Mirrlees, J. A. (1962) 'A new model of economic growth', *Review of Economic Studies*, 29, 174–92, reprinted in Kaldor (1978), 54–80

Kalecki, M. (1935a), 'A macro-dynamic theory of business cycles', *Econometrica*, 3, 327–44, reprinted in *CW*, vol. I, 1990, 12–43

(1935b), 'Essai d'une théorie du mouvement cyclique des affaires', *Revue d'Economie Politique*, 49, 285–305, reprinted in *CW*, vol. I, 1990, 67–81

(1936), 'Pare uwag o teorii Keynesa' ('Some remarks on Keynes' theory'), *Ekonomista*, 3, reprinted in *CW*, vol. I, 1990, 223–32, see also Targetti and Kinda-Hass (1982)

(1937), 'The principle of increasing risk', *Economica*, 4, 440–7, reprinted in Kalecki (1971) as 'Entrepreneurial capital and investment', 105–9 and *CW*, vol. I, 1990, 285–93

(1938), 'The determinants of distribution of the National Income', *Econometrica*, 6, 97–112, reprinted in Kalecki (1971), 62–77 and *CW*, vol. I, 1990, 235–52 and vol. II, 1991, 3–20

(1943), 'Political aspects of full employment,' *Political Quarterly*, 14, 322–31, reprinted in Kalecki (1971), 138–45 and *CW*, vol. I, 1990, 347–56

(1944), 'Professor Pigou on the classical stationary state: a comment', *Economica Journal*, 54, 131–2, reprinted in *CW*, vol. I, 1990, 342–43

(1968), 'Trend and business cycles reconsidered', *Economic Journal*, 78, 263–76, reprinted in Kalecki (1971), 165–83 and *CW*, vol. II, 1991, 435–50

(1971), *Selected Essays on the Dynamics of the Capitalist Economy, 1933–1970*, Cambridge: Cambridge University Press

(1990–7), *Collected Works of Michal Kalecki*, 7 vols., ed. Jerzy Osiatyński, Oxford: Oxford University Press

Kerr, Prue (1993), 'Adam Smith's theory of growth and technological change revisited', *Contributions to Political Economy*, 12, 1–27

(ed.), with the collaboration of G. C. Harcourt (2002), *Joan Robinson: Critical Assessments of Leading Economists*, 5 vols., London and New York: Routledge

Keynes, J. M. (1919), *The Economic Consequences of the Peace*, London: Macmillan, *CW*, vol. II, 1971

(1921), *A Treatise on Probability*, London: Macmillan: *CW*, vol. VIII, 1973

(1923), *A Tract on Monetary Reform*, London: Macmillan, *CW*, vol. IV, 1971

(1930), *A Treatise on Money*, 2 vols., London: Macmillan, *CW*, vol. V, VI, 1971

(1931), *Essays in Persuasion*, London: Macmillan: *CW*, vol. IX, 1972

(1933), *Essays in Biography*, London: Macmillan, *CW*, vol. X, 1972

(1936), *The General Theory of Employment, Interest and Money*, London: Macmillan, *CW*, vol. VII, 1973

(1937a), 'Alternative theories of the rate of interest', *Economic Journal*, 47, 241–52, *CW*, vol. XIV, 1973, 201–15

(1937b), 'The "ex ante" theory of the rate of interest', *Economic Journal*, 47, 663–9, *CW*, vol. XIV, 1973, 215–26

(1937c), 'The General Theory of Employment,' *Quarterly Journal of Economics*, 51, 209–23, *CW*, vol. XIV, 1973, 109–23

(1973), *The General Theory and After, Part II: Defence and Development*, *CW*, vol. XIV, London: Macmillan

Keynes, J. N. (1884), *Studies and Exercises in Formal Logic*, London: Macmillan

(1891), *The Scope and Method of Political Economy*, London: Macmillan

Keynes, M. (ed.) (1975), *Essays on John Maynard Keynes*, Cambridge: Cambridge University Press

King, J. E. (1988), *Economic Exiles*, New York: St Martin's Press

(2002), *A History of Post Keynesian Economics since 1936*, Cheltenham: Edward Elgar

Kregel, J. (1995), 'Causality and time in Asimakopulos's approach to saving and investment in the theory of distribution', in Harcourt, Roncaglia and Rowley (eds.) (1995), 67–82

Kriesler, P. (1987), *Kalecki's Microeconomics: The Development of Kalecki's Analysis of Pricing and Distribution*, Cambridge: Cambridge University Press

Kurz, H. D. (1997), 'What could the "new" growth theory tell Smith or Ricardo?', *Economic Issues*, 2, 1–20

Kurz, H. D. (forthcoming), 'Endogenous growth', in Clark (ed.) (forthcoming)

Kurz, H. D. and N. Salvadori (1995), *Theory of Production: A Long-Period Analysis*, Cambridge: Cambridge University Press

    (2003), 'Theories of economic growth: old and new', in Salvadori (ed.) (2003), 1–22

Laidler, D. (1999), *Fabricating the Keynesian Revolution: Studies of the Inter-War literature on Money, the Cycle and Unemployment*, Cambridge: Cambridge University Press

Lekachman, R. (ed.) (1964), *Keynes' General Theory: Reports of Three Decades*, London: Macmillan

Lerner, A. P. (1944), *The Economics of Control: Principles of Welfare Economics*, London: Macmillan

Lewis, W. A. (1954), 'Economic development with unlimited supplies of labour', *Manchester School*, 22, 139–91

    (1980), 'Sir Arthur Lewis', in *Les Prix Nobel 1979*, Stockholm, 255–8

Lucas, Robert E., Jr (1988), 'On the mechanics of economic development', *Journal of Monetary Economics*, 22, 3–42

Lutz, F. A. and D. C. Hague (eds.) (1961), *The Theory of Capital*, London: Macmillan

Luxemburg, R. (1913), *Akkumalation des Kapitals*, trans. D. Schwarzchild with an introduction by Joan Robinson (1951) as *The Accumulation of Capital*, London: Routledge & Kegan Paul

Marglin, S. A. (1984a), 'Growth, distribution and inflation: a centennial synthesis', *Cambridge Journal of Economics*, 8, 115–44

    (1984b), *Growth, Distribution and Prices*, Cambridge, MA: Harvard University Press

Marx, Karl (1867), *Das Kapital*, Band I; in English, *Capital*, vol. I (1976), Harmondsworth: Penguin

    (1885), *Das Kapital*, Band II, published by F. Engels; in English, *Capital*, vol. II (1978), Harmondsworth: Penguin

    (1894), *Das Kapital*, Band III, published by F. Engels; in English, *Capital*, vol. III (1981), Harmondsworth: Penguin

Marshall, A. (1890), *Principles of Economics: An Introductory Volume*, London: Macmillan, 8 edns. 1890–1920, ninth (variorum) edn. 1961

McCombie, J. S. L. and A. P. Thirlwall (1994), *Economic Growth and the Balance of Payments*, London: Macmillan

Meade, J. E. (1975), 'The Keynesian revolution', chapter 10 in M. Keynes (ed.) (1975), 82–8

Meek, R. L. (1961), 'Mr. Sraffa's rehabilitation of classical economics', *Scottish Journal of Political Economy*, 8, 119–36, reprinted in Meek (1967), 161–78

    (1967), *Economics and Ideology and Other Essays: Studies in the Development of Economic Thought*, London: Chapman & Hall

Meidner, R. (1993), 'Why did the Swedish model fail?', in Miliband and Panitch (eds.) (1993), 211–28

Michl, T. R. (2002), 'The fossil production function in a vintage model',
  Australian Economic Papers, 41, 53–68
Miliband, R. and L. Panitch (eds.) (1993), *Real Problems False Solutions, Socialist
  Register 1993*, London: Merlin Press
Minhas, B. S. (1963), *An International Comparison of Factor Costs and Factor Use*,
  Amsterdam: North-Holland
Moore, B. J. (1988), *Horizontalists and Verticalists: The Macroeconomics of Credit
  Money*, Cambridge: Cambridge University Press
Morishima, M. (1976), 'Positive profits with negative surplus value: a comment',
  Economic Journal, 86, 599–603
Pasinetti, L. L. (1960), 'A mathematical formulation of the Ricardian system',
  Review of Economic Studies, 27, 78–98
  (1962), 'Rate of profit and income distribution in relation to the rate of
  economic growth', *Review of Economic Studies*, 29, 267–79
  (1965), 'A new theoretical approach to the problems of economic growth',
  28, Pontificiae Academiae Scientiarum Scripta Varia, Vatican City, reprinted in L. Pasinetti, *Econometric Approach to Development Planning*
  (1965), Amsterdam: North-Holland, 571–69
  (1966), 'Changes in the rate of profit and switches of techniques', *Quarterly
  Journal of Economics*, 80, 503–17
  (1969), 'Switches of techniques and the "rate of return" in capital theory',
  Economic Journal, 79, 508–31
  (1970), 'Again on capital theory and Solow's "rate of return"', *Economic
  Journal*, 80, 428–31
  (1973), 'The notion of vertical integration in economic analysis', *Metroeconomica*, 25, 1–29
  (1974), *Growth and Income Distribution: Essays in Economic Theory*, Cambridge:
  Cambridge University Press
  (1980–1), 'The rate of interest and the distribution of income in a pure labour
  economy', *Journal of Post Keynesian Economics*, 3, 170–82
  (1981), *Structural Change and Economic Growth: A Theoretical Essay on the
  Dynamics of the Wealth of Nations*, Cambridge: Cambridge University
  Press
  (1986), 'Sraffa's circular process and the concept of vertical integration',
  Political Economy: Studies in the Surplus Approach, 3–16
  (1988), 'Growing sub-systems, vertically hyper-integrated sectors and the
  labour theory of value', *Cambridge Journal of Economics*, 12, 125–34
  (1990), 'At the roots of post-Keynesian thought: Keynes' break with tradition', Tenth Annual Conference of the Association of Post-Keynesian
  Studies, Amsterdam, mimeo
  (1993), *Structural Economic Dynamics: A Theory of the Economic Consequences of
  Human Learning*, Cambridge: Cambridge University Press
  (1997), 'The marginal efficiency of investment', in Harcourt and Riach (eds.)
  (1997), vol. 1, 198–218
Pekkarinen, J., M. Pohjola and B. Rowthorn (eds.) (1992), *Social Corporatism:
  A Superior Economic System?*, Oxford: Oxford University Press

Pitchford, John D. (2002), 'Trevor Swan's 1956 economic growth "seminar" and notes on growth', *Economic Record*, 78, 381–7

Reddaway, W. B. (1936), 'Review article of *The General Theory of Employment, Interest and Money*', *Economic Record*, 12, 28–36, reprinted in Lekachman (ed.) (1964), 99–108

Ricardo, D., *Works and Correspondence of*, 11 vols. (1957–73), ed. Piero Sraffa with the collaboration of M. H. Dobb, Cambridge: Cambridge University Press

Robertson, D. H. (later, Sir Dennis) (1956), *Economic Commentaries*, London: Staples Press

(1957), *Lectures on Economic Principles, Volume I*, London: Staples Press

(1958), *Lectures on Economic Principles, Volume II*, London: Staples Press

(1959), *Lectures on Economic Principles, Volume III*, London: Staples Press

Robinson, E. A. G. (1936), 'Mr. Keynes on money', *The Economist*, 24 February, 471–2

(1947), 'John Maynard Keynes 1883–1946', *Economic Journal*, 57, 1–68

(ed.) (1965), *Problems in Economic Development*, London: Macmillan

Robinson, Joan (1932), *Economics is a Serious Subject: The Apologia of an Economist to the Mathematician, the Scientist and the Plain Man*, Cambridge: Heffers

(1933a), *The Economics of Imperfect Competition*, London: Macmillan, 2nd edn. 1969

(1933b), 'A parable of saving and investment', *Economica*, 13, 75–84

(1933c), 'The theory of money and the analysis of output', *Review of Economic Studies*, 1, 22–6, reprinted in *CEP*, vol. I, 1951, 52–8

(1937), *Essays in the Theory of Employment*, Oxford: Basil Blackwell, 2nd edn. 1947

(1942), *An Essay on Marxian Economics*, London: Macmillan, 2nd edn. 1966

(1951–80), *Collected Economic Papers*, 6 vols., Oxford: Basil Blackwell

(1952), *The Rate of Interest and Other Essays*, London: Macmillan

(1953), *On Re-reading Marx.*, Cambridge: Students' Bookshop, reprinted in *CEP*, vol. IV, 1973, 247–68

(1953–4), 'The production function and the theory of capital,' *Review of Economic Studies*, 21, 81–106, reprinted in *CEP*, vol. II, 1960, 114–31

(1955), 'Marx, Marshall and Keynes', Delhi School of Economics, Occasional Reprint No. 9, reprinted in *CEP*, II, 1960, 1–17

(1956), *The Accumulation of Capital*, London: Macmillan, 2nd edn. 1965, 3rd edn. 1969

(1959), 'Accumulation and the production function', *Economic Journal*, 69, 433–42, reprinted in *CEP*, vol. II, 1960, 132–44

(1962a), *Essays in the Theory of Economic Growth*, London: Macmillan

(1962b), 'Review of H. G. Johnson, *Money, Trade and Economic Growth* (1962)', *Economic Journal*, 72, 690–2, reprinted in *CEP*, vol. III, 1965, 100–2

(1964), 'Solow on the rate of return', *Economic Journal*, 74, 410–17, reprinted in *CEP*, vol. III, 1965, 36–47

(1965a), 'Harrod's knife-edge', in *CEP*, vol. III, 1965, 52–5

(1965b), 'Piero Sraffa and the rate of exploitation', *New Left Review*, 5, 28–34, reprinted as 'A reconsideration of the theory of value', in *CEP*, vol. III, 1965, 173–81

(1974), 'History versus equilibrium', London: Thames Polytechnic, reprinted in *CEP*, vol. V, 1979, 48–58

(1975), 'The unimportance of reswitching', *Quarterly Journal of Economics*, 89, 32–9, reprinted in *CEP*, vol. V, 1979b, 76–89

(1977a), 'Michal Kalecki on the economics of capitalism', *Oxford Bulletin of Economics and Statistics*, 39, 7–17, reprinted as 'Michal Kalecki', in *CEP*, vol. V, 1979b, 184–96

(1977b), 'What are the questions?', *Journal of Economic Literature*, 15, 1318–39, reprinted in *CEP*, vol. V, 1979b, 1–31

(1978), 'Keynes and Ricardo', *Journal of Post Keynesian Economics*, 1, 12–18, reprinted in *CEP*, vol. V, 1979b, 210–16

(1979a), *Aspects of Development and Underdevelopment*, Cambridge: Cambridge University Press

(1979c), 'Thinking about thinking', *CEP*, vol. V, 1979b, 110–19

(1980), 'Spring cleaning', Cambridge, mimeo, published as 'The theory of normal prices and the reconstruction of economic theory', in Feiwel (ed.) (1985), 157–65

(1981), *The Arms Race* (The Tanner lectures on Human Values), Logan, UT: University of Utah

Romer, P. M. (1986), 'Increasing returns and long-run growth', *Journal of Political Economy*, 94, 1002–37

Rowthorn, B. (1977), 'Conflict, inflation and money', *Cambridge Journal of Economics*, 1, 215–39, reprinted in Rowthorn (1980), 148–81

(1980), *Capitalism, Conflict and Inflation: Essays in Political Economy*, London: Lawrence & Wishart

(1992), 'Corporatism and labour market performance', in Pekkarinen, Pohjola and Rowthorn (eds.) (1992), 82–131

Salter, W. E. G. (1960), *Productivity and Technical Change*, Cambridge: Cambridge University Press, 2nd edn. 1966

(1965), 'Productivity growth and accumulation as historical processes', in Robinson (ed.) (1965), 266–91

Salvadori, N. (ed.) (2003), *The Theory of Economic Growth: A 'Classical' Perspective*, Cheltenham and Northampton, MA: Edward Elgar

Samuelson, P. A. (1948), 'International trade and the equalisation of factor prices', *Economic Journal*, 58, 163–97

(1962), 'Parable and realism in capital theory: the surrogate production function', *Review of Economic Studies*, 29, 192–206

(1964) 'A brief survey of post-Keynesian developments [1963]', in Lekachman (ed.) (1964), 331–47

(1966), 'A summing up', *Quarterly Journal of Economics*, 80, 568–83

Sardoni, C. (1981), 'Multisectoral models of balanced growth and the Marxian schemes of expanded reproduction', *Australian Economic Papers*, 20, 383–97

(ed.) (1992), *On Political Economists and Modern Political Economy: Selected Essays of G. C. Harcourt*, London: Routledge

Sardoni, C. and Peter Kriesler (eds.) (1999), *Keynes, Post-Keynesianism and Political Economy: Essays in honour of Geoff Harcourt, Volume Three*, London: Routledge

Scazzieri, R. (1983), 'Economic dynamics and structural change: a comment on Pasinetti', *Rivista Internazionale di Scienze Economiche e Commerciali*, 73–90

Sen, Amartya (1960), *Choice of Techniques: An Aspect of the Theory of Planned Economic Development*, Oxford: Basil Blackwell

(ed.) (1970), *Growth Economics*, Harmondsworth: Penguin

Shapiro, N. (1997), 'Imperfect competition and Keynes', in Harcourt and Riach (eds.) (1997), vol. 1, 83–92

Shepherd, G. B. (1994), *Rejected: Leading Economists Ponder the Publication Process*, Texas, TX: Thomas Horton and Daughters

Shove, G. F. (1944), 'Mrs Robinson on Marxian economics', *Economic Journal*, 54, 47–61

Skidelsky, R. (1983), *John Maynard Keynes, Volume One: Hopes Betrayed 1883–1920*, London: Macmillan

(1992), *John Maynard Keynes, Volume Two: The Economist as Saviour 1920–1937*, London: Macmillan

(2000), *John Maynard Keynes, Volume Three: Fighting for Britain 1937–1946*, London: Macmillan

Smith, A. (1759a), *Theory of Moral Sentiments*, vol. I of the Glasgow Edition of Smith's *Works*

(1759b), *Lectures on Jurisprudence*, vol. V of the Glasgow Edition of Smith's *Works*

(1776), *An Inquiry into the Nature and Causes of the Wealth of Nations*, vol. II of the Glasgow Edition of Smith's *Works*

(n.d.) *Essays on Philosophical Subjects*, vol. III of the Glasgow Edition of Smith's *Works*

Smithies, A. (1962), 'Discussion', *American Economic Review, Papers and Proceedings*, 52, 91–2

Solow, R. M. (1956), 'A contribution to the theory of economic growth', *Quarterly Journal of Economics*, 70, 65–94

(1957), 'Technical change and the aggregate production function', *Review of Economics and Statistics*, 39, 312–20

(1963), *Capital Theory and the Rate of Return*, Amsterdam: North-Holland

(1970), 'On the rate of return: reply to Pasinetti', *Economic Journal*, 80, 423–8

(1974), 'Laws of production and laws of algebra: the Humbug production function: a comment', *Review of Economics and Statistics*, 56, 121

(1997a), *Learning from 'Learning by Doing': Lessons for Economic Growth*, Stanford, CA: Stanford University Press

(1997b), 'Thoughts inspired by reading an atypical paper by Harcourt', in Arestis, Palma and Sawyer (eds.) (1997a), 419–24

Sraffa, Piero (1920), 'L'inflazione monetaria in Italia durante e dopo la guerra', Turin, unpublished dissertation, trans. W. J. Harcourt and C. Sardoni (1993), 'Monetary inflation in Italy during the war', *Cambridge Joural of Economics*, 17, 7–26

(1922a), 'The bank crisis in Italy,' *Economic Journal*, 32, 178–97

(1922b), 'L'attuale situazione delle banche italiane', *Manchester Guardian Commercial – The Reconstruction of Europe*, 11, December, 694–5

(1926), 'The laws of returns under competitive conditions', *Economic Journal*, 36, 535–50

(1960), *Production of Commodities by Means of Commodities: Prelude to a Critique of Economic Theory*, Cambridge: Cambridge University Press

(1962), '*Production of Commodities*: a comment', *Economic Journal*, 72, 477–9

Sraffa, P. with the collaboration of M. H. Dobb (eds.) (1951–73), *Works and Correspondence of David Ricardo*, 12 vols., Cambridge: Cambridge University Press

Steedman, I. (1975), 'Positive profits with negative surplus value,' *Economic Journal*, 85, 114–23

(1977), *Marx after Sraffa*, London: New Left Books

Stegman, T. (1987), 'Incomes policy: some issues', in Stegman, Schott, Robson and Scott (eds.) (1987), 1–24

Stegman, T., K. Schott, P. Robson and G. Scott (eds.) (1987), *The Future of Incomes Policies in Australia*, CAER Paper, 24, Sydney: University of New South Wales

Steindl, J. (1981), 'A personal portrait of Michal Kalecki', *Journal of Post Keynesian Economics*, 3, 590–96

Stiglitz, J. E. and A. Weiss (1981) 'Credit rationing in markets with imperfect information', *American Economic Review*, 71, 393–410

(1983), 'Incentive effects of terminations: applications to the credit and labor markets,' *American Economic Review*, 73, 912–27

Swan, T. W. (1956), 'Economic growth and capital accumulation', *Economic Record*, 32, 334–61

(2002), 'Economic growth', *Economic Record*, 78, 375–80

Tahir, P. (1999), 'Joan Robinson: a neglected precursor of internal migration models', in Sardoni and Kriesler (eds.) (1999), 312–33

Tahir, P., G. C. Harcourt and P. Kerr (2002), 'On Joan Robinson and China', in P. Kerr (ed.), with the collaboration of G. C. Harcourt (2002), vol. V, 267–80

Targetti, F. and B. Kinda-Hass (1982), 'Kalecki's review of Keynes' *General Theory*', *Australian Economic Papers*, 21, 244–60

Targetti, F. and A. P. Thirlwall (eds.) (1989), *The Essential Kaldor*, London: Duckworth

Tarshis, L. (1939), 'The determinants of labour income', Cambridge: unpublished PhD dissertation

von Neumann, J. (1945–6), 'A model of general economic equilibrium', *Review of Economic Studies*, 13, 1–9

Warner, M. (ed.) (1996), *International Encyclopedia of Business and Management*, London: Routledge

Wicksell, Knut (1911 [1934]), *Lectures on Political Economy, Volume I*, London: George Routledge & Sons

Wittgenstein, Ludwig (1922), *Tractatus logico-philosophicus*, with an introduction by Bertrand Russell, London: Kegan Paul, Trench, Trübner

(1953), *Philosophical Investigations (Philosophische Untersuchungen)* trans. by G. E. M. Anscombe, Oxford: Blackwell

Wood, A. (1975), *A Theory of Profits*, Cambridge: Cambridge University Press

Worswick, G. D. N. (1959), 'Mrs. Robinson on simple accumulation: a comment', *Oxford Economic Papers*, 11, 125–41

Worswick, D. and J. Trevithick (eds.) (1983), *Keynes and the Modern World: Proceedings of the Keynes Centenary Conference, King's College, Cambridge*, Cambridge: Cambridge University Press

Young, A. (1928), 'Increasing returns and economic progress', *Economic Journal*, 38, 527–42

Index